OpenStack Operations Guide

by Tom Fifield, Diane Fleming, Anne Gentle, Lorin Hochstein, Jonathan Proulx, Everett Toews, and Joe Topjian

Beijing • Cambridge • Farnham • Köln • Sebastopol • Tokyo

OpenStack Operations Guide

by Tom Fifield, Diane Fleming, Anne Gentle, Lorin Hochstein, Jonathan Proulx, Everett Toews, and Joe Topjian

Printed in the United States of America.

Published by O'Reilly Media, Inc. , 1005 Gravenstein Highway North, Sebastopol, CA 95472.

O'Reilly books may be purchased for educational, business, or sales promotional use. Online editions are also available for most titles (*http://my.safaribooksonline.com*). For more information, contact our corporate/institutional sales department: 800-998-9938 or corporate@oreilly.com .

Editors: Andy Oram and Brian Anderson
Production Editor: Kristen Brown
Copyeditor: John Pierce
Proofreader: Amanda Kersey
Indexer: Judith McConville
Interior Designer: David Futato
Cover Designer: Karen Montgomery
Illustrator: Rebecca Demarest

May 2014: First Edition

Revision History for the First Edition

2014-04-21: First release

See *http://oreilly.com/catalog/errata.csp?isbn=9781491946954* for release details.

978-1-491-94695-4

[LSI]

Table of Contents

Part II. Operations

Preface

OpenStack is an open source platform that lets you build an Infrastructure as a Service (IaaS) cloud that runs on commodity hardware.

Introduction to OpenStack

OpenStack believes in open source, open design, open development, all in an open community that encourages participation by anyone. The long-term vision for OpenStack is to produce a ubiquitous open source cloud computing platform that meets the needs of public and private cloud providers regardless of size. OpenStack services control large pools of compute, storage, and networking resources throughout a data center.

The technology behind OpenStack consists of a series of interrelated projects delivering various components for a cloud infrastructure solution. Each service provides an open API so that all of these resources can be managed through a dashboard that gives administrators control while empowering users to provision resources through a web interface, a command-line client, or software development kits that support the API. Many OpenStack APIs are extensible, meaning you can keep compatibility with a core set of calls while providing access to more resources and innovating through API extensions. The OpenStack project is a global collaboration of developers and cloud computing technologists. The project produces an open standard cloud computing platform for both public and private clouds. By focusing on ease of implementation, massive scalability, a variety of rich features, and tremendous extensibility, the project aims to deliver a practical and reliable cloud solution for all types of organizations.

Getting Started with OpenStack

As an open source project, one of the unique aspects of OpenStack is that it has many different levels at which you can begin to engage with it—you don't have to do everything yourself.

Using OpenStack

You could ask, "Do I even need to build a cloud?" If you want to start using a compute or storage service by just swiping your credit card, you can go to eNovance, HP, Rackspace, or other organizations to start using their public OpenStack clouds. Using their OpenStack cloud resources is similar to accessing the publically available Amazon Web Services Elastic Compute Cloud (EC2) or Simple Storage Solution (S3).

Plug and Play OpenStack

However, the enticing part of OpenStack might be to build your own private cloud, and there are several ways to accomplish this goal. Perhaps the simplest of all is an appliance-style solution. You purchase an appliance, unpack it, plug in the power and the network, and watch it transform into an OpenStack cloud with minimal additional configuration. Few, if any, other open source cloud products have such turnkey options. If a turnkey solution is interesting to you, take a look at Nebula One.

However, hardware choice is important for many applications, so if that applies to you, consider that there are several software distributions available that you can run on servers, storage, and network products of your choosing. Canonical (where OpenStack replaced Eucalyptus as the default cloud option in 2011), Red Hat, and SUSE offer enterprise OpenStack solutions and support. You may also want to take a look at some of the specialized distributions, such as those from Rackspace, Piston, SwiftStack, or Cloudscaling. Also, a hat tip to Apache CloudStack, which Citrix donated to the Apache Foundation after its $200 million purchase of Cloud.com. While not currently packaged in any distributions, like Eucalyptus, it is an example of an alternative private cloud software developed in an open source–like manner.

Alternatively, if you want someone to help guide you through the decisions about the underlying hardware or your applications, perhaps adding in a few features or integrating components along the way, consider contacting one of the system integrators with OpenStack experience, such as Mirantis or Metacloud.

If your preference is to build your own OpenStack expertise internally, a good way to kick-start that might be to attend or arrange a training session. The OpenStack Foundation recently launched a Training Marketplace (*http://opsgui.de/NPH6JZ*) where you can look for nearby events. Also, the OpenStack community is working to produce (*http://opsgui.de/1eLCyio*) open source training materials.

Roll Your Own OpenStack

However, this guide has a different audience—those seeking to derive the most flexibility from the OpenStack framework by conducting do-it-yourself solutions.

OpenStack is designed for scalability, so you can easily add new compute, network, and storage resources to grow your cloud over time. In addition to several massive OpenStack public clouds, a considerable number of organizations (such as Paypal, Intel, and Comcast) have built large-scale private clouds. OpenStack offers much more than a typical software package because it lets you integrate a number of different technologies to construct a cloud. This approach provides great flexibility, but the number of options might be bewildering at first.

Who This Book Is For

This book is for those of you starting to run OpenStack clouds as well as those of you who were handed an operational one and want to keep it running well. Perhaps you're on a DevOps team, perhaps you are a system administrator starting to dabble in the cloud, or maybe you want to get on the OpenStack cloud team at your company. This book is for all of you.

This guide assumes that you are familiar with a Linux distribution that supports OpenStack, SQL databases, and virtualization. You must be comfortable administering and configuring multiple Linux machines for networking. You must install and maintain a MySQL database and occasionally run SQL queries against it.

One of the most complex aspects of an OpenStack cloud is the networking configuration. You should be familiar with concepts such as DHCP, Linux bridges, VLANs, and iptables. You must also have access to a network hardware expert who can configure the switches and routers required in your OpenStack cloud.

Cloud computing is a quite advanced topic, and this book requires a lot of background knowledge. However, if you are fairly new to cloud computing, we recommend that you make use of the Glossary at the back of the book, as well as the online documentation for OpenStack and additional resources mentioned in this book in Appendix E.

Further Reading

There are other books on the OpenStack documentation website (*http://docs.openstack.org*) that can help you get the job done.

OpenStack Installation Guides
: Describes a manual installation process, as in, by hand, without automation, for multiple distributions based on a packaging system:

  - Installation Guide for Debian 7.0 (*http://opsgui.de/1eLBGtX*)
  - Installation Guide for openSUSE and SUSE Linux Enterprise Server (*http://opsgui.de/1eLBI50*)
  - Installation Guide for Red Hat Enterprise Linux, CentOS, and Fedora (*http://opsgui.de/NPGvrs*)
  - Installation Guide for Ubuntu 12.04 (LTS) Server (*http://opsgui.de/NPGunp*)

OpenStack Configuration Reference (http://opsgui.de/1eLCDTf)
: Contains a reference listing of all configuration options for core and integrated OpenStack services by release version

OpenStack Cloud Administrator Guide (http://opsgui.de/1eLBLON)
: Contains how-to information for managing an OpenStack cloud as needed for your use cases, such as storage, computing, or software-defined-networking

OpenStack High Availability Guide (http://opsgui.de/1eLCEGD)
: Describes potential strategies for making your OpenStack services and related controllers and data stores highly available

OpenStack Security Guide (http://opsgui.de/NPG4NW)
: Provides best practices and conceptual information about securing an OpenStack cloud

Virtual Machine Image Guide (http://opsgui.de/1eLCHlR)
: Shows you how to obtain, create, and modify virtual machine images that are compatible with OpenStack

OpenStack End User Guide (http://opsgui.de/NPHaJI)
: Shows OpenStack end users how to create and manage resources in an OpenStack cloud with the OpenStack dashboard and OpenStack client commands

OpenStack Admin User Guide (http://opsgui.de/1eLBkDJ)
: Shows OpenStack administrators how to create and manage resources in an OpenStack cloud with the OpenStack dashboard and OpenStack client commands

OpenStack API Quick Start (http://opsgui.de/NPHdVO)
: A brief overview of how to send REST API requests to endpoints for OpenStack services

How This Book Is Organized

This book is organized in two parts: the architecture decisions for designing OpenStack clouds and the repeated operations for running OpenStack clouds.

Part I:

Chapter 1
: Because of all the decisions the other chapters discuss, this chapter describes the decisions made for this particular book and much of the justification for the example architecture.

Chapter 2
: While this book doesn't describe installation, we do recommend automation for deployment and configuration, discussed in this chapter.

Chapter 3
: The cloud controller is an invention for the sake of consolidating and describing which services run on which nodes. This chapter discusses hardware and network considerations as well as how to design the cloud controller for performance and separation of services.

Chapter 4
: This chapter describes the compute nodes, which are dedicated to running virtual machines. Some hardware choices come into play here, as well as logging and networking descriptions.

Chapter 5
: This chapter discusses the growth of your cloud resources through scaling and segregation considerations.

Chapter 6
: As with other architecture decisions, storage concepts within OpenStack take a lot of consideration, and this chapter lays out the choices for you.

Chapter 7
: Your OpenStack cloud networking needs to fit into your existing networks while also enabling the best design for your users and administrators, and this chapter gives you in-depth information about networking decisions.

Part II:

Chapter 8
: This chapter is written to let you get your hands wrapped around your OpenStack cloud through command-line tools and understanding what is already set up in your cloud.

Chapter 9
This chapter walks through user-enabling processes that all admins must face to manage users, give them quotas to parcel out resources, and so on.

Chapter 10
This chapter shows you how to use OpenStack cloud resources and train your users as well.

Chapter 11
This chapter goes into the common failures that the authors have seen while running clouds in production, including troubleshooting.

Chapter 12
Because network troubleshooting is especially difficult with virtual resources, this chapter is chock-full of helpful tips and tricks for tracing network traffic, finding the root cause of networking failures, and debugging related services, such as DHCP and DNS.

Chapter 13
This chapter shows you where OpenStack places logs and how to best read and manage logs for monitoring purposes.

Chapter 14
This chapter describes what you need to back up within OpenStack as well as best practices for recovering backups.

Chapter 15
For readers who need to get a specialized feature into OpenStack, this chapter describes how to use DevStack to write custom middleware or a custom scheduler to rebalance your resources.

Chapter 16
Because OpenStack is so, well, open, this chapter is dedicated to helping you navigate the community and find out where you can help and where you can get help.

Chapter 17
Much of OpenStack is driver-oriented, so you can plug in different solutions to the base set of services. This chapter describes some advanced configuration topics.

Chapter 18
This chapter provides upgrade information based on the architectures used in this book.

Backmatter:

Appendix A
: You can read a small selection of use cases from the OpenStack community with some technical details and further resources.

Appendix B
: These are shared legendary tales of image disappearances, VM massacres, and crazy troubleshooting techniques to share those hard-learned lessons and wisdom.

Appendix C
: Read about how to track the OpenStack roadmap through the open and transparent development processes.

Appendix D
: A preview of the new features in the Icehouse release of OpenStack.

Appendix E
: So many OpenStack resources are available online because of the fast-moving nature of the project, but there are also resources listed here that the authors found helpful while learning themselves.

Glossary
: A list of terms used in this book is included, which is a subset of the larger OpenStack glossary available online.

Why and How We Wrote This Book

We wrote this book because we have deployed and maintained OpenStack clouds for at least a year, and wanted to be able to distribute this knowledge to others. After months of being the point people for an OpenStack cloud, we also wanted to have a document to hand to our system administrators so that they'd know how to operate the cloud on a daily basis—both reactively and proactively. We wanted to provide more detailed technical information about the decisions that deployers make along the way.

We wrote this book to help you:

- Design and create an architecture for your first nontrivial OpenStack cloud. After you read this guide, you'll know which questions to ask and how to organize your compute, networking, and storage resources and the associated software packages.
- Perform the day-to-day tasks required to administer a cloud.

We wrote this book in a book sprint, which is a facilitated, rapid development production method for books. For more information, see the BookSprints site (*http://opsgui.de/1eLCIpY*). Your authors cobbled this book together in five days during February 2013, fueled by caffeine and the best takeout food that Austin, Texas, could offer.

On the first day, we filled white boards with colorful sticky notes to start to shape this nebulous book about how to architect and operate clouds:

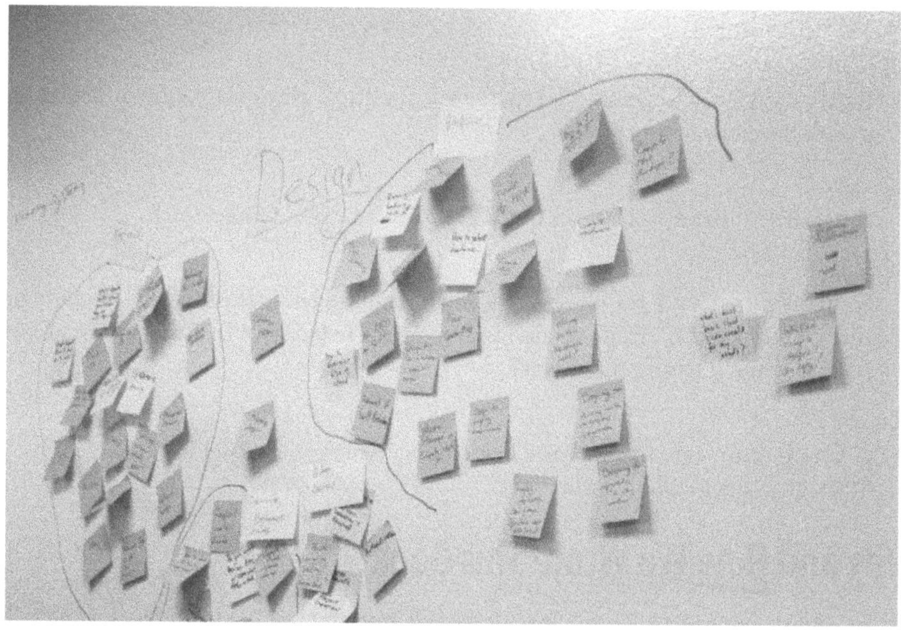

We wrote furiously from our own experiences and bounced ideas between each other. At regular intervals we reviewed the shape and organization of the book and further molded it, leading to what you see today.

The team includes:

Tom Fifield
: After learning about scalability in computing from particle physics experiments, such as ATLAS at the Large Hadron Collider (LHC) at CERN, Tom worked on OpenStack clouds in production to support the Australian public research sector. Tom currently serves as an OpenStack community manager and works on OpenStack documentation in his spare time.

Diane Fleming
: Diane works on the OpenStack API documentation tirelessly. She helped out wherever she could on this project.

Anne Gentle
: Anne is the documentation coordinator for OpenStack and also served as an individual contributor to the Google Documentation Summit in 2011, working with the Open Street Maps team. She has worked on book sprints in the past, with FLOSS Manuals' Adam Hyde facilitating. Anne lives in Austin, Texas.

Lorin Hochstein
: An academic turned software-developer-slash-operator, Lorin worked as the lead architect for Cloud Services at Nimbis Services, where he deploys OpenStack for technical computing applications. He has been working with OpenStack since the Cactus release. Previously, he worked on high-performance computing extensions for OpenStack at University of Southern California's Information Sciences Institute (USC-ISI).

Adam Hyde
: Adam facilitated this book sprint. He also founded the books sprint methodology and is the most experienced book-sprint facilitator around. See *http://www.booksprints.net* for more information. Adam founded FLOSS Manuals—a community of some 3,000 individuals developing Free Manuals about Free Software. He is also the founder and project manager for Booktype, an open source project for writing, editing, and publishing books online and in print.

Jonathan Proulx
: Jon has been piloting an OpenStack cloud as a senior technical architect at the MIT Computer Science and Artificial Intelligence Lab for his researchers to have as much computing power as they need. He started contributing to OpenStack documentation and reviewing the documentation so that he could accelerate his learning.

Everett Toews
: Everett is a developer advocate at Rackspace making OpenStack and the Rackspace Cloud easy to use. Sometimes developer, sometimes advocate, and sometimes operator, he's built web applications, taught workshops, given presentations around the world, and deployed OpenStack for production use by academia and business.

Joe Topjian
: Joe has designed and deployed several clouds at Cybera, a nonprofit where they are building e-infrastructure to support entrepreneurs and local researchers in Alberta, Canada. He also actively maintains and operates these clouds as a systems architect, and his experiences have generated a wealth of troubleshooting skills for cloud environments.

OpenStack community members

Many individual efforts keep a community book alive. Our community members updated content for this book year-round. Also, a year after the first sprint, Jon Proulx hosted a second two-day mini-sprint at MIT with the goal of updating the book for the latest release. Since the book's inception, more than 30 contributors have supported this book. We have a tool chain for reviews, continuous builds, and translations. Writers and developers continuously review patches, enter doc bugs, edit content, and fix doc bugs. We want to recognize their efforts!

The following people have contributed to this book: Akihiro Motoki, Alejandro Avella, Alexandra Settle, Andreas Jaeger, Andy McCallum, Benjamin Stassart, Chandan Kumar, Chris Ricker, David Cramer, David Wittman, Denny Zhang, Emilien Macchi, Gauvain Pocentek, Ignacio Barrio, James E. Blair, Jay Clark, Jeff White, Jeremy Stanley, K Jonathan Harker, KATO Tomoyuki, Lana Brindley, Laura Alves, Lee Li, Lukasz Jernas, Mario B. Codeniera, Matthew Kassawara, Michael Still, Monty Taylor, Nermina Miller, Nigel Williams, Phil Hopkins, Russell Bryant, Sahid Orentino Ferdjaoui, Sandy Walsh, Sascha Peilicke, Sean M. Collins, Sergey Lukjanov, Shilla Saebi, Stephen Gordon, Summer Long, Uwe Stuehler, Vaibhav Bhatkar, Veronica Musso, Ying Chun "Daisy" Guo, Zhengguang Ou, and ZhiQiang Fan.

How to Contribute to This Book

The genesis of this book was an in-person event, but now that the book is in your hands, we want you to contribute to it. OpenStack documentation follows the coding principles of iterative work, with bug logging, investigating, and fixing. We also store the source content on GitHub and invite collaborators through the OpenStack Gerrit installation, which offers reviews. For the O'Reilly edition of this book, we are using the company's Atlas system, which also stores source content on GitHub and enables collaboration among contributors.

Learn more about how to contribute to the OpenStack docs at Documentation How To (*http://opsgui.de/1eLCK10*).

If you find a bug and can't fix it or aren't sure it's really a doc bug, log a bug at OpenStack Manuals (*http://opsgui.de/NPHdoC*). Tag the bug under Extra options with the `ops-guide` tag to indicate that the bug is in this guide. You can assign the bug to yourself if you know how to fix it. Also, a member of the OpenStack doc-core team can triage the doc bug.

Conventions Used in This Book

The following typographical conventions are used in this book:

Italic
: Indicates new terms, URLs, email addresses, filenames, and file extensions.

`Constant width`
: Used for program listings, as well as within paragraphs to refer to program elements such as variable or function names, databases, data types, environment variables, statements, and keywords.

`Constant width bold`
: Shows commands or other text that should be typed literally by the user.

`Constant width italic`
: Shows text that should be replaced with user-supplied values or by values determined by context.

Command prompts
: Commands prefixed with the # prompt should be executed by the `root` user. These examples can also be executed using the `sudo` command, if available.

  Commands prefixed with the `$` prompt can be executed by any user, including `root`.

This element signifies a tip or suggestion.

This element signifies a general note.

This element indicates a warning or caution.

Using Code Examples

Supplemental material (code examples, exercises, etc.) is available for download at *https://github.com/openstack/openstack-manuals*.

This book is here to help you get your job done. In general, if example code is offered with this book, you may use it in your programs and documentation. You do not need to contact us for permission unless you're reproducing a significant portion of the code. For example, writing a program that uses several chunks of code from this book does not require permission. Selling or distributing a CD-ROM of examples from O'Reilly books does require permission. Answering a question by citing this book and quoting example code does not require permission. Incorporating a significant amount of example code from this book into your product's documentation does require permission.

We appreciate, but do not require, attribution. An attribution usually includes the title, author, publisher, and ISBN. For example: "*OpenStack Operations Guide* by Tom Fifield, Diane Fleming, Anne Gentle, Lorin Hochstein, Jonathan Proulx, Everett Toews, and Joe Topjian (O'Reilly). Copyright 2014 OpenStack Foundation, 978-1-491-94695-4."

If you feel your use of code examples falls outside fair use or the permission given above, feel free to contact us at *permissions@oreilly.com*.

Safari® Books Online

Safari Books Online (*www.safaribooksonline.com*) is an on-demand digital library that delivers expert content in both book and video form from the world's leading authors in technology and business.

Technology professionals, software developers, web designers, and business and creative professionals use Safari Books Online as their primary resource for research, problem solving, learning, and certification training.

Safari Books Online offers a range of product mixes and pricing programs for organizations, government agencies, and individuals. Subscribers have access to thousands of books, training videos, and prepublication manuscripts in one fully searchable database from publishers like O'Reilly Media, Prentice Hall Professional, Addison-Wesley Professional, Microsoft Press, Sams, Que, Peachpit Press, Focal Press, Cisco Press, John Wiley & Sons, Syngress, Morgan Kaufmann, IBM Redbooks, Packt, Adobe Press, FT Press, Apress, Manning, New Riders, McGraw-Hill, Jones & Bartlett, Course Technology, and dozens more. For more information about Safari Books Online, please visit us online.

How to Contact Us

Please address comments and questions concerning this book to the publisher:

O'Reilly Media, Inc.
1005 Gravenstein Highway North
Sebastopol, CA 95472
800-998-9938 (in the United States or Canada)
707-829-0515 (international or local)
707-829-0104 (fax)

We have a web page for this book, where we list errata, examples, and any additional information. You can access this page at *http://bit.ly/openstack-ops-guide*.

To comment or ask technical questions about this book, send email to *bookquestions@oreilly.com*.

For more information about our books, courses, conferences, and news, see our website at *http://www.oreilly.com*.

Find us on Facebook: *http://facebook.com/oreilly*

Follow us on Twitter: *http://twitter.com/oreillymedia*

Watch us on YouTube: *http://www.youtube.com/oreillymedia*

Acknowledgments

The OpenStack Foundation supported the creation of this book with plane tickets to Austin, lodging (including one adventurous evening without power after a windstorm), and delicious food. For about $10,000, we could collaborate intensively for a week in the same room at the Rackspace Austin office. The authors are all members of the OpenStack Foundation, which you can join. Go to the Foundation website (*http://opsgui.de/1eLCVcx*).

We want to acknowledge our excellent host, Rackers at Rackspace in Austin:

- Emma Richards of Rackspace guest relations took excellent care of our lunch orders and even set aside a pile of sticky notes that had fallen off the walls.
- Betsy Hagemeier, a fanatical executive assistant, took care of a room reshuffle and helped us settle in for the week.
- The real estate team at Rackspace in Austin, also known as "The Victors," were super responsive.
- Adam Powell in Racker IT supplied us with bandwidth each day and second monitors for those of us needing more screens.

- On Wednesday night we had a fun happy hour with the Austin OpenStack Meetup group, and Racker Katie Schmidt took great care of our group.

We also had some excellent input from outside the room:

- Tim Bell from CERN gave us feedback on the outline before we started and reviewed it midweek.
- Sébastien Han has written excellent blogs and generously gave his permission for reuse.
- Oisin Feeley read the book, made some edits, and emailed feedback right when we asked.

Inside the book-sprint room with us each day was our book-sprint facilitator, Adam Hyde. Without his tireless support and encouragement, we would have thought a book of this scope was impossible in five days. Adam has proven again and again that the book-sprint method is effective. He creates both tools and faith in collaborative authoring at *http://www.booksprints.net*.

We couldn't have pulled it off without so much supportive help and encouragement.

PART I
Architecture

Designing an OpenStack cloud is a great achievement. It requires a robust understanding of the requirements and needs of the cloud's users to determine the best possible configuration to meet them. OpenStack provides a great deal of flexibility to achieve your needs, and this part of the book aims to shine light on many of the decisions you need to make during the process.

To design, deploy, and configure OpenStack, administrators must understand the logical architecture. A diagram can help you envision all the integrated services within OpenStack and how they interact with each other.

OpenStack modules are one of the following types:

Daemon
: Runs as a background process. On Linux platforms, a daemon is usually installed as a service.

Script
: Installs a virtual environment and runs tests.

Command-line interface (CLI)
: Enables users to submit API calls to OpenStack services through commands.

As shown, end users can interact through the dashboard, CLIs, and APIs. All services authenticate through a common Identity Service, and individual services interact with each other through public APIs, except where privileged administrator commands are necessary. Figure I-1 shows the most common, but not the only logical architecture for an OpenStack cloud.

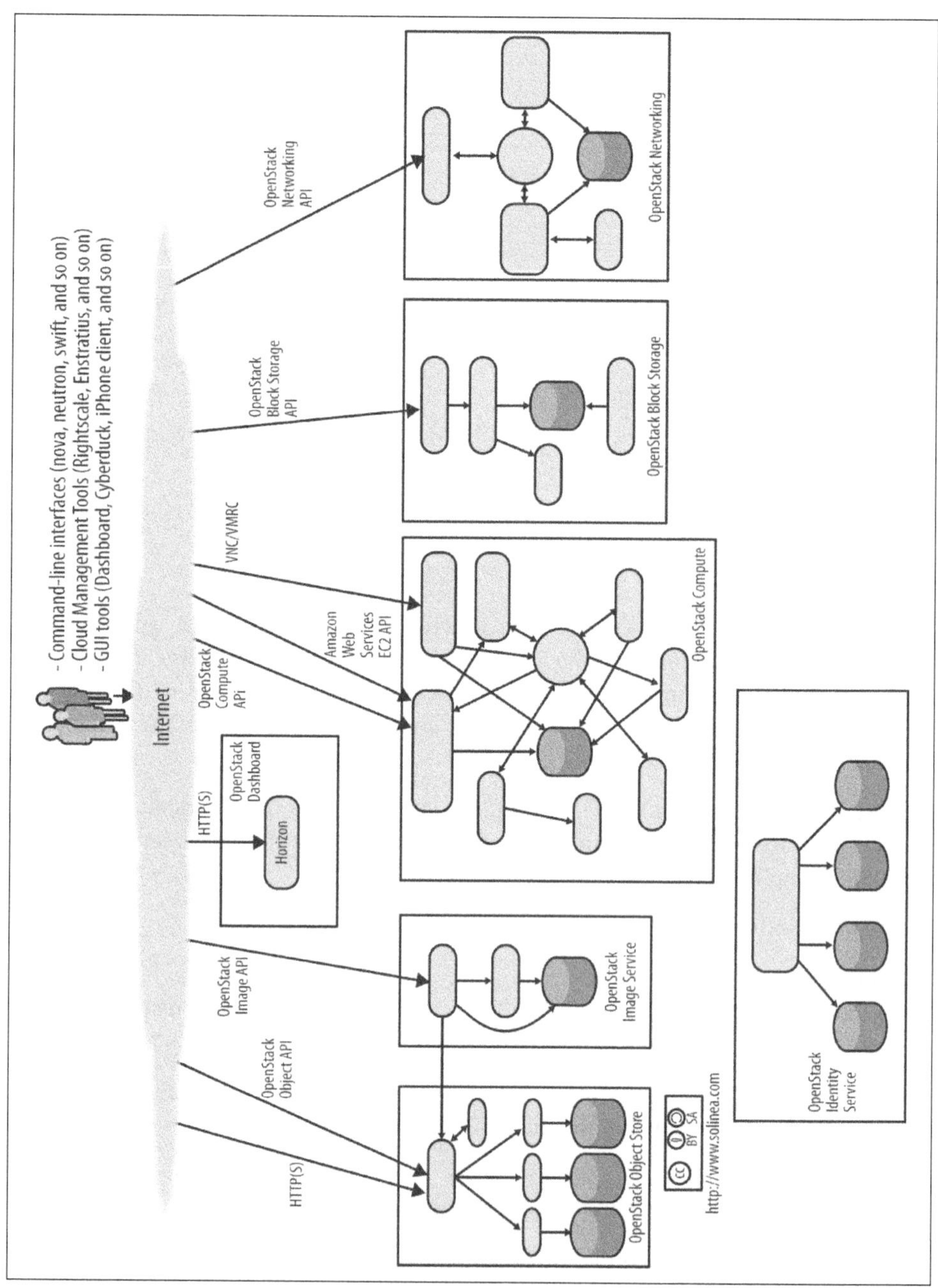

Figure I-1. OpenStack Havana Logical Architecture (http://opsgui.de/1kYnyy1)

CHAPTER 1
Example Architectures

To understand the possibilities OpenStack offers, it's best to start with basic architectures that are tried-and-true and have been tested in production environments. We offer two such examples with basic pivots on the base operating system (Ubuntu and Red Hat Enterprise Linux) and the networking architectures. There are other differences between these two examples, but you should find the considerations made for the choices in each as well as a rationale for why it worked well in a given environment.

Because OpenStack is highly configurable, with many different backends and network configuration options, it is difficult to write documentation that covers all possible OpenStack deployments. Therefore, this guide defines example architectures to simplify the task of documenting, as well as to provide the scope for this guide. Both of the offered architecture examples are currently running in production and serving users.

As always, refer to the Glossary if you are unclear about any of the terminology mentioned in these architectures.

Example Architecture—Legacy Networking (nova)

This particular example architecture has been upgraded from Grizzly to Havana and tested in production environments where many public IP addresses are available for assignment to multiple instances. You can find a second example architecture that uses OpenStack Networking (neutron) after this section. Each example offers high availability, meaning that if a particular node goes down, another node with the same configuration can take over the tasks so that service continues to be available.

Overview

The simplest architecture you can build upon for Compute has a single cloud controller and multiple compute nodes. The simplest architecture for Object Storage has five nodes: one for identifying users and proxying requests to the API, then four for storage itself to provide enough replication for eventual consistency. This example architecture does not dictate a particular number of nodes, but shows the thinking and considerations that went into choosing this architecture including the features offered.

Components

Component	Details
OpenStack release	Havana
Host operating system	Ubuntu 12.04 LTS or Red Hat Enterprise Linux 6.5, including derivatives such as CentOS and Scientific Linux
OpenStack package repository	Ubuntu Cloud Archive (*http://opsgui.de/NPHp7s*) or RDO (*http://opsgui.de/1eLCZcm*)*
Hypervisor	KVM
Database	MySQL*
Message queue	RabbitMQ for Ubuntu; Qpid for Red Hat Enterprise Linux and derivatives
Networking service	`nova-network`
Network manager	FlatDHCP
Single `nova-network` or multi-host?	multi-host*
Image Service (glance) backend	file
Identity Service (keystone) driver	SQL
Block Storage Service (cinder) backend	LVM/iSCSI
Live Migration backend	Shared storage using NFS*
Object storage	OpenStack Object Storage (swift)

An asterisk (*) indicates when the example architecture deviates from the settings of a default installation. We'll offer explanations for those deviations next.

The following features of OpenStack are supported by the example architecture documented in this guide, but are optional:

- Dashboard: You probably want to offer a dashboard, but your users may be more interested in API access only.
- Block storage: You don't have to offer users block storage if their use case only needs ephemeral storage on compute nodes, for example.
- Floating IP address: Floating IP addresses are public IP addresses that you allocate from a predefined pool to assign to virtual machines at launch. Floating IP address ensure that the public IP address is available whenever an instance is booted. Not every organization can offer thousands of public floating IP addresses for thousands of instances, so this feature is considered optional.
- Live migration: If you need to move running virtual machine instances from one host to another with little or no service interruption, you would enable live migration, but it is considered optional.
- Object storage: You may choose to store machine images on a file system rather than in object storage if you do not have the extra hardware for the required replication and redundancy that OpenStack Object Storage offers.

Rationale

This example architecture has been selected based on the current default feature set of OpenStack Havana, with an emphasis on stability. We believe that many clouds that currently run OpenStack in production have made similar choices.

You must first choose the operating system that runs on all of the physical nodes. While OpenStack is supported on several distributions of Linux, we used *Ubuntu 12.04 LTS (Long Term Support)*, which is used by the majority of the development community, has feature completeness compared with other distributions and has clear future support plans.

We recommend that you do not use the default Ubuntu OpenStack install packages and instead use the Ubuntu Cloud Archive (*http://opsgui.de/NPHp7s*). The Cloud Archive is a package repository supported by Canonical that allows you to upgrade to future OpenStack releases while remaining on Ubuntu 12.04.

KVM as a hypervisor complements the choice of Ubuntu—being a matched pair in terms of support, and also because of the significant degree of attention it garners from the OpenStack development community (including the authors, who mostly use KVM). It is also feature complete, free from licensing charges and restrictions.

MySQL follows a similar trend. Despite its recent change of ownership, this database is the most tested for use with OpenStack and is heavily documented. We deviate from the default database, *SQLite*, because SQLite is not an appropriate database for production usage.

The choice of *RabbitMQ* over other AMQP compatible options that are gaining support in OpenStack, such as ZeroMQ and Qpid, is due to its ease of use and significant testing in production. It also is the only option that supports features such as Compute cells. We recommend clustering with RabbitMQ, as it is an integral component of the system and fairly simple to implement due to its inbuilt nature.

As discussed in previous chapters, there are several options for networking in OpenStack Compute. We recommend *FlatDHCP* and to use *Multi-Host* networking mode for high availability, running one `nova-network` daemon per OpenStack compute host. This provides a robust mechanism for ensuring network interruptions are isolated to individual compute hosts, and allows for the direct use of hardware network gateways.

Live Migration is supported by way of shared storage, with *NFS* as the distributed file system.

Acknowledging that many small-scale deployments see running Object Storage just for the storage of virtual machine images as too costly, we opted for the file backend in the OpenStack Image Service (Glance). If your cloud will include Object Storage, you can easily add it as a backend.

We chose the *SQL backend for Identity Service (keystone)* over others, such as LDAP. This backend is simple to install and is robust. The authors acknowledge that many installations want to bind with existing directory services and caution careful understanding of the array of options available (*http://opsgui.de/1eLCZJr*).

Block Storage (cinder) is installed natively on external storage nodes and uses the *LVM/iSCSI plug-in*. Most Block Storage Service plug-ins are tied to particular vendor products and implementations limiting their use to consumers of those hardware platforms, but LVM/iSCSI is robust and stable on commodity hardware.

While the cloud can be run without the *OpenStack Dashboard*, we consider it to be indispensable, not just for user interaction with the cloud, but also as a tool for operators. Additionally, the dashboard's use of Django makes it a flexible framework for extension.

Why not use the OpenStack Network Service (neutron)?

This example architecture does not use the OpenStack Network Service (neutron), because it does not yet support multi-host networking and our organizations (university, government) have access to a large range of publicly-accessible IPv4 addresses.

Why use multi-host networking?

In a default OpenStack deployment, there is a single `nova-network` service that runs within the cloud (usually on the cloud controller) that provides services such as network address translation (NAT), DHCP, and DNS to the guest instances. If the single node that runs the `nova-network` service goes down, you cannot access your instances, and the instances cannot access the Internet. The single node that runs the `nova-network` service can become a bottleneck if excessive network traffic comes in and goes out of the cloud.

Multi-host (*http://opsgui.de/NPHqbu*) is a high-availability option for the network configuration, where the `nova-network` service is run on every compute node instead of running on only a single node.

Detailed Description

The reference architecture consists of multiple compute nodes, a cloud controller, an external NFS storage server for instance storage, and an OpenStack Block Storage server for volume storage. A network time service (Network Time Protocol, or NTP) synchronizes time on all the nodes. FlatDHCPManager in multi-host mode is used for the networking. A logical diagram for this example architecture shows which services are running on each node:

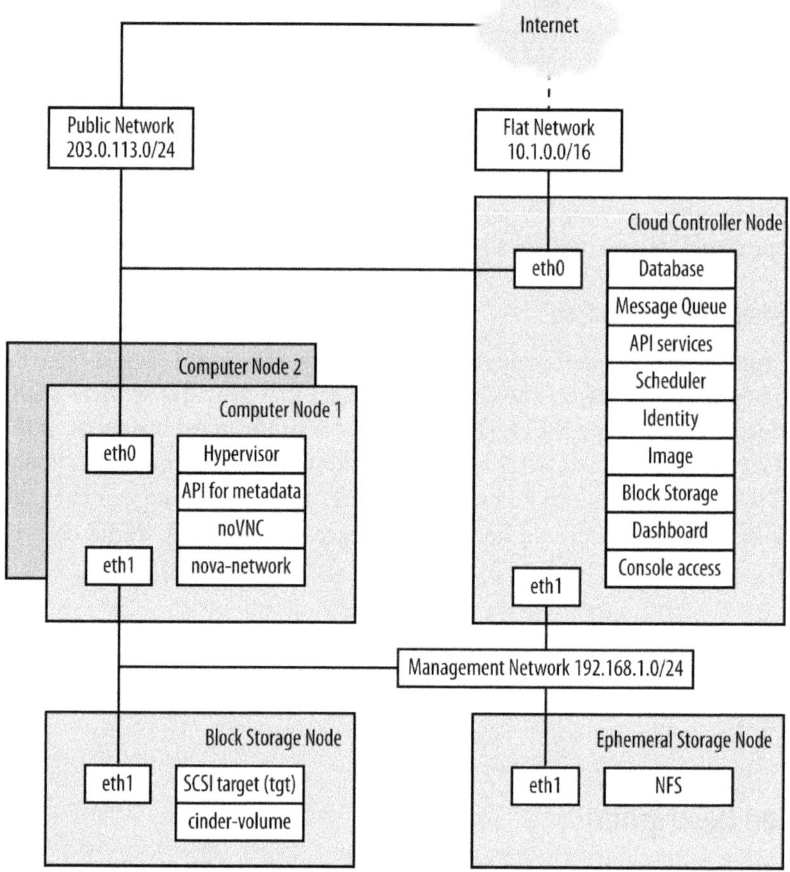

The cloud controller runs the dashboard, the API services, the database (MySQL), a message queue server (RabbitMQ), the scheduler for choosing compute resources (`nova-scheduler`), Identity services (keystone, `nova-consoleauth`), Image services (`glance-api`, `glance-registry`), services for console access of guests, and Block Storage services, including the scheduler for storage resources (`cinder-api` and `cinder-scheduler`).

Compute nodes are where the computing resources are held, and in our example architecture, they run the hypervisor (KVM), libvirt (the driver for the hypervisor, which enables live migration from node to node), `nova-compute`, `nova-api-metadata` (generally only used when running in multi-host mode, it retrieves instance-specific metadata), `nova-vncproxy`, and `nova-network`.

The network consists of two switches, one for the management or private traffic, and one that covers public access, including floating IPs. To support this, the cloud controller and the compute nodes have two network cards. The OpenStack Block Storage and NFS storage servers only need to access the private network and therefore only need one network card, but multiple cards run in a bonded configuration are recommended if possible. Floating IP access is direct to the Internet, whereas Flat IP access goes through a NAT. To envision the network traffic, use this diagram:

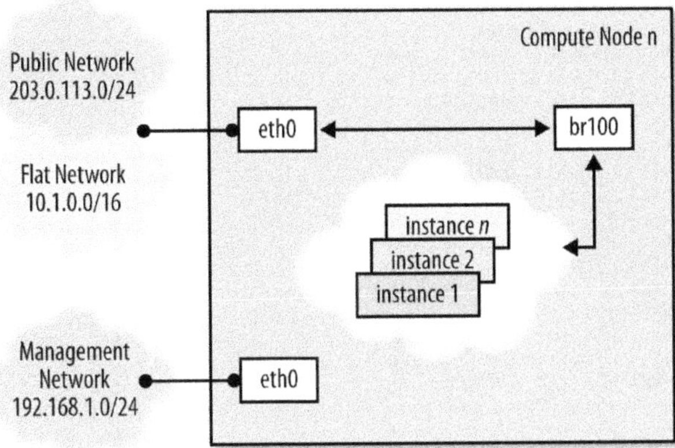

Optional Extensions

You can extend this reference architecture as follows:

- Add additional cloud controllers (see Chapter 11).
- Add an OpenStack Storage service (see the Object Storage chapter in the *OpenStack Installation Guide* for your distribution).
- Add additional OpenStack Block Storage hosts (see Chapter 11).

Example Architecture—OpenStack Networking

This chapter provides an example architecture using OpenStack Networking, also known as the Neutron project, in a highly available environment.

Overview

A highly-available environment can be put into place if you require an environment that can scale horizontally, or want your cloud to continue to be operational in case of node failure. This example architecture has been written based on the current default feature set of OpenStack Havana, with an emphasis on high availability.

Components

Component	Details
OpenStack release	Havana
Host operating system	Red Hat Enterprise Linux 6.5
OpenStack package repository	Red Hat Distributed OpenStack (RDO) (*http://opsgui.de/1eLCXBh*)
Hypervisor	KVM
Database	MySQL
Message queue	Qpid
Networking service	OpenStack Networking
Tenant Network Separation	VLAN
Image Service (glance) backend	GlusterFS
Identity Service (keystone) driver	SQL
Block Storage Service (cinder) backend	GlusterFS

Rationale

This example architecture has been selected based on the current default feature set of OpenStack Havana, with an emphasis on high availability. This architecture is currently being deployed in an internal Red Hat OpenStack cloud and used to run hosted and shared services, which by their nature must be highly available.

This architecture's components have been selected for the following reasons:

Red Hat Enterprise Linux
: You must choose an operating system that can run on all of the physical nodes. This example architecture is based on Red Hat Enterprise Linux, which offers reliability, long-term support, certified testing, and is hardened. Enterprise customers, now moving into OpenStack usage, typically require these advantages.

RDO
: The Red Hat Distributed OpenStack package offers an easy way to download the most current OpenStack release that is built for the Red Hat Enterprise Linux platform.

KVM
: KVM is the supported hypervisor of choice for Red Hat Enterprise Linux (and included in distribution). It is feature complete and free from licensing charges and restrictions.

MySQL
: MySQL is used as the database backend for all databases in the OpenStack environment. MySQL is the supported database of choice for Red Hat Enterprise Linux (and included in distribution); the database is open source, scalable, and handles memory well.

Qpid
: Apache Qpid offers 100 percent compatibility with the Advanced Message Queuing Protocol Standard, and its broker is available for both C++ and Java.

OpenStack Networking
: OpenStack Networking offers sophisticated networking functionality, including Layer 2 (L2) network segregation and provider networks.

VLAN
: Using a virtual local area network offers broadcast control, security, and physical layer transparency. If needed, use VXLAN to extend your address space.

GlusterFS
: GlusterFS offers scalable storage. As your environment grows, you can continue to add more storage nodes (instead of being restricted, for example, by an expensive storage array).

Detailed Description

Node types

This section gives you a breakdown of the different nodes that make up the OpenStack environment. A node is a physical machine that is provisioned with an operating system, and running a defined software stack on top of it. Table 1-1 provides node descriptions and specifications.

Table 1-1. Node types

Type	Description	Example hardware
Controller	Controller nodes are responsible for running the management software services needed for the OpenStack environment to function. These nodes: • Provide the front door that people access as well as the API services that all other components in the environment talk to. • Run a number of services in a highly available fashion, utilizing Pacemaker and HAProxy to provide a virtual IP and load-balancing functions so all controller nodes are being used. • Supply highly available "infrastructure" services, such as MySQL and Qpid, that underpin all the services. • Provide what is known as "persistent storage" through services run on the host as well. This persistent storage is backed onto the storage nodes for reliability. See Figure 1-3.	Model: Dell R620 CPU: 2 x Intel® Xeon® CPU E5-2620 0 @ 2.00 GHz Memory: 32 GB Disk: 2 x 300 GB 10000 RPM SAS Disks Network: 2 x 10G network ports
Compute	Compute nodes run the virtual machine instances in OpenStack. They: • Run the bare minimum of services needed to facilitate these instances. • Use local storage on the node for the virtual machines so that no VM migration or instance recovery at node failure is possible. See Figure 1-4.	Model: Dell R620 CPU: 2x Intel® Xeon® CPU E5-2650 0 @ 2.00 GHz Memory: 128 GB Disk: 2 x 600 GB 10000 RPM SAS Disks Network: 4 x 10G network ports (For future proofing expansion)
Storage	Storage nodes store all the data required for the environment, including disk images in the Image Service library, and the persistent storage volumes created by the Block Storage service. Storage nodes use GlusterFS technology to keep the data highly available and scalable. See Figure 1-6.	Model: Dell R720xd CPU: 2 x Intel® Xeon® CPU E5-2620 0 @ 2.00 GHz Memory: 64 GB Disk: 2 x 500 GB 7200 RPM SAS Disks + 24 x 600 GB 10000 RPM SAS Disks Raid Controller: PERC H710P Integrated RAID Controller, 1 GB NV Cache Network: 2 x 10G network ports

Type	Description	Example hardware
Network	Network nodes are responsible for doing all the virtual networking needed for people to create public or private networks and uplink their virtual machines into external networks. Network nodes: • Form the only ingress and egress point for instances running on top of OpenStack. • Run all of the environment's networking services, with the exception of the networking API service (which runs on the controller node). See Figure 1-5.	Model: Dell R620 CPU: 1 x Intel® Xeon® CPU E5-2620 0 @ 2.00 GHz Memory: 32 GB Disk: 2 x 300 GB 10000 RPM SAS Disks Network: 5 x 10G network ports
Utility	Utility nodes are used by internal administration staff only to provide a number of basic system administration functions needed to get the environment up and running and to maintain the hardware, OS, and software on which it runs. These nodes run services such as provisioning, configuration management, monitoring, or GlusterFS management software. They are not required to scale, although these machines are usually backed up.	Model: Dell R620 CPU: 2x Intel® Xeon® CPU E5-2620 0 @ 2.00 GHz Memory: 32 GB Disk: 2 x 500 GB 7200 RPM SAS Disks Network: 2 x 10G network ports

Networking layout

The network contains all the management devices for all hardware in the environment (for example, by including Dell iDrac7 devices for the hardware nodes, and management interfaces for network switches). The network is accessed by internal staff only when diagnosing or recovering a hardware issue.

OpenStack internal network. This network is used for OpenStack management functions and traffic, including services needed for the provisioning of physical nodes (`pxe`, `tftp`, `kickstart`), traffic between various OpenStack node types using OpenStack APIs and messages (for example, `nova-compute` talking to `keystone` or `cinder-volume` talking to `nova-api`), and all traffic for storage data to the storage layer underneath by the Gluster protocol. All physical nodes have at least one network interface (typically `eth0`) in this network. This network is only accessible from other VLANs on port 22 (for `ssh` access to manage machines).

Public Network. This network is a combination of:

- IP addresses for public-facing interfaces on the controller nodes (which end users will access the OpenStack services)
- A range of publicly routable, IPv4 network addresses to be used by OpenStack Networking for floating IPs. You may be restricted in your access to IPv4 addresses; a large range of IPv4 addresses is not necessary.
- Routers for private networks created within OpenStack.

This network is connected to the controller nodes so users can access the OpenStack interfaces, and connected to the network nodes to provide VMs with publicly routable traffic functionality. The network is also connected to the utility machines so that any utility services that need to be made public (such as system monitoring) can be accessed.

VM traffic network. This is a closed network that is not publicly routable and is simply used as a private, internal network for traffic between virtual machines in OpenStack, and between the virtual machines and the network nodes that provide l3 routes out to the public network (and floating IPs for connections back in to the VMs). Because this is a closed network, we are using a different address space to the others to clearly define the separation. Only Compute and OpenStack Networking nodes need to be connected to this network.

Node connectivity

The following section details how the nodes are connected to the different networks (see "Networking layout") and what other considerations need to take place (for example, bonding) when connecting nodes to the networks.

Initial deployment. Initially, the connection setup should revolve around keeping the connectivity simple and straightforward in order to minimize deployment complexity and time to deploy. The deployment shown in Figure 1-1 aims to have 1 x 10G connectivity available to all compute nodes, while still leveraging bonding on appropriate nodes for maximum performance.

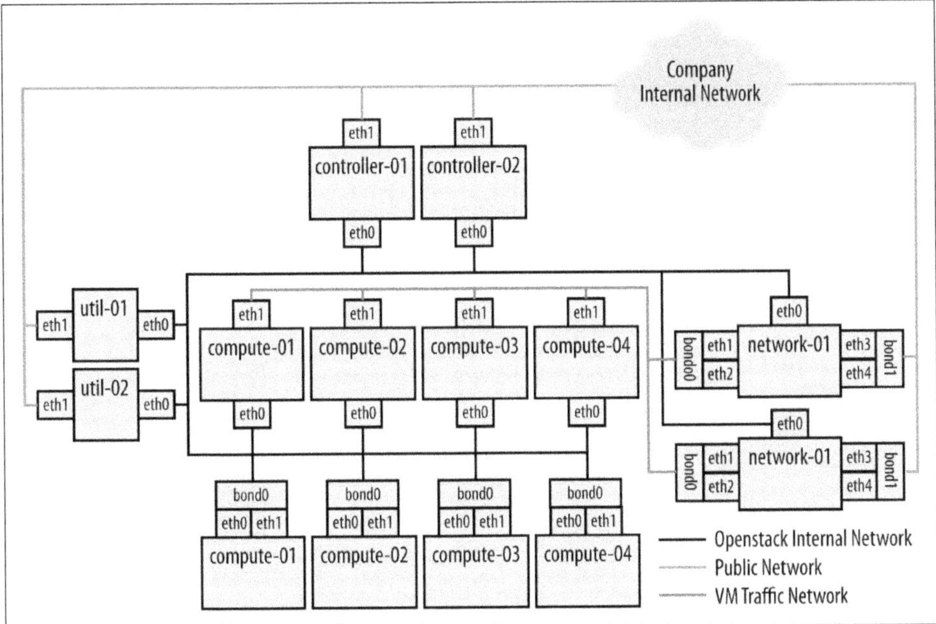

Figure 1-1. Basic node deployment

Connectivity for maximum performance. If the networking performance of the basic layout is not enough, you can move to Figure 1-2, which provides 2 x 10G network links to all instances in the environment as well as providing more network bandwidth to the storage layer.

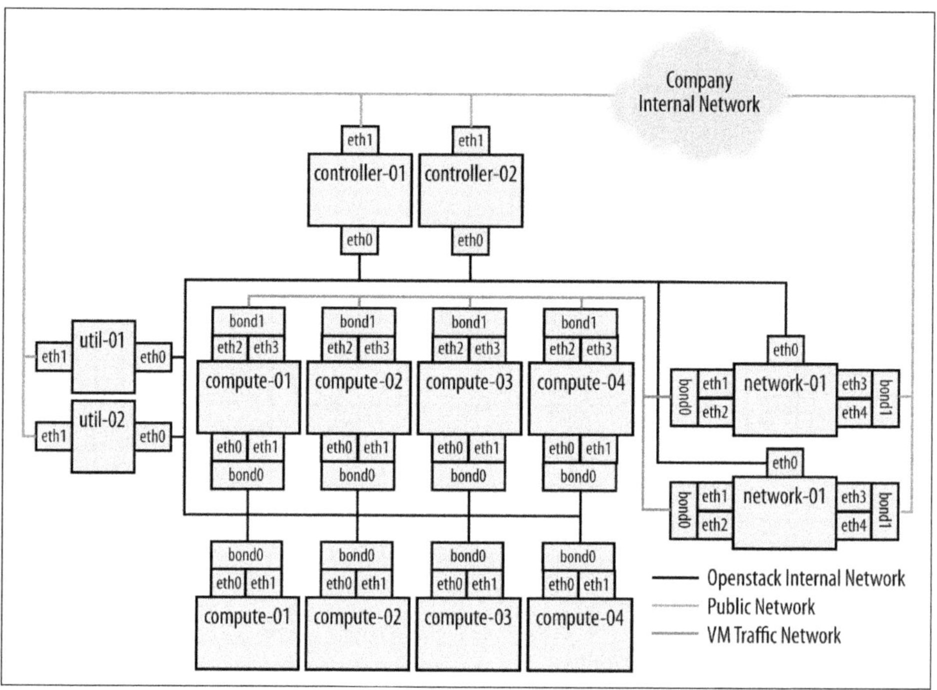

Figure 1-2. Performance node deployment

Node diagrams

The following diagrams (Figure 1-3 through Figure 1-6) include logical information about the different types of nodes, indicating what services will be running on top of them and how they interact with each other. The diagrams also illustrate how the availability and scalability of services are achieved.

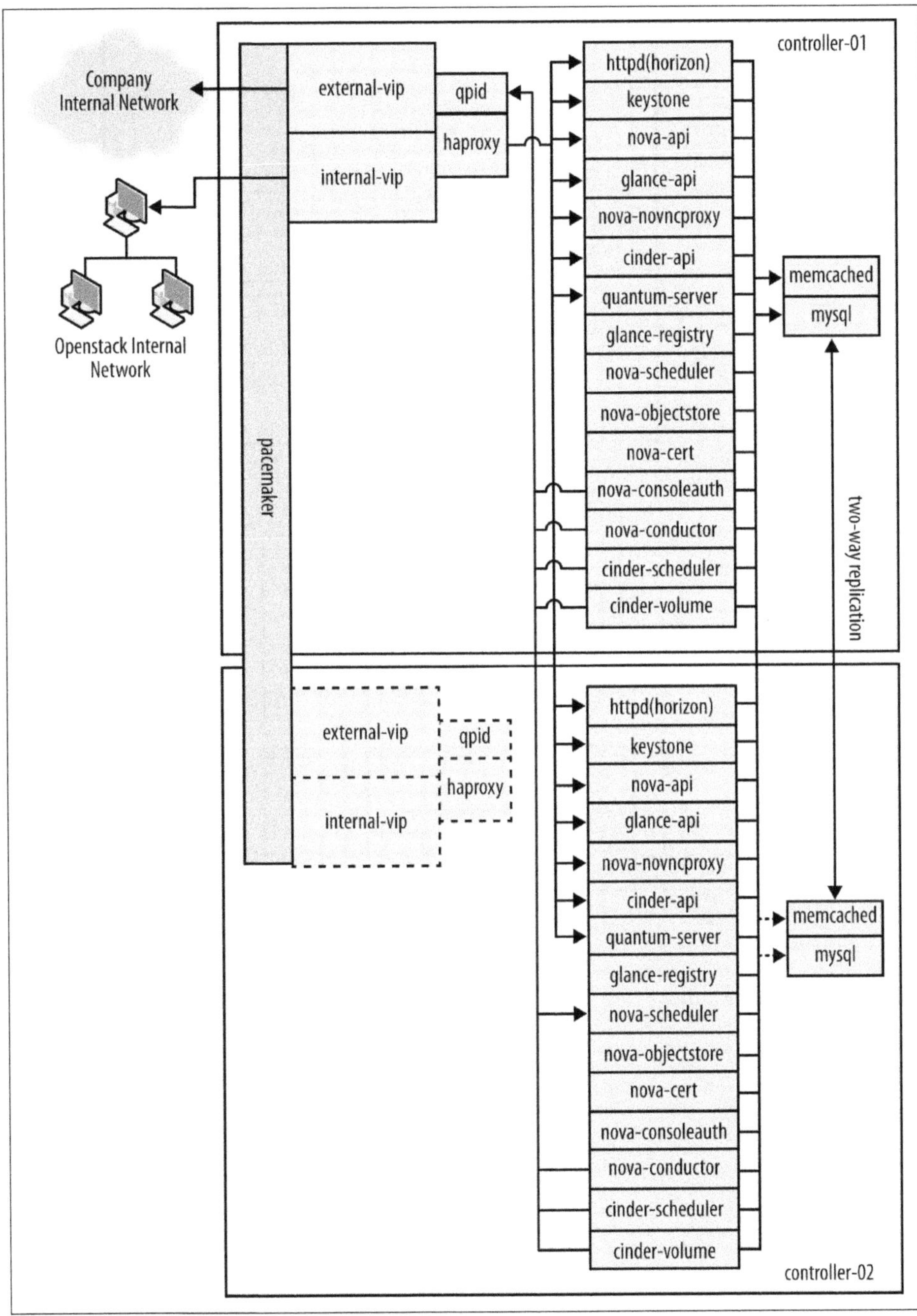

Figure 1-3. Controller node

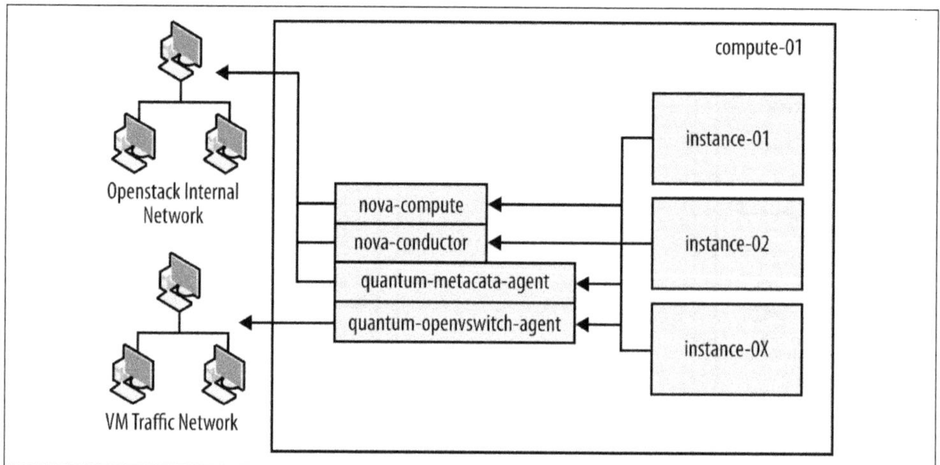

Figure 1-4. Compute node

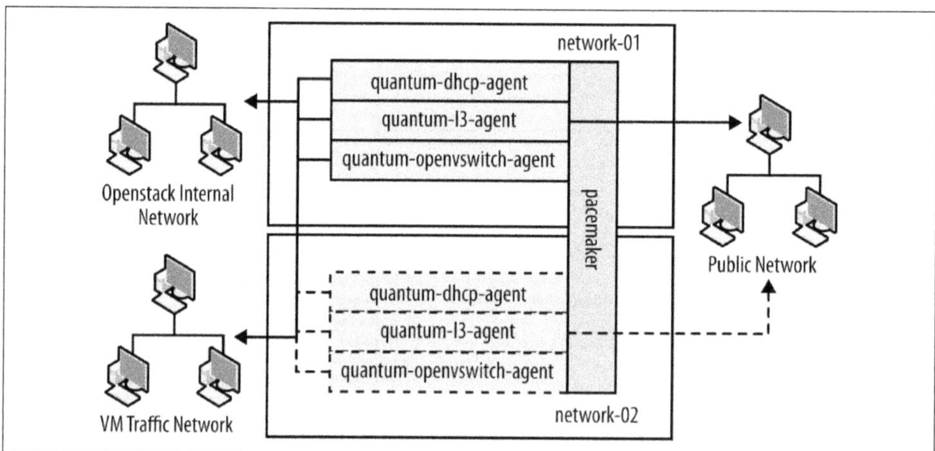

Figure 1-5. Network node

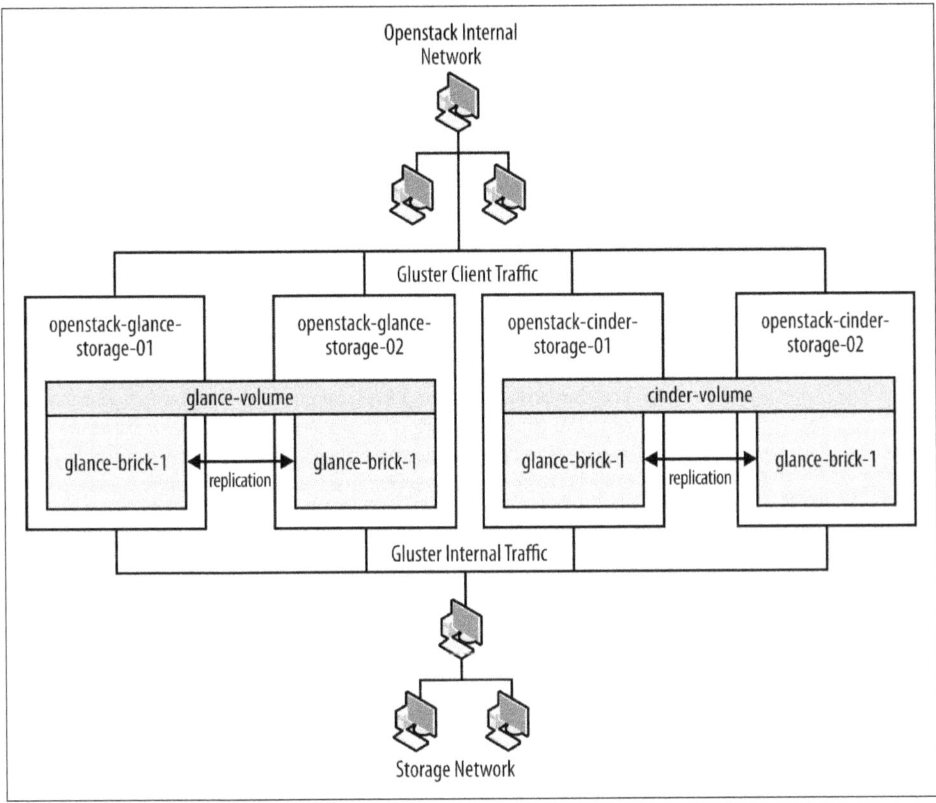

Figure 1-6. Storage node

Example Component Configuration

Table 1-2 and Table 1-3 include example configuration and considerations for both third-party and OpenStack components:

Table 1-2. Third-party component configuration

Component	Tuning	Availability	Scalability
MySQL	`binlog-format = row`	Master/master replication. However, both nodes are not used at the same time. Replication keeps all nodes as close to being up to date as possible (although the asynchronous nature of the replication means a fully consistent state is not possible). Connections to the database only happen through a Pacemaker virtual IP, ensuring that most problems that occur with master-master replication can be avoided.	Not heavily considered. Once load on the MySQL server increases enough that scalability needs to be considered, multiple masters or a master/slave setup can be used.

Component	Tuning	Availability	Scalability
Qpid	`max-connections=1000` `worker-threads=20` `connection-backlog=10`, sasl security enabled with SASL-BASIC authentication	Qpid is added as a resource to the Pacemaker software that runs on Controller nodes where Qpid is situated. This ensures only one Qpid instance is running at one time, and the node with the Pacemaker virtual IP will always be the node running Qpid.	Not heavily considered. However, Qpid can be changed to run on all controller nodes for scalability and availability purposes, and removed from Pacemaker.
HAProxy	`maxconn 3000`	HAProxy is a software layer-7 load balancer used to front door all clustered OpenStack API components and do SSL termination. HAProxy can be added as a resource to the Pacemaker software that runs on the Controller nodes where HAProxy is situated. This ensures that only one HAProxy instance is running at one time, and the node with the Pacemaker virtual IP will always be the node running HAProxy.	Not considered. HAProxy has small enough performance overheads that a single instance should scale enough for this level of workload. If extra scalability is needed, `keepalived` or other Layer-4 load balancing can be introduced to be placed in front of multiple copies of HAProxy.
Memcached	`MAXCONN="8192"` `CACHE SIZE="30457"`	Memcached is a fast in-memory key-value cache software that is used by OpenStack components for caching data and increasing performance. Memcached runs on all controller nodes, ensuring that should one go down, another instance of Memcached is available.	Not considered. A single instance of Memcached should be able to scale to the desired workloads. If scalability is desired, HAProxy can be placed in front of Memcached (in raw `tcp` mode) to utilize multiple Memcached instances for scalability. However, this might cause cache consistency issues.

Component	Tuning	Availability	Scalability
Pacemaker	Configured to use `corosync` and `cman` as a cluster communication stack/ quorum manager, and as a two-node cluster.	Pacemaker is the clustering software used to ensure the availability of services running on the controller and network nodes: • Because Pacemaker is cluster software, the software itself handles its own availability, leveraging `corosync` and `cman` underneath. • If you use the GlusterFS native client, no virtual IP is needed, since the client knows all about nodes after initial connection and automatically routes around failures on the client side. • If you use the NFS or SMB adaptor, you will need a virtual IP on which to mount the GlusterFS volumes.	If more nodes need to be made cluster aware, Pacemaker can scale to 64 nodes.
GlusterFS	`glusterfs` performance profile "virt" enabled on all volumes. Volumes are setup in two-node replication.	Glusterfs is a clustered file system that is run on the storage nodes to provide persistent scalable data storage in the environment. Because all connections to gluster use the `gluster` native mount points, the `gluster` instances themselves provide availability and failover functionality.	The scalability of GlusterFS storage can be achieved by adding in more storage volumes.

Table 1-3. OpenStack component configuration

Component	Node type	Tuning	Availability	Scalability
Dashboard (horizon)	Controller	Configured to use Memcached as a session store, `neutron` support is enabled, `can_set_mount_point = False`	The dashboard is run on all controller nodes, ensuring at least once instance will be available in case of node failure. It also sits behind HAProxy, which detects when the software fails and routes requests around the failing instance.	The dashboard is run on all controller nodes, so scalability can be achieved with additional controller nodes. HAProxy allows scalability for the dashboard as more nodes are added.
Identity (keystone)	Controller	Configured to use Memcached for caching and PKI for tokens.	Identity is run on all controller nodes, ensuring at least once instance will be available in case of node failure. Identity also sits behind HAProxy, which detects when the software fails and routes requests around the failing instance.	Identity is run on all controller nodes, so scalability can be achieved with additional controller nodes. HAProxy allows scalability for Identity as more nodes are added.

Component	Node type	Tuning	Availability	Scalability
Image Service (glance)	Controller	`/var/lib/glance/images` is a GlusterFS native mount to a Gluster volume off the storage layer.	The Image Service is run on all controller nodes, ensuring at least once instance will be available in case of node failure. It also sits behind HAProxy, which detects when the software fails and routes requests around the failing instance.	The Image Service is run on all controller nodes, so scalability can be achieved with additional controller nodes. HAProxy allows scalability for the Image Service as more nodes are added.
Compute (nova)	Controller, Compute	Configured to use Qpid, `qpid_heartbeat = 10`, configured to use Memcached for caching, configured to use `libvirt`, configured to use `neutron`. Configured `nova-consoleauth` to use Memcached for session management (so that it can have multiple copies and run in a load balancer).	The nova API, scheduler, objectstore, cert, consoleauth, conductor, and vncproxy services are run on all controller nodes, ensuring at least once instance will be available in case of node failure. Compute is also behind HAProxy, which detects when the software fails and routes requests around the failing instance. Compute's compute and conductor services, which run on the compute nodes, are only needed to run services on that node, so availability of those services is coupled tightly to the nodes that are available. As long as a compute node is up, it will have the needed services running on top of it.	The nova API, scheduler, objectstore, cert, consoleauth, conductor, and vncproxy services are run on all controller nodes, so scalability can be achieved with additional controller nodes. HAProxy allows scalability for Compute as more nodes are added. The scalability of services running on the compute nodes (compute, conductor) is achieved linearly by adding in more compute nodes.
Block Storage (cinder)	Controller	Configured to use Qpid, `qpid_heartbeat = 10`, configured to use a Gluster volume from the storage layer as the backend for Block Storage, using the Gluster native client.	Block Storage API, scheduler, and volume services are run on all controller nodes, ensuring at least once instance will be available in case of node failure. Block Storage also sits behind HAProxy, which detects if the software fails and routes requests around the failing instance.	Block Storage API, scheduler and volume services are run on all controller nodes, so scalability can be achieved with additional controller nodes. HAProxy allows scalability for Block Storage as more nodes are added.

Component	Node type	Tuning	Availability	Scalability
OpenStack Networking (neutron)	Controller, Compute, Network	Configured to use QPID, `qpid_heartbeat = 10`, kernel namespace support enabled, `tenant_network_type = vlan`, `allow_overlapping_ips = true`, `tenant_network_type = vlan`, `bridge_uplinks = br-ex:em2`, `bridge_mappings = physnet1:br-ex`	The OpenStack Networking service is run on all controller nodes, ensuring at least one instance will be available in case of node failure. It also sits behind HAProxy, which detects if the software fails and routes requests around the failing instance. OpenStack Networking's `ovs-agent`, `l3-agent-dhcp-agent`, and `metadata-agent` services run on the network nodes, as `lsb` resources inside of Pacemaker. This means that in the case of network node failure, services are kept running on another node. Finally, the `ovs-agent` service is also run on all compute nodes, and in case of compute node failure, the other nodes will continue to function using the copy of the service running on them.	The OpenStack Networking server service is run on all controller nodes, so scalability can be achieved with additional controller nodes. HAProxy allows scalability for OpenStack Networking as more nodes are added. Scalability of services running on the network nodes is not currently supported by OpenStack Networking, so they are not be considered. One copy of the services should be sufficient to handle the workload. Scalability of the `ovs-agent` running on compute nodes is achieved by adding in more compute nodes as necessary.

Parting Thoughts on Architectures

With so many considerations and options available, our hope is to provide a few clearly-marked and tested paths for your OpenStack exploration. If you're looking for additional ideas, check out Appendix A, the OpenStack Installation Guides (*http://opsgui.de/NPFTC8*), or the OpenStack User Stories page (*http://opsgui.de/1eLAAhX*).

CHAPTER 2

Provisioning and Deployment

A critical part of a cloud's scalability is the amount of effort that it takes to run your cloud. To minimize the operational cost of running your cloud, set up and use an automated deployment and configuration infrastructure with a configuration management system, such as Puppet or Chef. Combined, these systems greatly reduce manual effort and the chance for operator error.

This infrastructure includes systems to automatically install the operating system's initial configuration and later coordinate the configuration of all services automatically and centrally, which reduces both manual effort and the chance for error. Examples include Ansible, Chef, Puppet, and Salt. You can even use OpenStack to deploy OpenStack, fondly named TripleO, for OpenStack On OpenStack.

Automated Deployment

An automated deployment system installs and configures operating systems on new servers, without intervention, after the absolute minimum amount of manual work, including physical racking, MAC-to-IP assignment, and power configuration. Typically, solutions rely on wrappers around PXE boot and TFTP servers for the basic operating system install and then hand off to an automated configuration management system.

Both Ubuntu and Red Hat Linux include mechanisms for configuring the operating system, including preseed and kickstart, that you can use after a network boot. Typically, these are used to bootstrap an automated configuration system. Alternatively, you can use an image-based approach for deploying the operating system, such as systemimager. You can use both approaches with a virtualized infrastructure, such as when you run VMs to separate your control services and physical infrastructure.

When you create a deployment plan, focus on a few vital areas because they are very hard to modify post deployment. The next two sections talk about configurations for:

- Disk partioning and disk array setup for scalability
- Networking configuration just for PXE booting

Disk Partitioning and RAID

At the very base of any operating system are the hard drives on which the operating system (OS) is installed.

You must complete the following configurations on the server's hard drives:

- Partitioning, which provides greater flexibility for layout of operating system and swap space, as described below.
- Adding to a RAID array (RAID stands for redundant array of independent disks), based on the number of disks you have available, so that you can add capacity as your cloud grows. Some options are described in more detail below.

The simplest option to get started is to use one hard drive with two partitions:

- File system to store files and directories, where all the data lives, including the root partition that starts and runs the system
- Swap space to free up memory for processes, as an independent area of the physical disk used only for swapping and nothing else

RAID is not used in this simplistic one-drive setup because generally for production clouds, you want to ensure that if one disk fails, another can take its place. Instead, for production, use more than one disk. The number of disks determine what types of RAID arrays to build.

We recommend that you choose one of the following multiple disk options:

Option 1

Partition all drives in the same way in a horizontal fashion, as shown in Figure 2-1.

With this option, you can assign different partitions to different RAID arrays. You can allocate partition 1 of disk one and two to the `/boot` partition mirror. You can make partition 2 of all disks the root partition mirror. You can use partition 3 of all disks for a `cinder-volumes` LVM partition running on a RAID 10 array.

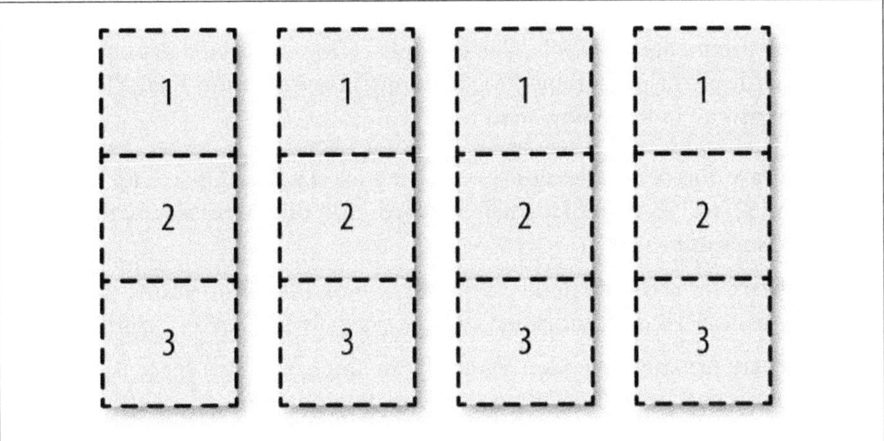

Figure 2-1. Partition setup of drives

While you might end up with unused partitions, such as partition 1 in disk three and four of this example, this option allows for maximum utilization of disk space. I/O performance might be an issue as a result of all disks being used for all tasks.

Option 2
: Add all raw disks to one large RAID array, either hardware or software based. You can partition this large array with the boot, root, swap, and LVM areas. This option is simple to implement and uses all partitions. However, disk I/O might suffer.

Option 3
: Dedicate entire disks to certain partitions. For example, you could allocate disk one and two entirely to the boot, root, and swap partitions under a RAID 1 mirror. Then, allocate disk three and four entirely to the LVM partition, also under a RAID 1 mirror. Disk I/O should be better because I/O is focused on dedicated tasks. However, the LVM partition is much smaller.

You may find that you can automate the partitioning itself. For example, MIT uses Fully Automatic Installation (FAI) (*http://fai-project.org/*) to do the initial PXE-based partition and then install using a combination of min/max and percentage-based partitioning.

As with most architecture choices, the right answer depends on your environment. If you are using existing hardware, you know the disk density of your servers and can determine some decisions based on the options above. If you are going through a procurement process, your user's requirements also help you determine hardware purchases. Here are some examples from a private cloud providing web developers custom environments at AT&T. This example is from a specific deployment, so your existing hardware or procurement opportunity may vary from this. AT&T uses three types of hardware in its deployment:

- Hardware for controller nodes, used for all stateless OpenStack API services. About 32–64 GB memory, small attached disk, one processor, varied number of cores, such as 6–12.
- Hardware for compute nodes. Typically 256 or 144 GB memory, two processors, 24 cores. 4–6 TB direct attached storage, typically in a RAID 5 configuration.
- Hardware for storage nodes. Typically for these, the disk space is optimized for the lowest cost per GB of storage while maintaining rack-space efficiency.

Again, the right answer depends on your environment. You have to make your decision based on the trade-offs between space utilization, simplicity, and I/O performance.

Network Configuration

Network configuration is a very large topic that spans multiple areas of this book. For now, make sure that your servers can PXE boot and successfully communicate with the deployment server.

For example, you usually cannot configure NICs for VLANs when PXE booting. Additionally, you usually cannot PXE boot with bonded NICs. If you run into this scenario, consider using a simple 1 GB switch in a private network on which only your cloud communicates.

Automated Configuration

The purpose of automatic configuration management is to establish and maintain the consistency of a system without using human intervention. You want to maintain consistency in your deployments so that you can have the same cloud every time, repeatably. Proper use of automatic configuration-management tools ensures that components of the cloud systems are in particular states, in addition to simplifying deployment, and configuration change propagation.

These tools also make it possible to test and roll back changes, as they are fully repeatable. Conveniently, a large body of work has been done by the OpenStack community in this space. Puppet, a configuration management tool, even provides official modules for OpenStack in an OpenStack infrastructure system known as Stackforge (*http://opsgui.de/NPFUpL*). Chef configuration management is provided within *https://github.com/stackforge/openstack-chef-repo*. Additional configuration management systems include Juju, Ansible, and Salt. Also, PackStack is a command-line utility for Red Hat Enterprise Linux and derivatives that uses Puppet modules to support rapid deployment of OpenStack on existing servers over an SSH connection.

An integral part of a configuration-management system is the items that it controls. You should carefully consider all of the items that you want, or do not want, to be automatically managed. For example, you may not want to automatically format hard drives with user data.

Remote Management

In our experience, most operators don't sit right next to the servers running the cloud, and many don't necessarily enjoy visiting the data center. OpenStack should be entirely remotely configurable, but sometimes not everything goes according to plan.

In this instance, having an out-of-band access into nodes running OpenStack components is a boon. The IPMI protocol is the de facto standard here, and acquiring hardware that supports it is highly recommended to achieve that lights-out data center aim.

In addition, consider remote power control as well. While IPMI usually controls the server's power state, having remote access to the PDU that the server is plugged into can really be useful for situations when everything seems wedged.

Parting Thoughts for Provisioning and Deploying OpenStack

You can save time by understanding the use cases for the cloud you want to create. Use cases for OpenStack are varied. Some include object storage only; others require preconfigured compute resources to speed development-environment set up; and others need fast provisioning of compute resources that are already secured per tenant with private networks. Your users may have need for highly redundant servers to make sure their legacy applications continue to run. Perhaps a goal would be to architect these legacy applications so that they run on multiple instances in a cloudy, fault-tolerant way, but not make it a goal to add to those clusters over time. Your users may indicate that they need scaling considerations because of heavy Windows server use.

You can save resources by looking at the best fit for the hardware you have in place already. You might have some high-density storage hardware available. You could format and repurpose those servers for OpenStack Object Storage. All of these considerations and input from users help you build your use case and your deployment plan.

For further research about OpenStack deployment, investigate the supported and documented preconfigured, prepackaged installers for OpenStack from companies such as Canonical (*http://opsgui.de/NPFSy7*), Cisco (*http://opsgui.de/1gwRmlS*), Cloudscaling (*http://opsgui.de/1eLAFSL*), IBM (*http://opsgui.de/NPFYG3*), Metacloud (*http://opsgui.de/1eLAGWE*), Mirantis (*http://opsgui.de/NPFWOy*), Piston (*http://opsgui.de/1eLAHKd*), Rackspace (*http://opsgui.de/1gwRm58*), Red Hat (*http://opsgui.de/NPFXlq*), SUSE (*http://opsgui.de/1eLALK5*), and SwiftStack (*http://opsgui.de/NPG0hb*).

Conclusion

The decisions you make with respect to provisioning and deployment will affect your day-to-day, week-to-week, and month-to-month maintenance of the cloud. Your configuration management will be able to evolve over time. However, more thought and design need to be done for upfront choices about deployment, disk partitioning, and network configuration.

CHAPTER 3

Designing for Cloud Controllers and Cloud Management

OpenStack is designed to be massively horizontally scalable, which allows all services to be distributed widely. However, to simplify this guide, we have decided to discuss services of a more central nature, using the concept of a *cloud controller*. A cloud controller is just a conceptual simplification. In the real world, you design an architecture for your cloud controller that enables high availability so that if any node fails, another can take over the required tasks. In reality, cloud controller tasks are spread out across more than a single node.

The cloud controller provides the central management system for OpenStack deployments. Typically, the cloud controller manages authentication and sends messaging to all the systems through a message queue.

For many deployments, the cloud controller is a single node. However, to have high availability, you have to take a few considerations into account, which we'll cover in this chapter.

The cloud controller manages the following services for the cloud:

Databases
: Tracks current information about users and instances, for example, in a database, typically one database instance managed per service

Message queue services
: All AMQP—Advanced Message Queue Protocol—messages for services are received and sent according to the queue broker

Conductor services
: Proxy requests to a database

Authentication and authorization for identity management
: Indicates which users can do what actions on certain cloud resources; quota management is spread out among services, however

Image-management services
: Stores and serves images with metadata on each, for launching in the cloud

Scheduling services
: Indicates which resources to use first; for example, spreading out where instances are launched based on an algorithm

User dashboard
: Provides a web-based frontend for users to consume OpenStack cloud services

API endpoints
: Offers each service's REST API access, where the API endpoint catalog is managed by the Identity Service

For our example, the cloud controller has a collection of `nova-*` components that represent the global state of the cloud; talks to services such as authentication; maintains information about the cloud in a database; communicates to all compute nodes and storage workers through a queue; and provides API access. Each service running on a designated cloud controller may be broken out into separate nodes for scalability or availability.

As another example, you could use pairs of servers for a collective cloud controller—one active, one standby—for redundant nodes providing a given set of related services, such as:

- Frontend web for API requests, the scheduler for choosing which compute node to boot an instance on, Identity services, and the dashboard
- Database and message queue server (such as MySQL, RabbitMQ)
- Image Service for the image management

Now that you see the myriad designs for controlling your cloud, read more about the further considerations to help with your design decisions.

Hardware Considerations

A cloud controller's hardware can be the same as a compute node, though you may want to further specify based on the size and type of cloud that you run.

It's also possible to use virtual machines for all or some of the services that the cloud controller manages, such as the message queuing. In this guide, we assume that all services are running directly on the cloud controller.

Table 3-1 contains common considerations to review when sizing hardware for the cloud controller design.

Table 3-1. Cloud controller hardware sizing considerations

Consideration	Ramification
How many instances will run at once?	Size your database server accordingly, and scale out beyond one cloud controller if many instances will report status at the same time and scheduling where a new instance starts up needs computing power.
How many compute nodes will run at once?	Ensure that your messaging queue handles requests successfully and size accordingly.
How many users will access the API?	If many users will make multiple requests, make sure that the CPU load for the cloud controller can handle it.
How many users will access the dashboard versus the REST API directly?	The dashboard makes many requests, even more than the API access, so add even more CPU if your dashboard is the main interface for your users.
How many `nova-api` services do you run at once for your cloud?	You need to size the controller with a core per service.
How long does a single instance run?	Starting instances and deleting instances is demanding on the compute node but also demanding on the controller node because of all the API queries and scheduling needs.
Does your authentication system also verify externally?	External systems such as LDAP or Active Directory require network connectivity between the cloud controller and an external authentication system. Also ensure that the cloud controller has the CPU power to keep up with requests.

Separation of Services

While our example contains all central services in a single location, it is possible and indeed often a good idea to separate services onto different physical servers. Table 3-2 is a list of deployment scenarios we've seen and their justifications.

Table 3-2. Deployment scenarios

Scenario	Justification
Run `glance-*` servers on the `swift-proxy` server.	This deployment felt that the spare I/O on the Object Storage proxy server was sufficient and that the Image Delivery portion of glance benefited from being on physical hardware and having good connectivity to the Object Storage backend it was using.

Scenario	Justification
Run a central dedicated database server.	This deployment used a central dedicated server to provide the databases for all services. This approach simplified operations by isolating database server updates and allowed for the simple creation of slave database servers for failover.
Run one VM per service.	This deployment ran central services on a set of servers running KVM. A dedicated VM was created for each service (`nova-scheduler`, rabbitmq, database, etc). This assisted the deployment with scaling because administrators could tune the resources given to each virtual machine based on the load it received (something that was not well understood during installation).
Use an external load balancer.	This deployment had an expensive hardware load balancer in its organization. It ran multiple `nova-api` and `swift-proxy` servers on different physical servers and used the load balancer to switch between them.

One choice that always comes up is whether to virtualize. Some services, such as `nova-compute`, `swift-proxy` and `swift-object` servers, should not be virtualized. However, control servers can often be happily virtualized—the performance penalty can usually be offset by simply running more of the service.

Database

OpenStack Compute uses a SQL database to store and retrieve stateful information. MySQL is the popular database choice in the OpenStack community.

Loss of the database leads to errors. As a result, we recommend that you cluster your database to make it failure tolerant. Configuring and maintaining a database cluster is done outside OpenStack and is determined by the database software you choose to use in your cloud environment. MySQL/Galera is a popular option for MySQL-based databases.

Message Queue

Most OpenStack services communicate with each other using the *message queue*. For example, Compute communicates to block storage services and networking services through the message queue. Also, you can optionally enable notifications for any service. RabbitMQ, Qpid, and 0mq are all popular choices for a message-queue service. In general, if the message queue fails or becomes inaccessible, the cluster grinds to a halt and ends up in a read-only state, with information stuck at the point where the last message was sent. Accordingly, we recommend that you cluster the message queue. Be aware that clustered message queues can be a pain point for many OpenStack deployments. While RabbitMQ has native clustering support, there have been reports of issues when running it at a large scale. While other queuing solutions are available, such as 0mq and Qpid, 0mq does not offer stateful queues. Qpid is the messaging system of choice for Red Hat and its derivatives. Qpid does not have native clustering capabilities and requires a supplemental service, such as Pacemaker or Corsync. For your message queue, you need to determine what level of data loss you are comfortable with and whether to use an OpenStack project's ability to retry multiple MQ hosts in the event of a failure, such as using Compute's ability to do so.

Conductor Services

In the previous version of OpenStack, all `nova-compute` services required direct access to the database hosted on the cloud controller. This was problematic for two reasons: security and performance. With regard to security, if a compute node is compromised, the attacker inherently has access to the database. With regard to performance, `nova-compute` calls to the database are single-threaded and blocking. This creates a performance bottleneck because database requests are fulfilled serially rather than in parallel.

The conductor service resolves both of these issues by acting as a proxy for the `nova-compute` service. Now, instead of `nova-compute` directly accessing the database, it contacts the `nova-conductor` service, and `nova-conductor` accesses the database on `nova-compute`'s behalf. Since `nova-compute` no longer has direct access to the database, the security issue is resolved. Additionally, `nova-conductor` is a nonblocking service, so requests from all compute nodes are fulfilled in parallel.

If you are using `nova-network` and multi-host networking in your cloud environment, `nova-compute` still requires direct access to the database.

The `nova-conductor` service is horizontally scalable. To make `nova-conductor` highly available and fault tolerant, just launch more instances of the `nova-conductor` process, either on the same server or across multiple servers.

Application Programming Interface (API)

All public access, whether direct, through a command-line client, or through the web-based dashboard, uses the API service. Find the API reference at *http://api.openstack.org/*.

You must choose whether you want to support the Amazon EC2 compatibility APIs, or just the OpenStack APIs. One issue you might encounter when running both APIs is an inconsistent experience when referring to images and instances.

For example, the EC2 API refers to instances using IDs that contain hexadecimal, whereas the OpenStack API uses names and digits. Similarly, the EC2 API tends to rely on DNS aliases for contacting virtual machines, as opposed to OpenStack, which typically lists IP addresses.

If OpenStack is not set up in the right way, it is simple to have scenarios in which users are unable to contact their instances due to having only an incorrect DNS alias. Despite this, EC2 compatibility can assist users migrating to your cloud.

As with databases and message queues, having more than one API server is a good thing. Traditional HTTP load-balancing techniques can be used to achieve a highly available `nova-api` service.

Extensions

The API Specifications (*http://opsgui.de/NPFK1H*) define the core actions, capabilities, and mediatypes of the OpenStack API. A client can always depend on the availability of this core API, and implementers are always required to support it in its entirety. Requiring strict adherence to the core API allows clients to rely upon a minimal level of functionality when interacting with multiple implementations of the same API.

The OpenStack Compute API is extensible. An extension adds capabilities to an API beyond those defined in the core. The introduction of new features, MIME types, actions, states, headers, parameters, and resources can all be accomplished by means of extensions to the core API. This allows the introduction of new features in the API without requiring a version change and allows the introduction of vendor-specific niche functionality.

Scheduling

The scheduling services are responsible for determining the compute or storage node where a virtual machine or block storage volume should be created. The scheduling services receive creation requests for these resources from the message queue and then begin the process of determining the appropriate node where the resource should reside. This process is done by applying a series of user-configurable filters against the available collection of nodes.

There are currently two schedulers: `nova-scheduler` for virtual machines and `cinder-scheduler` for block storage volumes. Both schedulers are able to scale horizontally, so for high-availability purposes, or for very large or high-schedule-frequency installations, you should consider running multiple instances of each scheduler. The schedulers all listen to the shared message queue, so no special load balancing is required.

Images

The OpenStack Image Service consists of two parts: `glance-api` and `glance-registry`. The former is responsible for the delivery of images; the compute node uses it to download images from the backend. The latter maintains the metadata information associated with virtual machine images and requires a database.

The `glance-api` part is an abstraction layer that allows a choice of backend. Currently, it supports:

OpenStack Object Storage
: Allows you to store images as objects.

File system
: Uses any traditional file system to store the images as files.

S3
: Allows you to fetch images from Amazon S3.

HTTP
: Allows you to fetch images from a web server. You cannot write images by using this mode.

If you have an OpenStack Object Storage service, we recommend using this as a scalable place to store your images. You can also use a file system with sufficient performance or Amazon S3—unless you do not need the ability to upload new images through OpenStack.

Dashboard

The OpenStack dashboard (horizon) provides a web-based user interface to the various OpenStack components. The dashboard includes an end-user area for users to manage their virtual infrastructure and an admin area for cloud operators to manage the OpenStack environment as a whole.

The dashboard is implemented as a Python web application that normally runs in Apache `httpd`. Therefore, you may treat it the same as any other web application, provided it can reach the API servers (including their admin endpoints) over the network.

Authentication and Authorization

The concepts supporting OpenStack's authentication and authorization are derived from well-understood and widely used systems of a similar nature. Users have credentials they can use to authenticate, and they can be a member of one or more groups (known as projects or tenants, interchangeably).

For example, a cloud administrator might be able to list all instances in the cloud, whereas a user can see only those in his current group. Resources quotas, such as the number of cores that can be used, disk space, and so on, are associated with a project.

The OpenStack Identity Service (keystone) is the point that provides the authentication decisions and user attribute information, which is then used by the other OpenStack services to perform authorization. Policy is set in the `policy.json` file. For information on how to configure these, see Chapter 9.

The Identity Service supports different plug-ins for authentication decisions and identity storage. Examples of these plug-ins include:

- In-memory key-value Store (a simplified internal storage structure)
- SQL database (such as MySQL or PostgreSQL)
- PAM (Pluggable Authentication Module)
- LDAP (such as OpenLDAP or Microsoft's Active Directory)

Many deployments use the SQL database; however, LDAP is also a popular choice for those with existing authentication infrastructure that needs to be integrated.

Network Considerations

Because the cloud controller handles so many different services, it must be able to handle the amount of traffic that hits it. For example, if you choose to host the OpenStack Imaging Service on the cloud controller, the cloud controller should be able to support the transferring of the images at an acceptable speed.

As another example, if you choose to use single-host networking where the cloud controller is the network gateway for all instances, then the cloud controller must support the total amount of traffic that travels between your cloud and the public Internet.

We recommend that you use a fast NIC, such as 10 GB. You can also choose to use two 10 GB NICs and bond them together. While you might not be able to get a full bonded 20 GB speed, different transmission streams use different NICs. For example, if the cloud controller transfers two images, each image uses a different NIC and gets a full 10 GB of bandwidth.

CHAPTER 4
Compute Nodes

In this chapter, we discuss some of the choices you need to consider when building out your compute nodes. Compute nodes form the resource core of the OpenStack Compute cloud, providing the processing, memory, network and storage resources to run instances.

Choosing a CPU

The type of CPU in your compute node is a very important choice. First, ensure that the CPU supports virtualization by way of *VT-x* for Intel chips and *AMD-v* for AMD chips.

Consult the vendor documentation to check for virtualization support. For Intel, read "Does my processor support Intel® Virtualization Technology?" (*http://opsgui.de/1eLAoiC*). For AMD, read AMD Virtualization (*http://opsgui.de/NPFI9Z*). Note that your CPU may support virtualization but it may be disabled. Consult your BIOS documentation for how to enable CPU features.

The number of cores that the CPU has also affects the decision. It's common for current CPUs to have up to 12 cores. Additionally, if an Intel CPU supports hyperthreading, those 12 cores are doubled to 24 cores. If you purchase a server that supports multiple CPUs, the number of cores is further multiplied.

Multithread Considerations

Hyper-Threading is Intel's proprietary simultaneous multithreading implementation used to improve parallelization on their CPUs. You might consider enabling Hyper-Threading to improve the performance of multithreaded applications.

Whether you should enable Hyper-Threading on your CPUs depends upon your use case. For example, disabling Hyper-Threading can be beneficial in intense computing environments. We recommend that you do performance testing with your local workload with both Hyper-Threading on and off to determine what is more appropriate in your case.

Choosing a Hypervisor

A hypervisor provides software to manage virtual machine access to the underlying hardware. The hypervisor creates, manages, and monitors virtual machines. OpenStack Compute supports many hypervisors to various degrees, including:

- KVM (*http://opsgui.de/1eLApTQ*)
- LXC (*http://opsgui.de/NPFL5O*)
- QEMU (*http://opsgui.de/1eLAs1W*)
- VMWare ESX/ESXi (*http://opsgui.de/NPFOyn*)
- Xen (*http://opsgui.de/1eLAt5Z*)
- Hyper-V (*http://opsgui.de/NPFMXx*)
- Docker (*http://opsgui.de/1eLAxm5*)

Probably the most important factor in your choice of hypervisor is your current usage or experience. Aside from that, there are practical concerns to do with feature parity, documentation, and the level of community experience.

For example, KVM is the most widely adopted hypervisor in the OpenStack community. Besides KVM, more deployments run Xen, LXC, VMWare, and Hyper-V than the others listed. However, each of these are lacking some feature support or the documentation on how to use them with OpenStack is out of date.

The best information available to support your choice is found on the Hypervisor Support Matrix (*http://opsgui.de/NPFQ9w*) and in the configuration reference (*http://opsgui.de/1eLAwP2*).

It is also possible to run multiple hypervisors in a single deployment using host aggregates or cells. However, an individual compute node can run only a single hypervisor at a time.

Instance Storage Solutions

As part of the procurement for a compute cluster, you must specify some storage for the disk on which the instantiated instance runs. There are three main approaches to providing this temporary-style storage, and it is important to understand the implications of the choice.

They are:

- Off compute node storage—shared file system
- On compute node storage—shared file system
- On compute node storage—nonshared file system

In general, the questions you should ask when selecting storage are as follows:

- What is the platter count you can achieve?
- Do more spindles result in better I/O despite network access?
- Which one results in the best cost-performance scenario you're aiming for?
- How do you manage the storage operationally?

Many operators use separate compute and storage hosts. Compute services and storage services have different requirements, and compute hosts typically require more CPU and RAM than storage hosts. Therefore, for a fixed budget, it makes sense to have different configurations for your compute nodes and your storage nodes. Compute nodes will be invested in CPU and RAM, and storage nodes will be invested in block storage.

However, if you are more restricted in the number of physical hosts you have available for creating your cloud and you want to be able to dedicate as many of your hosts as possible to running instances, it makes sense to run compute and storage on the same machines.

We'll discuss the three main approaches to instance storage in the next few sections.

Off Compute Node Storage—Shared File System

In this option, the disks storing the running instances are hosted in servers outside of the compute nodes.

If you use separate compute and storage hosts, you can treat your compute hosts as "stateless." As long as you don't have any instances currently running on a compute host, you can take it offline or wipe it completely without having any effect on the rest of your cloud. This simplifies maintenance for the compute hosts.

There are several advantages to this approach:

- If a compute node fails, instances are usually easily recoverable.
- Running a dedicated storage system can be operationally simpler.
- You can scale to any number of spindles.
- It may be possible to share the external storage for other purposes.

The main downsides to this approach are:

- Depending on design, heavy I/O usage from some instances can affect unrelated instances.
- Use of the network can decrease performance.

On Compute Node Storage—Shared File System

In this option, each compute node is specified with a significant amount of disk space, but a distributed file system ties the disks from each compute node into a single mount.

The main advantage of this option is that it scales to external storage when you require additional storage.

However, this option has several downsides:

- Running a distributed file system can make you lose your data locality compared with nonshared storage.
- Recovery of instances is complicated by depending on multiple hosts.
- The chassis size of the compute node can limit the number of spindles able to be used in a compute node.
- Use of the network can decrease performance.

On Compute Node Storage—Nonshared File System

In this option, each compute node is specified with enough disks to store the instances it hosts.

There are two main reasons why this is a good idea:

- Heavy I/O usage on one compute node does not affect instances on other compute nodes.
- Direct I/O access can increase performance.

This has several downsides:

- If a compute node fails, the instances running on that node are lost.
- The chassis size of the compute node can limit the number of spindles able to be used in a compute node.
- Migrations of instances from one node to another are more complicated and rely on features that may not continue to be developed.
- If additional storage is required, this option does not scale.

Running a shared file system on a storage system apart from the computes nodes is ideal for clouds where reliability and scalability are the most important factors. Running a shared file system on the compute nodes themselves may be best in a scenario where you have to deploy to preexisting servers for which you have little to no control over their specifications. Running a nonshared file system on the compute nodes themselves is a good option for clouds with high I/O requirements and low concern for reliability.

Issues with Live Migration

We consider live migration an integral part of the operations of the cloud. This feature provides the ability to seamlessly move instances from one physical host to another, a necessity for performing upgrades that require reboots of the compute hosts, but only works well with shared storage.

Live migration can also be done with nonshared storage, using a feature known as *KVM live block migration*. While an earlier implementation of block-based migration in KVM and QEMU was considered unreliable, there is a newer, more reliable implementation of block-based live migration as of QEMU 1.4 and libvirt 1.0.2 that is also compatible with OpenStack. However, none of the authors of this guide have firsthand experience using live block migration.

Choice of File System

If you want to support shared-storage live migration, you need to configure a distributed file system.

Possible options include:

- NFS (default for Linux)
- GlusterFS
- MooseFS
- Lustre

We've seen deployments with all, and recommend that you choose the one you are most familiar with operating. If you are not familiar with any of these, choose NFS, as it is the easiest to set up and there is extensive community knowledge about it.

Overcommitting

OpenStack allows you to overcommit CPU and RAM on compute nodes. This allows you to increase the number of instances you can have running on your cloud, at the cost of reducing the performance of the instances. OpenStack Compute uses the following ratios by default:

- CPU allocation ratio: 16:1
- RAM allocation ratio: 1.5:1

The default CPU allocation ratio of 16:1 means that the scheduler allocates up to 16 virtual cores per physical core. For example, if a physical node has 12 cores, the scheduler sees 192 available virtual cores. With typical flavor definitions of 4 virtual cores per instance, this ratio would provide 48 instances on a physical node.

The formula for the number of virtual instances on a compute node is *(OR*PC)/VC*, where:

OR
: CPU overcommit ratio (virtual cores per physical core)

PC
: Number of physical cores

VC
: Number of virtual cores per instance

Similarly, the default RAM allocation ratio of 1.5:1 means that the scheduler allocates instances to a physical node as long as the total amount of RAM associated with the instances is less than 1.5 times the amount of RAM available on the physical node.

For example, if a physical node has 48 GB of RAM, the scheduler allocates instances to that node until the sum of the RAM associated with the instances reaches 72 GB (such as nine instances, in the case where each instance has 8 GB of RAM).

You must select the appropriate CPU and RAM allocation ratio for your particular use case.

Logging

Logging is detailed more fully in Chapter 13. However, it is an important design consideration to take into account before commencing operations of your cloud.

OpenStack produces a great deal of useful logging information, however; but for the information to be useful for operations purposes, you should consider having a central logging server to send logs to, and a log parsing/analysis system (such as logstash).

Networking

Networking in OpenStack is a complex, multifaceted challenge. See Chapter 7.

Conclusion

Compute nodes are the workhorse of your cloud and the place where your users' applications will run. They are likely to be affected by your decisions on what to deploy and how you deploy it. Their requirements should be reflected in the choices you make.

CHAPTER 5

Scaling

Whereas traditional applications required larger hardware to scale ("vertical scaling"), cloud-based applications typically request more, discrete hardware ("horizontal scaling"). If your cloud is successful, eventually you must add resources to meet the increasing demand.

To suit the cloud paradigm, OpenStack itself is designed to be horizontally scalable. Rather than switching to larger servers, you procure more servers and simply install identically configured services. Ideally, you scale out and load balance among groups of functionally identical services (for example, compute nodes or `nova-api` nodes), that communicate on a message bus.

The Starting Point

Determining the scalability of your cloud and how to improve it is an exercise with many variables to balance. No one solution meets everyone's scalability goals. However, it is helpful to track a number of metrics. Since you can define virtual hardware templates, called "flavors" in OpenStack, you can start to make scaling decisions based on the flavors you'll provide. These templates define sizes for memory in RAM, root disk size, amount of ephemeral data disk space available, and number of cores for starters.

The default OpenStack flavors are shown in Table 5-1.

Table 5-1. OpenStack default flavors

Name	Virtual cores	Memory	Disk	Ephemeral
m1.tiny	1	512 MB	1 GB	0 GB
m1.small	1	2 GB	10 GB	20 GB
m1.medium	2	4 GB	10 GB	40 GB
m1.large	4	8 GB	10 GB	80 GB
m1.xlarge	8	16 GB	10 GB	160 GB

The starting point for most is the core count of your cloud. By applying some ratios, you can gather information about:

- The number of virtual machines (VMs) you expect to run, `((overcommit fraction × cores) / virtual cores per instance)`
- How much storage is required `(flavor disk size × number of instances)`

You can use these ratios to determine how much additional infrastructure you need to support your cloud.

Here is an example using the ratios for gathering scalability information for the number of VMs expected as well as the storage needed. The following numbers support (200 / 2) × 16 = 1600 VM instances and require 80 TB of storage for `/var/lib/nova/instances`:

- 200 physical cores.
- Most instances are size m1.medium (two virtual cores, 50 GB of storage).
- Default CPU overcommit ratio (`cpu_allocation_ratio` in nova.conf) of 16:1.

However, you need more than the core count alone to estimate the load that the API services, database servers, and queue servers are likely to encounter. You must also consider the usage patterns of your cloud.

As a specific example, compare a cloud that supports a managed web-hosting platform with one running integration tests for a development project that creates one VM per code commit. In the former, the heavy work of creating a VM happens only every few months, whereas the latter puts constant heavy load on the cloud controller. You must consider your average VM lifetime, as a larger number generally means less load on the cloud controller.

Aside from the creation and termination of VMs, you must consider the impact of users accessing the service—particularly on `nova-api` and its associated database. Listing instances garners a great deal of information and, given the frequency with which users run this operation, a cloud with a large number of users can increase the load significantly. This can occur even without their knowledge—leaving the OpenStack dashboard instances tab open in the browser refreshes the list of VMs every 30 seconds.

After you consider these factors, you can determine how many cloud controller cores you require. A typical eight core, 8 GB of RAM server is sufficient for up to a rack of compute nodes — given the above caveats.

You must also consider key hardware specifications for the performance of user VMs, as well as budget and performance needs, including storage performance (spindles/core), memory availability (RAM/core), network bandwidth (Gbps/core), and overall CPU performance (CPU/core).

For a discussion of metric tracking, including how to extract metrics from your cloud, see Chapter 13.

Adding Cloud Controller Nodes

You can facilitate the horizontal expansion of your cloud by adding nodes. Adding compute nodes is straightforward—they are easily picked up by the existing installation. However, you must consider some important points when you design your cluster to be highly available.

Recall that a cloud controller node runs several different services. You can install services that communicate only using the message queue internally—`nova-scheduler` and `nova-console`—on a new server for expansion. However, other integral parts require more care.

You should load balance user-facing services such as dashboard, `nova-api`, or the Object Storage proxy. Use any standard HTTP load-balancing method (DNS round robin, hardware load balancer, or software such as Pound or HAProxy). One caveat with dashboard is the VNC proxy, which uses the WebSocket protocol—something that an L7 load balancer might struggle with. See also Horizon session storage (*http://opsgui.de/1eLAOFE*).

You can configure some services, such as `nova-api` and `glance-api`, to use multiple processes by changing a flag in their configuration file—allowing them to share work between multiple cores on the one machine.

Several options are available for MySQL load balancing, and the supported AMQP brokers have built-in clustering support. Information on how to configure these and many of the other services can be found in Part II.

Segregating Your Cloud

When you want to offer users different regions to provide legal considerations for data storage, redundancy across earthquake fault lines, or for low-latency API calls, you segregate your cloud. Use one of the following OpenStack methods to segregate your cloud: *cells*, *regions*, *availability zones*, or *host aggregates*.

Each method provides different functionality and can be best divided into two groups:

- Cells and regions, which segregate an entire cloud and result in running separate Compute deployments.
- Availability zones and host aggregates, which merely divide a single Compute deployment.

Table 5-2 provides a comparison view of each segregation method currently provided by OpenStack Compute.

Table 5-2. OpenStack segregation methods

	Cells	Regions	Availability zones	Host aggregates
Use when you need	A single API endpoint for compute, or you require a second level of scheduling.	Discrete regions with separate API endpoints and no coordination between regions.	Logical separation within your nova deployment for physical isolation or redundancy.	To schedule a group of hosts with common features.
Example	A cloud with multiple sites where you can schedule VMs "anywhere" or on a particular site.	A cloud with multiple sites, where you schedule VMs to a particular site and you want a shared infrastructure.	A single-site cloud with equipment fed by separate power supplies.	Scheduling to hosts with trusted hardware support.
Overhead	Considered experimental. A new service, nova-cells. Each cell has a full nova installation except nova-api.	A different API endpoint for every region. Each region has a full nova installation.	Configuration changes to nova.conf.	Configuration changes to nova.conf.
Shared services	Keystone `nova-api`	Keystone	Keystone All nova services	Keystone All nova services

Cells and Regions

OpenStack Compute cells are designed to allow running the cloud in a distributed fashion without having to use more complicated technologies, or be invasive to existing nova installations. Hosts in a cloud are partitioned into groups called *cells*. Cells are configured in a tree. The top-level cell ("API cell") has a host that runs the `nova-api` service, but no `nova-compute` services. Each child cell runs all of the other typical `nova-*` services found in a regular installation, except for the `nova-api` service. Each cell has its own message queue and database service and also runs `nova-cells`, which manages the communication between the API cell and child cells.

This allows for a single API server being used to control access to multiple cloud installations. Introducing a second level of scheduling (the cell selection), in addition to the regular `nova-scheduler` selection of hosts, provides greater flexibility to control where virtual machines are run.

Contrast this with regions. Regions have a separate API endpoint per installation, allowing for a more discrete separation. Users wanting to run instances across sites have to explicitly select a region. However, the additional complexity of a running a new service is not required.

The OpenStack dashboard (horizon) currently uses only a single region, so one dashboard service should be run per region. Regions are a robust way to share some infrastructure between OpenStack Compute installations, while allowing for a high degree of failure tolerance.

Availability Zones and Host Aggregates

You can use availability zones, host aggregates, or both to partition a nova deployment.

Availability zones are implemented through and configured in a similar way to host aggregates.

However, you use them for different reasons.

Availability zone

This enables you to arrange OpenStack compute hosts into logical groups and provides a form of physical isolation and redundancy from other availability zones, such as by using a separate power supply or network equipment.

You define the availability zone in which a specified compute host resides locally on each server. An availability zone is commonly used to identify a set of servers that have a common attribute. For instance, if some of the racks in your data center are on a separate power source, you can put servers in those racks in their own availability zone. Availability zones can also help separate different classes of hardware.

When users provision resources, they can specify from which availability zone they want their instance to be built. This allows cloud consumers to ensure that their application resources are spread across disparate machines to achieve high availability in the event of hardware failure.

Host aggregates zone

This enables you to partition OpenStack Compute deployments into logical groups for load balancing and instance distribution. You can use host aggregates to further partition an availability zone. For example, you might use host aggregates to partition an availability zone into groups of hosts that either share common resources, such as storage and network, or have a special property, such as trusted computing hardware.

A common use of host aggregates is to provide information for use with the `nova-scheduler`. For example, you might use a host aggregate to group a set of hosts that share specific flavors or images.

The general case for this is setting key-value pairs in the aggregate metadata and matching key-value pairs in instance type extra specs. The `AggregateInstanceExtraSpecsFilter` in the filter scheduler will enforce that instances be scheduled only on hosts in aggregates that define the same key to the same value.

An advanced use of this general concept allows different instance types to run with different CPU and RAM allocation rations so that high-intensity computing loads and low-intensity development and testing systems can share the same cloud without either starving the high-use systems or wasting resources on low-utilization systems. This works by setting `metadata` in your host aggregates and matching `extra_specs` in your instance types.

The first step is setting the aggregate metadata keys `cpu_allocation_ratio` and `ram_allocation_ration` to a floating-point value. The filter schedulers `AggregateCoreFilter` and `AggregateRamFilter` will use those values rather than the global defaults in `nova.conf` when scheduling to hosts in the aggregate. It is important to be cautious when using this feature, since each host can be in multiple aggregates but should have only one allocation ratio for each resources. It is up to you to avoid putting a host in multiple aggregates that define different values for the same resource.

This is the first half of the equation. To get instance types that are guaranteed a particular ratio, you must set the `extra_specs` in the instance type to the key-value pair you want to match in the aggregate. For example, if you define `extra specs cpu_allocation_ratio` to "1.0", then instances of that type will run in aggregates only where the metadata key `cpu_allocation_ratio` is also defined as "1.0." In practice, it is better to define an additional key-value pair in the aggregate metadata to match on rather than match directly on `cpu_allocation_ratio` or `core_allocation_ratio`. This allows better abstraction. For example, by defining a key `overcommit` and setting a value of "high," "medium," or "low," you could then tune the numeric allocation ratios in the aggregates without also needing to change all instance types relating to them.

> Previously, all services had an availability zone. Currently, only the `nova-compute` service has its own availability zone. Services such as `nova-scheduler`, `nova-network`, and `nova-conductor` have always spanned all availability zones.
>
> When you run any of the following operations, the services appear in their own internal availability zone (CONF.internal_service_availability_zone):
>
> - nova host-list (os-hosts)
> - euca-describe-availability-zones verbose
> - `nova-manage` service list
>
> The internal availability zone is hidden in euca-describe-availability_zones (nonverbose).
>
> CONF.node_availability_zone has been renamed to CONF.default_availability_zone and is used only by the `nova-api` and `nova-scheduler` services.
>
> CONF.node_availability_zone still works but is deprecated.

Scalable Hardware

While several resources already exist to help with deploying and installing OpenStack, it's very important to make sure that you have your deployment planned out ahead of time. This guide presumes that you have at least set aside a rack for the OpenStack cloud but also offers suggestions for when and what to scale.

Hardware Procurement

"The Cloud" has been described as a volatile environment where servers can be created and terminated at will. While this may be true, it does not mean that your servers must be volatile. Ensuring that your cloud's hardware is stable and configured correctly means that your cloud environment remains up and running. Basically, put effort into creating a stable hardware environment so that you can host a cloud that users may treat as unstable and volatile.

OpenStack can be deployed on any hardware supported by an OpenStack-compatible Linux distribution.

Hardware does not have to be consistent, but it should at least have the same type of CPU to support instance migration.

The typical hardware recommended for use with OpenStack is the standard value-for-money offerings that most hardware vendors stock. It should be straightforward to divide your procurement into building blocks such as "compute," "object storage," and "cloud controller," and request as many of these as you need. Alternatively, should you be unable to spend more, if you have existing servers—provided they meet your performance requirements and virtualization technology—they are quite likely to be able to support OpenStack.

Capacity Planning

OpenStack is designed to increase in size in a straightforward manner. Taking into account the considerations that we've mentioned in this chapter—particularly on the sizing of the cloud controller—it should be possible to procure additional compute or object storage nodes as needed. New nodes do not need to be the same specification, or even vendor, as existing nodes.

For compute nodes, `nova-scheduler` will take care of differences in sizing having to do with core count and RAM amounts; however, you should consider that the user experience changes with differing CPU speeds. When adding object storage nodes, a weight should be specified that reflects the capability of the node.

Monitoring the resource usage and user growth will enable you to know when to procure. Chapter 13 details some useful metrics.

Burn-in Testing

Server hardware's chance of failure is high at the start and the end of its life. As a result, much effort in dealing with hardware failures while in production can be avoided by appropriate burn-in testing to attempt to trigger the early-stage failures. The general principle is to stress the hardware to its limits. Examples of burn-in tests include running a CPU or disk benchmark for several days.

CHAPTER 6

Storage Decisions

Storage is found in many parts of the OpenStack stack, and the differing types can cause confusion to even experienced cloud engineers. This section focuses on persistent storage options you can configure with your cloud. It's important to understand the distinction between ephemeral storage and persistent storage.

Ephemeral Storage

If you deploy only the OpenStack Compute Service (nova), your users do not have access to any form of persistent storage by default. The disks associated with VMs are "ephemeral," meaning that (from the user's point of view) they effectively disappear when a virtual machine is terminated.

Persistent Storage

Persistent storage means that the storage resource outlives any other resource and is always available, regardless of the state of a running instance.

Today, OpenStack clouds explicitly support two types of persistent storage: *object storage* and *block storage*.

Object Storage

With object storage, users access binary objects through a REST API. You may be familiar with Amazon S3, which is a well-known example of an object storage system. Object storage is implemented in OpenStack by the OpenStack Object Storage (swift) project. If your intended users need to archive or manage large datasets, you want to provide them with object storage. In addition, OpenStack can store your virtual machine (VM) images inside of an object storage system, as an alternative to storing the images on a file system.

OpenStack Object Storage provides a highly scalable, highly available storage solution by relaxing some of the constraints of traditional file systems. In designing and procuring for such a cluster, it is important to understand some key concepts about its operation. Essentially, this type of storage is built on the idea that all storage hardware fails, at every level, at some point. Infrequently encountered failures that would hamstring other storage systems, such as issues taking down RAID cards or entire servers, are handled gracefully with OpenStack Object Storage.

A good document describing the Object Storage architecture is found within the developer documentation (*http://opsgui.de/NPG0xO*)—read this first. Once you understand the architecture, you should know what a proxy server does and how zones work. However, some important points are often missed at first glance.

When designing your cluster, you must consider durability and availability. Understand that the predominant source of these is the spread and placement of your data, rather than the reliability of the hardware. Consider the default value of the number of replicas, which is three. This means that before an object is marked as having been written, at least two copies exist—in case a single server fails to write, the third copy may or may not yet exist when the write operation initially returns. Altering this number increases the robustness of your data, but reduces the amount of storage you have available. Next, look at the placement of your servers. Consider spreading them widely throughout your data center's network and power-failure zones. Is a zone a rack, a server, or a disk?

Object Storage's network patterns might seem unfamiliar at first. Consider these main traffic flows:

- Among object, container, and account servers
- Between those servers and the proxies
- Between the proxies and your users

Object Storage is very "chatty" among servers hosting data—even a small cluster does megabytes/second of traffic, which is predominantly, "Do you have the object?"/"Yes I have the object!" Of course, if the answer to the aforementioned question is negative or the request times out, replication of the object begins.

Consider the scenario where an entire server fails and 24 TB of data needs to be transferred "immediately" to remain at three copies—this can put significant load on the network.

Another fact that's often forgotten is that when a new file is being uploaded, the proxy server must write out as many streams as there are replicas—giving a multiple of network traffic. For a three-replica cluster, 10 Gbps in means 30 Gbps out. Combining this with the previous high bandwidth demands of replication is what results in the recommendation that your private network be of significantly higher bandwidth than your public need be. Oh, and OpenStack Object Storage communicates internally with unencrypted, unauthenticated rsync for performance—you do want the private network to be private.

The remaining point on bandwidth is the public-facing portion. The `swift-proxy` service is stateless, which means that you can easily add more and use HTTP load-balancing methods to share bandwidth and availability between them.

More proxies means more bandwidth, if your storage can keep up.

Block Storage

Block storage (sometimes referred to as volume storage) provides users with access to block-storage devices. Users interact with block storage by attaching volumes to their running VM instances.

These volumes are persistent: they can be detached from one instance and re-attached to another, and the data remains intact. Block storage is implemented in OpenStack by the OpenStack Block Storage (cinder) project, which supports multiple backends in the form of drivers. Your choice of a storage backend must be supported by a Block Storage driver.

Most block storage drivers allow the instance to have direct access to the underlying storage hardware's block device. This helps increase the overall read/write IO.

Experimental support for utilizing files as volumes began in the Folsom release. This initially started as a reference driver for using NFS with cinder. By Grizzly's release, this has expanded into a full NFS driver as well as a GlusterFS driver.

These drivers work a little differently than a traditional "block" storage driver. On an NFS or GlusterFS file system, a single file is created and then mapped as a "virtual" volume into the instance. This mapping/translation is similar to how OpenStack utilizes QEMU's file-based virtual machines stored in `/var/lib/nova/instances`.

OpenStack Storage Concepts

Table 6-1 explains the different storage concepts provided by OpenStack.

Table 6-1. OpenStack storage

	Ephemeral storage	Block storage	Object storage
Used to...	Run operating system and scratch space	Add additional persistent storage to a virtual machine (VM)	Store data, including VM images
Accessed through...	A file system	A block device that can be partitioned, formatted, and mounted (such as, /dev/vdc)	The REST API
Accessible from...	Within a VM	Within a VM	Anywhere
Managed by...	OpenStack Compute (nova)	OpenStack Block Storage (cinder)	OpenStack Object Storage (swift)
Persists until...	VM is terminated	Deleted by user	Deleted by user
Sizing determined by...	Administrator configuration of size settings, known as *flavors*	User specification in initial request	Amount of available physical storage
Example of typical usage...	10 GB first disk, 30 GB second disk	1 TB disk	10s of TBs of dataset storage

File-level Storage (for Live Migration)

With file-level storage, users access stored data using the operating system's file system interface. Most users, if they have used a network storage solution before, have encountered this form of networked storage. In the Unix world, the most common form of this is NFS. In the Windows world, the most common form is called CIFS (previously, SMB).

OpenStack clouds do not present file-level storage to end users. However, it is important to consider file-level storage for storing instances under `/var/lib/nova/instances` when designing your cloud, since you must have a shared file system if you want to support live migration.

Choosing Storage Backends

Users will indicate different needs for their cloud use cases. Some may need fast access to many objects that do not change often, or want to set a time-to-live (TTL) value on a file. Others may access only storage that is mounted with the file system itself, but want it to be replicated instantly when starting a new instance. For other systems, ephemeral storage—storage that is released when a VM attached to it is shut down—

is the preferred way. When you select storage backends, ask the following questions on behalf of your users:

- Do my users need block storage?
- Do my users need object storage?
- Do I need to support live migration?
- Should my persistent storage drives be contained in my compute nodes, or should I use external storage?
- What is the platter count I can achieve? Do more spindles result in better I/O despite network access?
- Which one results in the best cost-performance scenario I'm aiming for?
- How do I manage the storage operationally?
- How redundant and distributed is the storage? What happens if a storage node fails? To what extent can it mitigate my data-loss disaster scenarios?

To deploy your storage by using only commodity hardware, you can use a number of open-source packages, as shown in Table 6-2.

Table 6-2. Persistent file-based storage support

	Object	Block	File-level[a]
Swift	✓		
LVM		✓	
Ceph	✓	✓	Experimental
Gluster	✓		✓
NFS		✓	✓
ZFS		✓	

[a] This list of open source file-level shared storage solutions is not exhaustive; other open source solutions exist (MooseFS). Your organization may already have deployed a file-level shared storage solution that you can use.

> **Storage Driver Support**
>
> In addition to the open source technologies, there are a number of proprietary solutions that are officially supported by OpenStack Block Storage. They are offered by the following vendors:
>
> - IBM (Storwize family/SVC, XIV)
> - NetApp
> - Nexenta
> - SolidFire
>
> You can find a matrix of the functionality provided by all of the supported Block Storage drivers on the OpenStack wiki (*http://opsgui.de/1eLAQxg*).

Also, you need to decide whether you want to support object storage in your cloud. The two common use cases for providing object storage in a compute cloud are:

- To provide users with a persistent storage mechanism
- As a scalable, reliable data store for virtual machine images

Commodity Storage Backend Technologies

This section provides a high-level overview of the differences among the different commodity storage backend technologies. Depending on your cloud user's needs, you can implement one or many of these technologies in different combinations:

OpenStack Object Storage (swift)
: The official OpenStack Object Store implementation. It is a mature technology that has been used for several years in production by Rackspace as the technology behind Rackspace Cloud Files. As it is highly scalable, it is well-suited to managing petabytes of storage. OpenStack Object Storage's advantages are better integration with OpenStack (integrates with OpenStack Identity, works with the OpenStack dashboard interface) and better support for multiple data center deployment through support of asynchronous eventual consistency replication.

  Therefore, if you eventually plan on distributing your storage cluster across multiple data centers, if you need unified accounts for your users for both compute and object storage, or if you want to control your object storage with the OpenStack dashboard, you should consider OpenStack Object Storage. More detail can be found about OpenStack Object Storage in the section below.

Ceph

A scalable storage solution that replicates data across commodity storage nodes. Ceph was originally developed by one of the founders of DreamHost and is currently used in production there.

Ceph was designed to expose different types of storage interfaces to the end user: it supports object storage, block storage, and file-system interfaces, although the file-system interface is not yet considered production-ready. Ceph supports the same API as swift for object storage and can be used as a backend for cinder block storage as well as backend storage for glance images. Ceph supports "thin provisioning," implemented using copy-on-write.

This can be useful when booting from volume because a new volume can be provisioned very quickly. Ceph also supports keystone-based authentication (as of version 0.56), so it can be a seamless swap in for the default OpenStack swift implementation.

Ceph's advantages are that it gives the administrator more fine-grained control over data distribution and replication strategies, enables you to consolidate your object and block storage, enables very fast provisioning of boot-from-volume instances using thin provisioning, and supports a distributed file-system interface, though this interface is not yet recommended (*http://opsgui.de/NPG1BD*) for use in production deployment by the Ceph project.

If you want to manage your object and block storage within a single system, or if you want to support fast boot-from-volume, you should consider Ceph.

Gluster

A distributed, shared file system. As of Gluster version 3.3, you can use Gluster to consolidate your object storage and file storage into one unified file and object storage solution, which is called Gluster For OpenStack (GFO). GFO uses a customized version of swift that enables Gluster to be used as the backend storage.

The main reason to use GFO rather than regular swift is if you also want to support a distributed file system, either to support shared storage live migration or to provide it as a separate service to your end users. If you want to manage your object and file storage within a single system, you should consider GFO.

LVM

The Logical Volume Manager is a Linux-based system that provides an abstraction layer on top of physical disks to expose logical volumes to the operating system. The LVM backend implements block storage as LVM logical partitions.

On each host that will house block storage, an administrator must initially create a volume group dedicated to Block Storage volumes. Blocks are created from LVM logical volumes.

LVM does *not* provide any replication. Typically, administrators configure RAID on nodes that use LVM as block storage to protect against failures of individual hard drives. However, RAID does not protect against a failure of the entire host.

ZFS

The Solaris iSCSI driver for OpenStack Block Storage implements blocks as ZFS entities. ZFS is a file system that also has the functionality of a volume manager. This is unlike on a Linux system, where there is a separation of volume manager (LVM) and file system (such as, ext3, ext4, xfs, and btrfs). ZFS has a number of advantages over ext4, including improved data-integrity checking.

The ZFS backend for OpenStack Block Storage supports only Solaris-based systems, such as Illumos. While there is a Linux port of ZFS, it is not included in any of the standard Linux distributions, and it has not been tested with OpenStack Block Storage. As with LVM, ZFS does not provide replication across hosts on its own; you need to add a replication solution on top of ZFS if your cloud needs to be able to handle storage-node failures.

We don't recommend ZFS unless you have previous experience with deploying it, since the ZFS backend for Block Storage requires a Solaris-based operating system, and we assume that your experience is primarily with Linux-based systems.

Conclusion

We hope that you now have some considerations in mind and questions to ask your future cloud users about their storage use cases. As you can see, your storage decisions will also influence your network design for performance and security needs. Continue with us to make more informed decisions about your OpenStack cloud design.

CHAPTER 7
Network Design

OpenStack provides a rich networking environment, and this chapter details the requirements and options to deliberate when designing your cloud.

If this is the first time you are deploying a cloud infrastructure in your organization, after reading this section, your first conversations should be with your networking team. Network usage in a running cloud is vastly different from traditional network deployments and has the potential to be disruptive at both a connectivity and a policy level.

For example, you must plan the number of IP addresses that you need for both your guest instances as well as management infrastructure. Additionally, you must research and discuss cloud network connectivity through proxy servers and firewalls.

In this chapter, we'll give some examples of network implementations to consider and provide information about some of the network layouts that OpenStack uses. Finally, we have some brief notes on the networking services that are essential for stable operation.

Management Network

A management network (a separate network for use by your cloud operators) typically consists of a separate switch and separate NICs (network interface cards), and is a recommended option. This segregation prevents system administration and the monitoring of system access from being disrupted by traffic generated by guests.

Consider creating other private networks for communication between internal components of OpenStack, such as the message queue and OpenStack Compute. Using a virtual local area network (VLAN) works well for these scenarios because it provides a method for creating multiple virtual networks on a physical network.

Public Addressing Options

There are two main types of IP addresses for guest virtual machines: fixed IPs and floating IPs. Fixed IPs are assigned to instances on boot, whereas floating IP addresses can change their association between instances by action of the user. Both types of IP addresses can be either public or private, depending on your use case.

Fixed IP addresses are required, whereas it is possible to run OpenStack without floating IPs. One of the most common use cases for floating IPs is to provide public IP addresses to a private cloud, where there are a limited number of IP addresses available. Another is for a public cloud user to have a "static" IP address that can be reassigned when an instance is upgraded or moved.

Fixed IP addresses can be private for private clouds, or public for public clouds. When an instance terminates, its fixed IP is lost. It is worth noting that newer users of cloud computing may find their ephemeral nature frustrating.

IP Address Planning

An OpenStack installation can potentially have many subnets (ranges of IP addresses) and different types of services in each. An IP address plan can assist with a shared understanding of network partition purposes and scalability. Control services can have public and private IP addresses, and as noted above, there are a couple of options for an instance's public addresses.

An IP address plan might be broken down into the following sections:

Subnet router
: Packets leaving the subnet go via this address, which could be a dedicated router or a `nova-network` service.

Control services public interfaces
: Public access to `swift-proxy`, `nova-api`, `glance-api`, and horizon come to these addresses, which could be on one side of a load balancer or pointing at individual machines.

Object Storage cluster internal communications
: Traffic among object/account/container servers and between these and the proxy server's internal interface uses this private network.

Compute and storage communications
: If ephemeral or block storage is external to the compute node, this network is used.

Out-of-band remote management
: If a dedicated remote access controller chip is included in servers, often these are on a separate network.

In-band remote management
: Often, an extra (such as 1 GB) interface on compute or storage nodes is used for system administrators or monitoring tools to access the host instead of going through the public interface.

Spare space for future growth
: Adding more public-facing control services or guest instance IPs should always be part of your plan.

For example, take a deployment that has both OpenStack Compute and Object Storage, with private ranges 172.22.42.0/24 and 172.22.87.0/26 available. One way to segregate the space might be as follows:

```
172.22.42.0/24:
172.22.42.1   - 172.22.42.3   - subnet routers
172.22.42.4   - 172.22.42.20  - spare for networks
172.22.42.21  - 172.22.42.104 - Compute node remote access controllers
                                (inc spare)
172.22.42.105 - 172.22.42.188 - Compute node management interfaces (inc spare)
172.22.42.189 - 172.22.42.208 - Swift proxy remote access controllers
                                (inc spare)
172.22.42.209 - 172.22.42.228 - Swift proxy management interfaces (inc spare)
172.22.42.229 - 172.22.42.252 - Swift storage servers remote access controllers
                                (inc spare)
172.22.42.253 - 172.22.42.254 - spare
172.22.87.0/26:
172.22.87.1  - 172.22.87.3    - subnet routers
172.22.87.4  - 172.22.87.24   - Swift proxy server internal interfaces
                                (inc spare)
172.22.87.25 - 172.22.87.63   - Swift object server internal interfaces
                                (inc spare)
```

A similar approach can be taken with public IP addresses, taking note that large, flat ranges are preferred for use with guest instance IPs. Take into account that for some OpenStack networking options, a public IP address in the range of a guest instance public IP address is assigned to the `nova-compute` host.

Network Topology

OpenStack Compute with `nova-network` provides predefined network deployment models, each with its own strengths and weaknesses. The selection of a network manager changes your network topology, so the choice should be made carefully. You also have a choice between the tried-and-true legacy `nova-network` settings or the neutron project for OpenStack Networking. Both offer networking for launched instances with different implementations and requirements.

For OpenStack Networking with the neutron project, typical configurations are documented with the idea that any setup you can configure with real hardware you can re-create with a software-defined equivalent. Each tenant can contain typical network elements such as routers, and services such as DHCP.

Table 7-1 discusses the networking deployment options for both legacy `nova-network` options and an equivalent neutron configuration.

Table 7-1. Networking deployment options

Network deployment model	Strengths	Weaknesses	Neutron equivalent
Flat	Extremely simple topology. No DHCP overhead.	Requires file injection into the instance to configure network interfaces.	Configure a single bridge as the integration bridge (br-int) and connect it to a physical network interface with the Modular Layer 2 (ML2) plug-in, which uses Open vSwitch by default.
FlatDHCP	Relatively simple to deploy. Standard networking. Works with all guest operating systems.	Requires its own DHCP broadcast domain.	Configure DHCP agents and routing agents. Network Address Translation (NAT) performed outside of compute nodes, typically on one or more network nodes.
VlanManager	Each tenant is isolated to its own VLANs.	More complex to set up. Requires its own DHCP broadcast domain. Requires many VLANs to be trunked onto a single port. Standard VLAN number limitation. Switches must support 802.1q VLAN tagging.	Isolated tenant networks implement some form of isolation of layer 2 traffic between distinct networks. VLAN tagging is key concept, where traffic is "tagged" with an ordinal identifier for the VLAN. Isolated network implementations may or may not include additional services like DHCP, NAT, and routing.

Network deployment model	Strengths	Weaknesses	Neutron equivalent
FlatDHCP Multi-host with high availability (HA)	Networking failure is isolated to the VMs running on the affected hypervisor. DHCP traffic can be isolated within an individual host. Network traffic is distributed to the compute nodes.	More complex to set up. Compute nodes typically need IP addresses accessible by external networks. Options must be carefully configured for live migration to work with networking services.	Configure neutron with multiple DHCP and layer-3 agents. Network nodes are not able to failover to each other, so the controller runs networking services, such as DHCP. Compute nodes run the ML2 plug-in with support for agents such as Open vSwitch or Linux Bridge.

Both `nova-network` and neutron services provide similar capabilities, such as VLAN between VMs. You also can provide multiple NICs on VMs with either service. Further discussion follows.

VLAN Configuration Within OpenStack VMs

VLAN configuration can be as simple or as complicated as desired. The use of VLANs has the benefit of allowing each project its own subnet and broadcast segregation from other projects. To allow OpenStack to efficiently use VLANs, you must allocate a VLAN range (one for each project) and turn each compute node switch port into a trunk port.

For example, if you estimate that your cloud must support a maximum of 100 projects, pick a free VLAN range that your network infrastructure is currently not using (such as VLAN 200–299). You must configure OpenStack with this range and also configure your switch ports to allow VLAN traffic from that range.

Multi-NIC Provisioning

OpenStack Compute has the ability to assign multiple NICs to instances on a per-project basis. This is generally an advanced feature and not an everyday request. This can easily be done on a per-request basis, though. However, be aware that a second NIC uses up an entire subnet or VLAN. This decrements your total number of supported projects by one.

Multi-Host and Single-Host Networking

The `nova-network` service has the ability to operate in a multi-host or single-host mode. Multi-host is when each compute node runs a copy of `nova-network` and the instances on that compute node use the compute node as a gateway to the Internet.

The compute nodes also host the floating IPs and security groups for instances on that node. Single-host is when a central server—for example, the cloud controller—runs the `nova-network` service. All compute nodes forward traffic from the instances to the cloud controller. The cloud controller then forwards traffic to the Internet. The cloud controller hosts the floating IPs and security groups for all instances on all compute nodes in the cloud.

There are benefits to both modes. Single-node has the downside of a single point of failure. If the cloud controller is not available, instances cannot communicate on the network. This is not true with multi-host, but multi-host requires that each compute node has a public IP address to communicate on the Internet. If you are not able to obtain a significant block of public IP addresses, multi-host might not be an option.

Services for Networking

OpenStack, like any network application, has a number of standard considerations to apply, such as NTP and DNS.

NTP

Time synchronization is a critical element to ensure continued operation of OpenStack components. Correct time is necessary to avoid errors in instance scheduling, replication of objects in the object store, and even matching log timestamps for debugging.

All servers running OpenStack components should be able to access an appropriate NTP server. You may decide to set up one locally or use the public pools available from the Network Time Protocol project (*http://opsgui.de/NPFRua*).

DNS

OpenStack does not currently provide DNS services, aside from the dnsmasq daemon, which resides on `nova-network` hosts. You could consider providing a dynamic DNS service to allow instances to update a DNS entry with new IP addresses. You can also consider making a generic forward and reverse DNS mapping for instances' IP addresses, such as vm-203-0-113-123.example.com.

Conclusion

Armed with your IP address layout and numbers and knowledge about the topologies and services you can use, it's now time to prepare the network for your installation. Be sure to also check out the *OpenStack Security Guide* (*http://opsgui.de/NPG4NW*) for tips on securing your network. We wish you a good relationship with your networking team!

PART II
Operations

Congratulations! By now, you should have a solid design for your cloud. We now recommend that you turn to the OpenStack Installation Guide (*http://opsgui.de/1eLCvD8* for Ubuntu, for example), which contains a step-by-step guide on how to manually install the OpenStack packages and dependencies on your cloud.

While it is important for an operator to be familiar with the steps involved in deploying OpenStack, we also strongly encourage you to evaluate configuration-management tools, such as Puppet or Chef, which can help automate this deployment process.

In the remainder of this guide, we assume that you have successfully deployed an OpenStack cloud and are able to perform basic operations such as adding images, booting instances, and attaching volumes.

As your focus turns to stable operations, we recommend that you do skim the remainder of this book to get a sense of the content. Some of this content is useful to read in advance so that you can put best practices into effect to simplify your life in the long run. Other content is more useful as a reference that you might turn to when an unexpected event occurs (such as a power failure), or to troubleshoot a particular problem.

CHAPTER 8

Lay of the Land

This chapter helps you set up your working environment and use it to take a look around your cloud.

Using the OpenStack Dashboard for Administration

As a cloud administrative user, you can use the OpenStack dashboard to create and manage projects, users, images, and flavors. Users are allowed to create and manage images within specified projects and to share images, depending on the Image Service configuration. Typically, the policy configuration allows admin users only to set quotas and create and manage services. The dashboard provides an Admin tab with a System Panel and Identity Panel. These interfaces give you access to system information and usage as well as to settings for configuring what end users can do. Refer to the OpenStack Admin User Guide (*http://opsgui.de/NPGcgz*) for detailed how-to information about using the dashboard as an admin user.

Command-Line Tools

We recommend using a combination of the OpenStack command-line interface (CLI) tools and the OpenStack dashboard for administration. Some users with a background in other cloud technologies may be using the EC2 Compatibility API, which uses naming conventions somewhat different from the native API. We highlight those differences.

We strongly suggest that you install the command-line clients from the Python Package Index (*http://opsgui.de/1eLBdb8*) (PyPI) instead of from the distribution packages. The clients are under heavy development, and it is very likely at any given time that the version of the packages distributed by your operating-system vendor are out of date.

The pip utility is used to manage package installation from the PyPI archive and is available in the python-pip package in most Linux distributions. Each OpenStack project has its own client, so depending on which services your site runs, install some or all of the following packages:

- python-novaclient (nova CLI)
- python-glanceclient (glance CLI)
- python-keystoneclient (keystone CLI)
- python-cinderclient (cinder CLI)
- python-swiftclient (swift CLI)
- python-neutronclient (neutron CLI)

Installing the Tools

To install (or upgrade) a package from the PyPI archive with pip, as root:

```
# pip install [--upgrade] <package-name>
```

To remove the package:

```
# pip uninstall <package-name>
```

If you need even newer versions of the clients, pip can install directly from the upstream git repository using the `-e` flag. You must specify a name for the Python egg that is installed. For example:

```
# pip install -e git+https://github.com/openstack/
                 python-novaclient.git#egg=python-novaclient
```

If you support the EC2 API on your cloud, you should also install the euca2ools package or some other EC2 API tool so that you can get the same view your users have. Using EC2 API-based tools is mostly out of the scope of this guide, though we discuss getting credentials for use with it.

Administrative Command-Line Tools

There are also several `*-manage` command-line tools. These are installed with the project's services on the cloud controller and do not need to be installed separately:

- `nova-manage`
- `glance-manage`
- `keystone-manage`
- `cinder-manage`

Unlike the CLI tools mentioned above, the `*-manage` tools must be run from the cloud controller, as root, because they need read access to the config files such as `/etc/nova/nova.conf` and to make queries directly against the database rather than against the OpenStack API endpoints.

The existence of the `*-manage` tools is a legacy issue. It is a goal of the OpenStack project to eventually migrate all of the remaining functionality in the `*-manage` tools into the API-based tools. Until that day, you need to SSH into the cloud controller node to perform some maintenance operations that require one of the `*-manage` tools.

Getting Credentials

You must have the appropriate credentials if you want to use the command-line tools to make queries against your OpenStack cloud. By far, the easiest way to obtain authentication credentials to use with command-line clients is to use the OpenStack dashboard. From the top-right navigation row, select Project, then Access & Security, then API Access to access the user settings page where you can set your language and timezone preferences for the dashboard view. This action displays two buttons, Download OpenStack RC File and Download EC2 Credentials, which let you generate files that you can source in your shell to populate the environment variables the command-line tools require to know where your service endpoints and your authentication information are. The user you logged in to the dashboard dictates the filename for the openrc file, such as `demo-openrc.sh`. When logged in as admin, the file is named `admin-openrc.sh`.

The generated file looks something like this:

```
#!/bin/bash

# With the addition of Keystone, to use an openstack cloud you should
# authenticate against keystone, which returns a **Token** and **Service
# Catalog**. The catalog contains the endpoint for all services the
# user/tenant has access to--including nova, glance, keystone, swift.
#
# *NOTE*: Using the 2.0 *auth api* does not mean that compute api is 2.0.
# We use the 1.1 *compute api*
export OS_AUTH_URL=http://203.0.113.10:5000/v2.0

# With the addition of Keystone we have standardized on the term **tenant**
# as the entity that owns the resources.
export OS_TENANT_ID=98333aba48e756fa8f629c83a818ad57
export OS_TENANT_NAME="test-project"

# In addition to the owning entity (tenant), openstack stores the entity
# performing the action as the **user**.
```

```
export OS_USERNAME=demo

# With Keystone you pass the keystone password.
echo "Please enter your OpenStack Password: "
read -s OS_PASSWORD_INPUT
export OS_PASSWORD=$OS_PASSWORD_INPUT
```

This does not save your password in plain text, which is a good thing. But when you source or run the script, it prompts you for your password and then stores your response in the environment variable `OS_PASSWORD`. It is important to note that this does require interactivity. It is possible to store a value directly in the script if you require a noninteractive operation, but you then need to be extremely cautious with the security and permissions of this file.

EC2 compatibility credentials can be downloaded by selecting Project, then Access & Security, then API Access to display the Download EC2 Credentials button. Click the button to generate a ZIP file with server x509 certificates and a shell script fragment. Create a new directory in a secure location because these are live credentials containing all the authentication information required to access your cloud identity, unlike the default `user-openrc`. Extract the ZIP file here. You should have `cacert.pem`, `cert.pem`, `ec2rc.sh`, and `pk.pem`. The `ec2rc.sh` is similar to this:

```
#!/bin/bash

NOVARC=$(readlink -f "${BASH_SOURCE:-${0}}" 2>/dev/null) ||\
NOVARC=$(python -c 'import os,sys; \
print os.path.abspath(os.path.realpath(sys.argv[1]))' "${BASH_SOURCE:-${0}}")
NOVA_KEY_DIR=${NOVARC%/*}
export EC2_ACCESS_KEY=df7f93ec47e84ef8a347bbb3d598449a
export EC2_SECRET_KEY=ead2fff9f8a344e489956deacd47e818
export EC2_URL=http://203.0.113.10:8773/services/Cloud
export EC2_USER_ID=42 # nova does not use user id, but bundling requires it
export EC2_PRIVATE_KEY=${NOVA_KEY_DIR}/pk.pem
export EC2_CERT=${NOVA_KEY_DIR}/cert.pem
export NOVA_CERT=${NOVA_KEY_DIR}/cacert.pem
export EUCALYPTUS_CERT=${NOVA_CERT} # euca-bundle-image seems to require this

alias ec2-bundle-image="ec2-bundle-image --cert $EC2_CERT --privatekey \
$EC2_PRIVATE_KEY --user 42 --ec2cert $NOVA_CERT"
alias ec2-upload-bundle="ec2-upload-bundle -a $EC2_ACCESS_KEY -s \
$EC2_SECRET_KEY --url $S3_URL --ec2cert $NOVA_CERT"
```

To put the EC2 credentials into your environment, source the `ec2rc.sh` file.

Inspecting API Calls

The command-line tools can be made to show the OpenStack API calls they make by passing the `--debug` flag to them. For example:

```
# nova --debug list
```

This example shows the HTTP requests from the client and the responses from the endpoints, which can be helpful in creating custom tools written to the OpenStack API.

Keyring Support (*http://opsgui.de/NPGeVy*) enables you to securely save your OpenStack password in an encrypted file.

This feature is disabled by default. To enable it, add the `--os-cache` flag or set the environment variable `OS_CACHE=1`.

Configuring `OS_CACHE` causes the command-line tool to authenticate on each and every interaction with the cloud. This can assist with working around this scenario. However, it increases the time taken to run commands and also the load on the server.

Using cURL for further inspection

Underlying the use of the command-line tools is the OpenStack API, which is a RESTful API that runs over HTTP. There may be cases where you want to interact with the API directly or need to use it because of a suspected bug in one of the CLI tools. The best way to do this is to use a combination of cURL (*http://opsgui.de/1eLBfQy*) and another tool, such as jq (*http://opsgui.de/NPGdB5*), to parse the JSON from the responses.

The first thing you must do is authenticate with the cloud using your credentials to get an authentication token.

Your credentials are a combination of username, password, and tenant (project). You can extract these values from the `openrc.sh` discussed above. The token allows you to interact with your other service endpoints without needing to reauthenticate for every request. Tokens are typically good for 24 hours, and when the token expires, you are alerted with a 401 (Unauthorized) response and you can request another token.

1. Look at your OpenStack service catalog:

```
$ curl -s -X POST http://203.0.113.10:35357/v2.0/tokens \
-d '{"auth": {"passwordCredentials": {"username":"test-user", \
                                     "password":"test-password"},  \
                                     "tenantName":"test-project"}}' \
-H "Content-type: application/json" | jq .
```

2. Read through the JSON response to get a feel for how the catalog is laid out.

   To make working with subsequent requests easier, store the token in an environment variable:

   ```
   $ TOKEN=`curl -s -X POST http://203.0.113.10:35357/v2.0/tokens \
   -d '{"auth": {"passwordCredentials": {"username":"test-user", \
                                         "password":"test-password"}, \
                                         "tenantName":"test-project"}}' \
   -H "Content-type: application/json" |  jq -r .access.token.id`
   ```

   Now you can refer to your token on the command line as `$TOKEN`.

3. Pick a service endpoint from your service catalog, such as compute. Try a request, for example, listing instances (servers):

   ```
   $ curl -s \
   -H "X-Auth-Token: $TOKEN" \
   http://203.0.113.10:8774/v2/98333aba48e756fa8f629c83a818ad57/servers | jq .
   ```

To discover how API requests should be structured, read the OpenStack API Reference (*http://opsgui.de/1eLBhrz*). To chew through the responses using jq, see the jq Manual (*http://opsgui.de/NPGeoH*).

The `-s flag` used in the cURL commands above are used to prevent the progress meter from being shown. If you are having trouble running cURL commands, you'll want to remove it. Likewise, to help you troubleshoot cURL commands, you can include the `-v` flag to show you the verbose output. There are many more extremely useful features in cURL; refer to the man page for all the options.

Servers and Services

As an administrator, you have a few ways to discover what your OpenStack cloud looks like simply by using the OpenStack tools available. This section gives you an idea of how to get an overview of your cloud, its shape, size, and current state.

First, you can discover what servers belong to your OpenStack cloud by running:

```
# nova-manage service list | sort
```

The output looks like the following:

```
Binary           Host              Zone Status  State Updated_At
nova-cert        cloud.example.com nova enabled  :-)  2013-02-25 19:32:38
nova-compute     c01.example.com   nova enabled  :-)  2013-02-25 19:32:35
nova-compute     c02.example.com   nova enabled  :-)  2013-02-25 19:32:32
nova-compute     c03.example.com   nova enabled  :-)  2013-02-25 19:32:36
nova-compute     c04.example.com   nova enabled  :-)  2013-02-25 19:32:32
nova-compute     c05.example.com   nova enabled  :-)  2013-02-25 19:32:41
nova-conductor   cloud.example.com nova enabled  :-)  2013-02-25 19:32:40
nova-consoleauth cloud.example.com nova enabled  :-)  2013-02-25 19:32:36
```

```
nova-network     cloud.example.com nova enabled  :-)  2013-02-25 19:32:32
nova-scheduler   cloud.example.com nova enabled  :-)  2013-02-25 19:32:33
```

The output shows that there are five compute nodes and one cloud controller. You see a smiley face, such as `:-)`, which indicates that the services are up and running. If a service is no longer available, the `:-)` symbol changes to `XXX`. This is an indication that you should troubleshoot why the service is down.

If you are using cinder, run the following command to see a similar listing:

```
# cinder-manage host list | sort

host              zone
c01.example.com   nova
c02.example.com   nova
c03.example.com   nova
c04.example.com   nova
c05.example.com   nova
cloud.example.com nova
```

With these two tables, you now have a good overview of what servers and services make up your cloud.

You can also use the Identity Service (keystone) to see what services are available in your cloud as well as what endpoints have been configured for the services.

The following command requires you to have your shell environment configured with the proper administrative variables:

```
$ keystone catalog

Service: image
+-------------+----------------------------------------+
|   Property  |                 Value                  |
+-------------+----------------------------------------+
|   adminURL  | http://cloud.internal.example.com:9292 |
| internalURL | http://cloud.example.com:9292          |
|  publicURL  | http://cloud.example.com:9292          |
|    region   |               RegionOne                |
+-------------+----------------------------------------+

Service: identity
+-------------+----------------------------------------------+
|   Property  |                    Value                     |
+-------------+----------------------------------------------+
|   adminURL  | http://cloud.internal.example.com:35357/v2.0 |
| internalURL | http://cloud.example.com:5000/v2.0           |
|  publicURL  | http://cloud.example.com:5000/v2.0           |
|    region   |                  RegionOne                   |
+-------------+----------------------------------------------+
```

The preceding output has been truncated to show only two services. You will see one service block for each service that your cloud provides. Note how the endpoint domain can be different depending on the endpoint type. Different endpoint domains per type are not required, but this can be done for different reasons, such as endpoint privacy or network traffic segregation.

You can find the version of the Compute installation by using the `nova-manage` command:

```
# nova-manage version list
```

Diagnose Your Compute Nodes

You can obtain extra information about virtual machines that are running—their CPU usage, the memory, the disk I/O or network I/O—per instance, by running the `nova diagnostics` command with a server ID:

```
$ nova diagnostics <serverID>
```

The output of this command varies depending on the hypervisor because hypervisors support different attributes. The following demonstrates the difference between the two most popular hypervisors. Here is example output when the hypervisor is Xen:

```
+----------------+-----------------+
|    Property    |      Value      |
+----------------+-----------------+
| cpu0           | 4.3627          |
| memory         | 1171088064.0000 |
| memory_target  | 1171088064.0000 |
| vbd_xvda_read  | 0.0             |
| vbd_xvda_write | 0.0             |
| vif_0_rx       | 3223.6870       |
| vif_0_tx       | 0.0             |
| vif_1_rx       | 104.4955        |
| vif_1_tx       | 0.0             |
+----------------+-----------------+
```

While the command should work with any hypervisor that is controlled through libvirt (e.g., KVM, QEMU, or LXC), it has been tested only with KVM. Here is example output when the hypervisor is KVM:

```
+-------------------+------------+
| Property          | Value      |
+-------------------+------------+
| cpu0_time         | 2870000000 |
| memory            | 524288     |
| vda_errors        | -1         |
| vda_read          | 262144     |
| vda_read_req      | 112        |
| vda_write         | 5606400    |
| vda_write_req     | 376        |
| vnet0_rx          | 63343      |
| vnet0_rx_drop     | 0          |
| vnet0_rx_errors   | 0          |
| vnet0_rx_packets  | 431        |
| vnet0_tx          | 4905       |
| vnet0_tx_drop     | 0          |
| vnet0_tx_errors   | 0          |
| vnet0_tx_packets  | 45         |
+-------------------+------------+
```

Network Inspection

To see which fixed IP networks are configured in your cloud, you can use the `nova` command-line client to get the IP ranges:

```
$ nova network-list
+--------------------------------------+--------+--------------+
| ID                                   | Label  | Cidr         |
+--------------------------------------+--------+--------------+
| 3df67919-9600-4ea8-952e-2a7be6f70774 | test01 |  10.1.0.0/24 |
| 8283efb2-e53d-46e1-a6bd-bb2bdef9cb9a | test02 |  10.1.1.0/24 |
+--------------------------------------+--------+--------------+
```

The `nova-manage` tool can provide some additional details:

```
# nova-manage network list
id IPv4        IPv6 start address DNS1 DNS2 VlanID project   uuid
1  10.1.0.0/24 None 10.1.0.3      None None 300    2725bbd   beacb3f2
2  10.1.1.0/24 None 10.1.1.3      None None 301    none      d0b1a796
```

This output shows that two networks are configured, each network containing 255 IPs (a /24 subnet). The first network has been assigned to a certain project, while the second network is still open for assignment. You can assign this network manually; otherwise, it is automatically assigned when a project launches its first instance.

To find out whether any floating IPs are available in your cloud, run:

```
# nova-manage floating list

2725bb...59f43f 1.2.3.4 None            nova vlan20
None            1.2.3.5 48a415...b010ff nova vlan20
```

Here, two floating IPs are available. The first has been allocated to a project, while the other is unallocated.

Users and Projects

To see a list of projects that have been added to the cloud, run:

```
$ keystone tenant-list

+-----+----------+---------+
| id  | name     | enabled |
+-----+----------+---------+
| ... | jtopjian | True    |
| ... | alvaro   | True    |
| ... | everett  | True    |
| ... | admin    | True    |
| ... | services | True    |
| ... | jonathan | True    |
| ... | lorin    | True    |
| ... | anne     | True    |
| ... | rhulsker | True    |
| ... | tom      | True    |
| ... | adam     | True    |
+-----+----------+---------+
```

To see a list of users, run:

```
$ keystone user-list

+-----+----------+---------+------------------------------+
| id  | name     | enabled | email                        |
+-----+----------+---------+------------------------------+
| ... | everett  | True    | everett.towne@backspace.com  |
| ... | jonathan | True    | jon@sfcu.edu                 |
| ... | nova     | True    | nova@localhost               |
| ... | rhulsker | True    | ryan.hulkster@cyberalbert.ca |
| ... | lorin    | True    | lorinhoch@nsservices.com     |
| ... | alvaro   | True    | Alvaro.Perry@cyberalbert.ca  |
| ... | anne     | True    | anne.green@backspace.com     |
| ... | admin    | True    | root@localhost               |
| ... | cinder   | True    | cinder@localhost             |
| ... | glance   | True    | glance@localhost             |
| ... | jtopjian | True    | joe.topjian@cyberalbert.com  |
| ... | adam     | True    | adam@ossmanuals.net          |
| ... | tom      | True    | fafield@univm.edu.au         |
+-----+----------+---------+------------------------------+
```

Sometimes a user and a group have a one-to-one mapping. This happens for standard system accounts, such as cinder, glance, nova, and swift, or when only one user is part of a group.

Running Instances

To see a list of running instances, run:

```
$ nova list --all-tenants

+-----+------------------+--------+-------------------------------------------+
| ID  | Name             | Status | Networks                                  |
+-----+------------------+--------+-------------------------------------------+
| ... | Windows          | ACTIVE | novanetwork_1=10.1.1.3, 199.116.232.39    |
| ... | cloud controller | ACTIVE | novanetwork_0=10.1.0.6; jtopjian=10.1.2.3 |
| ... | compute node 1   | ACTIVE | novanetwork_0=10.1.0.4; jtopjian=10.1.2.4 |
| ... | devbox           | ACTIVE | novanetwork_0=10.1.0.3                    |
| ... | devstack         | ACTIVE | novanetwork_0=10.1.0.5                    |
| ... | initial          | ACTIVE | nova_network=10.1.7.4, 10.1.8.4           |
| ... | lorin-head       | ACTIVE | nova_network=10.1.7.3, 10.1.8.3           |
+-----+------------------+--------+-------------------------------------------+
```

Unfortunately, this command does not tell you various details about the running instances, such as what compute node the instance is running on, what flavor the instance is, and so on. You can use the following command to view details about individual instances:

```
$ nova show <uuid>
```

For example:

```
# nova show 81db556b-8aa5-427d-a95c-2a9a6972f630

+-------------------------------------+-----------------------------------+
| Property                            | Value                             |
+-------------------------------------+-----------------------------------+
| OS-DCF:diskConfig                   | MANUAL                            |
| OS-EXT-SRV-ATTR:host                | c02.example.com                   |
| OS-EXT-SRV-ATTR:hypervisor_hostname | c02.example.com                   |
| OS-EXT-SRV-ATTR:instance_name       | instance-00000029                 |
| OS-EXT-STS:power_state              | 1                                 |
| OS-EXT-STS:task_state               | None                              |
| OS-EXT-STS:vm_state                 | active                            |
| accessIPv4                          |                                   |
| accessIPv6                          |                                   |
| config_drive                        |                                   |
| created                             | 2013-02-13T20:08:36Z              |
| flavor                              | m1.small (6)                      |
| hostId                              | ...                               |
| id                                  | ...                               |
| image                               | Ubuntu 12.04 cloudimg amd64 (...) |
| key_name                            | jtopjian-sandbox                  |
| metadata                            | {}                                |
| name                                | devstack                          |
| novanetwork_0 network               | 10.1.0.5                          |
| progress                            | 0                                 |
| security_groups                     | [{u'name': u'default'}]           |
```

```
| status                              | ACTIVE                              |
| tenant_id                           | ...                                 |
| updated                             | 2013-02-13T20:08:59Z                |
| user_id                             | ...                                 |
+-------------------------------------+-------------------------------------+
```

This output shows that an instance named **devstack** was created from an Ubuntu 12.04 image using a flavor of `m1.small` and is hosted on the compute node `c02.example.com`.

Summary

We hope you have enjoyed this quick tour of your working environment, including how to interact with your cloud and extract useful information. From here, you can use the *Admin User Guide (http://opsgui.de/1eLBkDJ)* as your reference for all of the command-line functionality in your cloud.

CHAPTER 9

Managing Projects and Users

An OpenStack cloud does not have much value without users. This chapter covers topics that relate to managing users, projects, and quotas. This chapter describes users and projects as described by version 2 of the OpenStack Identity API.

While version 3 of the Identity API is available, the client tools do not yet implement those calls, and most OpenStack clouds are still implementing Identity API v2.0.

Projects or Tenants?

In OpenStack user interfaces and documentation, a group of users is referred to as a project or tenant. These terms are interchangeable.

The initial implementation of the OpenStack Compute Service (nova) had its own authentication system and used the term `project`. When authentication moved into the OpenStack Identity Service (keystone) project, it used the term `tenant` to refer to a group of users. Because of this legacy, some of the OpenStack tools refer to projects and some refer to tenants.

This guide uses the term `project`, unless an example shows interaction with a tool that uses the term `tenant`.

Managing Projects

Users must be associated with at least one project, though they may belong to many. Therefore, you should add at least one project before adding users.

Adding Projects

To create a project through the OpenStack dashboard:

1. Log in as an administrative user.
2. Select the Admin tab in the left navigation bar.
3. Under Identity Panel, click Projects.
4. Click the Create Project button.

You are prompted for a project name and an optional, but recommended, description. Select the checkbox at the bottom of the form to enable this project. By default, it is enabled, as shown in Figure 9-1.

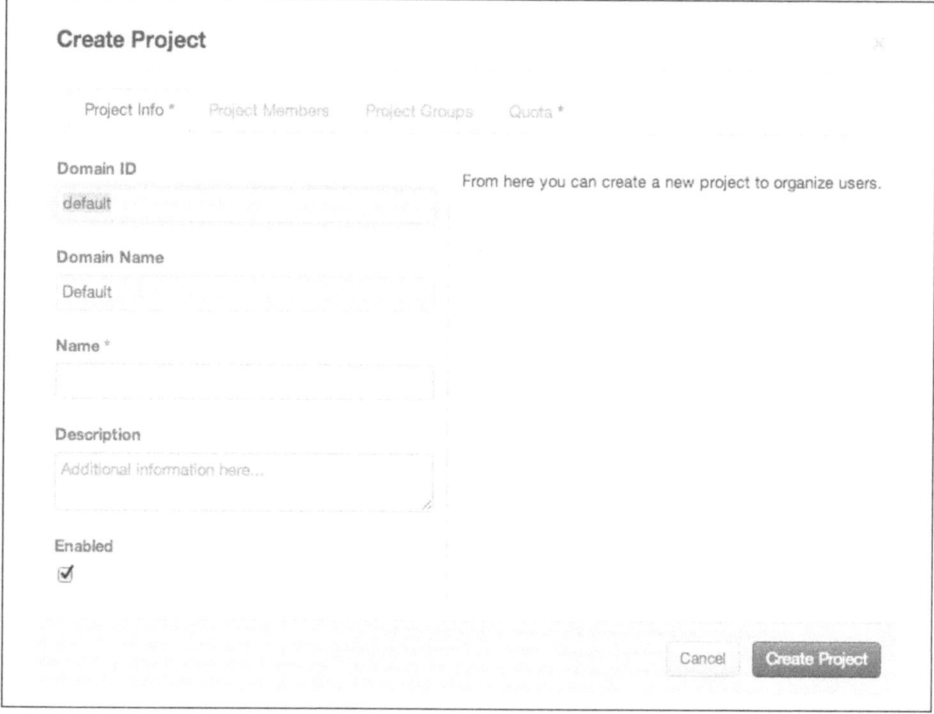

Figure 9-1. Dashboard's Create Project form

It is also possible to add project members and adjust the project quotas. We'll discuss those actions later, but in practice, it can be quite convenient to deal with all these operations at one time.

To add a project through the command line, you must use the keystone utility, which uses `tenant` in place of `project`:

```
# keystone tenant-create --name=demo
```

This command creates a project named "demo." Optionally, you can add a description string by appending `--description` *`tenant-description`*, which can be very useful. You can also create a group in a disabled state by appending `--enabled false` to the command. By default, projects are created in an enabled state.

Quotas

To prevent system capacities from being exhausted without notification, you can set up quotas. Quotas are operational limits. For example, the number of gigabytes allowed per tenant can be controlled to ensure that a single tenant cannot consume all of the disk space. Quotas are currently enforced at the tenant (or project) level, rather than by users.

Because without sensible quotas a single tenant could use up all the available resources, default quotas are shipped with OpenStack. You should pay attention to which quota settings make sense for your hardware capabilities.

Using the command-line interface, you can manage quotas for the OpenStack Compute Service and the Block Storage Service.

Typically, default values are changed because a tenant requires more than the OpenStack default of 10 volumes per tenant, or more than the OpenStack default of 1 TB of disk space on a compute node.

To view all tenants, run:

```
$ keystone tenant-list
```

```
+----------------------------------+----------+---------+
|                id                |   name   | enabled |
+----------------------------------+----------+---------+
| a981642d22c94e159a4a6540f70f9f8  |  admin   |   True  |
| 934b662357674c7b9f5e4ec6ded4d0e  | tenant01 |   True  |
| 7bc1dbfd7d284ec4a856ea1eb82dca8  | tenant02 |   True  |
| 9c554aaef7804ba49e1b21cbd97d218  | services |   True  |
+----------------------------------+----------+---------+
```

Set Image Quotas

OpenStack Havana introduced a basic quota feature for the Image service, so you can now restrict a project's image storage by total number of bytes. Currently, this quota is applied cloud-wide, so if you were to set an Image quota limit of 5 GB, then all projects in your cloud will be able to store only 5 GB of images and snapshots.

To enable this feature, edit the `/etc/glance/glance-api.conf` file, and under the [DEFAULT] section, add:

```
user_storage_quota = <bytes>
```

For example, to restrict a project's image storage to 5 GB, do this:

```
user_storage_quota = 5368709120
```

In the Icehouse release, there is a configuration option in `glance-api.conf` that limits the number of members allowed per image, called `image_member_quota`, set to 128 by default. That setting is a different quota from the storage quota.

Set Compute Service Quotas

As an administrative user, you can update the Compute Service quotas for an existing tenant, as well as update the quota defaults for a new tenant. See Table 9-1.

Table 9-1. Compute quota descriptions

Quota	Description	Property name
Fixed IPs	Number of fixed IP addresses allowed per tenant. This number must be equal to or greater than the number of allowed instances.	`fixed-ips`
Floating IPs	Number of floating IP addresses allowed per tenant.	`floating-ips`
Injected file content bytes	Number of content bytes allowed per injected file.	`injected-file-content-bytes`
Injected file path bytes	Number of bytes allowed per injected file path.	`injected-file-path-bytes`
Injected files	Number of injected files allowed per tenant.	`injected-files`
Instances	Number of instances allowed per tenant.	`instances`
Key pairs	Number of key pairs allowed per user.	`key-pairs`
Metadata items	Number of metadata items allowed per instance.	`metadata-items`

Quota	Description	Property name
RAM	Megabytes of instance RAM allowed per tenant.	`ram`
Security group rules	Number of rules per security group.	`security-group-rules`
Security groups	Number of security groups per tenant.	`security-groups`
VCPUs	Number of instance cores allowed per tenant.	`cores`

View and update compute quotas for a tenant (project)

As an administrative user, you can use the `nova quota-*` commands, which are provided by the `python-novaclient` package, to view and update tenant quotas.

To view and update default quota values

1. List all default quotas for all tenants, as follows:

   ```
   $ nova quota-defaults
   ```

   For example:

   ```
   $ nova quota-defaults
   +-----------------------------+-------+
   | Property                    | Value |
   +-----------------------------+-------+
   | metadata_items              | 128   |
   | injected_file_content_bytes | 10240 |
   | ram                         | 51200 |
   | floating_ips                | 10    |
   | key_pairs                   | 100   |
   | instances                   | 10    |
   | security_group_rules        | 20    |
   | injected_files              | 5     |
   | cores                       | 20    |
   | fixed_ips                   | -1    |
   | injected_file_path_bytes    | 255   |
   | security_groups             | 10    |
   +-----------------------------+-------+
   ```

2. Update a default value for a new tenant, as follows:

   ```
   $ nova quota-class-update default key value
   ```

   For example:

   ```
   $ nova quota-class-update default instances 15
   ```

To view quota values for a tenant (project)

1. Place the tenant ID in a useable variable, as follows:

   ```
   $ tenant=$(keystone tenant-list | awk '/tenantName/ {print $2}')
   ```

2. List the currently set quota values for a tenant, as follows:

   ```
   $ nova quota-show --tenant $tenant
   ```

   For example:

   ```
   $ nova quota-show --tenant $tenant
   +-----------------------------+-------+
   | Property                    | Value |
   +-----------------------------+-------+
   | metadata_items              | 128   |
   | injected_file_content_bytes | 10240 |
   | ram                         | 51200 |
   | floating_ips                | 12    |
   | key_pairs                   | 100   |
   | instances                   | 10    |
   | security_group_rules        | 20    |
   | injected_files              | 5     |
   | cores                       | 20    |
   | fixed_ips                   | -1    |
   | injected_file_path_bytes    | 255   |
   | security_groups             | 10    |
   +-----------------------------+-------+
   ```

To update quota values for a tenant (project)

1. Obtain the tenant ID, as follows:

   ```
   $ tenant=$(keystone tenant-list | awk '/tenantName/ {print $2}')
   ```

2. Update a particular quota value, as follows:

   ```
   # nova quota-update --quotaName quotaValue tenantID
   ```

   For example:

   ```
   # nova quota-update --floating-ips 20 $tenant
   # nova quota-show --tenant $tenant
   +-----------------------------+-------+
   | Property                    | Value |
   +-----------------------------+-------+
   | metadata_items              | 128   |
   | injected_file_content_bytes | 10240 |
   | ram                         | 51200 |
   | floating_ips                | 20    |
   | key_pairs                   | 100   |
   | instances                   | 10    |
   | security_group_rules        | 20    |
   | injected_files              | 5     |
   | cores                       | 20    |
   ```

```
| fixed_ips                  | -1    |
| injected_file_path_bytes   | 255   |
| security_groups            | 10    |
+----------------------------+-------+
```

To view a list of options for the `quota-update` command, run:

```
$ nova help quota-update
```

Set Object Storage Quotas

Object Storage quotas were introduced in Swift 1.8 (OpenStack Grizzly). There are currently two categories of quotas for Object Storage:

Container quotas
: Limit the total size (in bytes) or number of objects that can be stored in a single container.

Account quotas
: Limit the total size (in bytes) that a user has available in the Object Storage service.

To take advantage of either container quotas or account quotas, your Object Storage proxy server must have `container_quotas` or `account_quotas` (or both) added to the `[pipeline:main]` pipeline. Each quota type also requires its own section in the `proxy-server.conf` file:

```
[pipeline:main]
pipeline = healthcheck [...] container_quotas account_quotas proxy-server

[filter:account_quotas]
use = egg:swift#account_quotas

[filter:container_quotas]
use = egg:swift#container_quotas
```

To view and update Object Storage quotas, use the `swift` command provided by the `python-swiftclient` package. Any user included in the project can view the quotas placed on their project. To update Object Storage quotas on a project, you must have the role of ResellerAdmin in the project that the quota is being applied to.

To view account quotas placed on a project:

```
$ swift stat

   Account: AUTH_b36ed2d326034beba0a9dd1fb19b70f9
Containers: 0
   Objects: 0
     Bytes: 0
Meta Quota-Bytes: 214748364800
X-Timestamp: 1351050521.29419
Content-Type: text/plain; charset=utf-8
Accept-Ranges: bytes
```

To apply or update account quotas on a project:

```
$ swift post -m quota-bytes:
     <bytes>
```

For example, to place a 5 GB quota on an account:

```
$ swift post -m quota-bytes:
     5368709120
```

To verify the quota, run the `swift stat` command again:

```
$ swift stat

   Account: AUTH_b36ed2d326034beba0a9dd1fb19b70f9
Containers: 0
   Objects: 0
     Bytes: 0
Meta Quota-Bytes: 5368709120
X-Timestamp: 1351541410.38328
Content-Type: text/plain; charset=utf-8
Accept-Ranges: bytes
```

Set Block Storage Quotas

As an administrative user, you can update the Block Storage Service quotas for a tenant, as well as update the quota defaults for a new tenant. See Table 9-2.

Table 9-2. Block Storage quota descriptions

Property name	Description
gigabytes	Number of volume gigabytes allowed per tenant
snapshots	Number of Block Storage snapshots allowed per tenant.
volumes	Number of Block Storage volumes allowed per tenant

View and update Block Storage quotas for a tenant (project)

As an administrative user, you can use the `cinder quota-*` commands, which are provided by the `python-cinderclient` package, to view and update tenant quotas.

To view and update default Block Storage quota values

1. List all default quotas for all tenants, as follows:

   ```
   $ cinder quota-defaults
   ```

   For example:

   ```
   $ cinder quota-defaults
   +-----------+-------+
   |  Property | Value |
   +-----------+-------+
   | gigabytes |  1000 |
   | snapshots |   10  |
   |  volumes  |   10  |
   +-----------+-------+
   ```

2. To update a default value for a new tenant, update the property in the `/etc/cinder/cinder.conf` file.

To view Block Storage quotas for a tenant

1. View quotas for the tenant, as follows:

   ```
   # cinder quota-show tenantName
   ```

   For example:

   ```
   # cinder quota-show tenant01
   +-----------+-------+
   |  Property | Value |
   +-----------+-------+
   | gigabytes |  1000 |
   | snapshots |   10  |
   |  volumes  |   10  |
   +-----------+-------+
   ```

To update Compute Service quotas

1. Place the tenant ID in a useable variable, as follows:

   ```
   $ tenant=$(keystone tenant-list | awk '/tenantName/ {print $2}')
   ```

2. Update a particular quota value, as follows:

   ```
   # cinder quota-update --quotaName NewValue tenantID
   ```

   For example:

```
# cinder quota-update --volumes 15 $tenant
# cinder quota-show tenant01
+-----------+-------+
|  Property | Value |
+-----------+-------+
| gigabytes |  1000 |
| snapshots |   10  |
|  volumes  |   15  |
+-----------+-------+
```

User Management

The command-line tools for managing users are inconvenient to use directly. They require issuing multiple commands to complete a single task, and they use UUIDs rather than symbolic names for many items. In practice, humans typically do not use these tools directly. Fortunately, the OpenStack dashboard provides a reasonable interface to this. In addition, many sites write custom tools for local needs to enforce local policies and provide levels of self-service to users that aren't currently available with packaged tools.

Creating New Users

To create a user, you need the following information:

- Username
- Email address
- Password
- Primary project
- Role

Username and email address are self-explanatory, though your site may have local conventions you should observe. Setting and changing passwords in the Identity service requires administrative privileges. As of the Folsom release, users cannot change their own passwords. This is a large driver for creating local custom tools, and must be kept in mind when assigning and distributing passwords. The primary project is simply the first project the user is associated with and must exist prior to creating the user. Role is almost always going to be "member." Out of the box, OpenStack comes with two roles defined:

member
: A typical user

admin
: An administrative super user, which has full permissions across all projects and should be used with great care

It is possible to define other roles, but doing so is uncommon.

Once you've gathered this information, creating the user in the dashboard is just another web form similar to what we've seen before and can be found by clicking the Users link in the Admin navigation bar and then clicking the Create User button at the top right.

Modifying users is also done from this Users page. If you have a large number of users, this page can get quite crowded. The Filter search box at the top of the page can be used to limit the users listing. A form very similar to the user creation dialog can be pulled up by selecting Edit from the actions dropdown menu at the end of the line for the user you are modifying.

Associating Users with Projects

Many sites run with users being associated with only one project. This is a more conservative and simpler choice both for administration and for users. Administratively, if a user reports a problem with an instance or quota, it is obvious which project this relates to. Users needn't worry about what project they are acting in if they are only in one project. However, note that, by default, any user can affect the resources of any other user within their project. It is also possible to associate users with multiple projects if that makes sense for your organization.

Associating existing users with an additional project or removing them from an older project is done from the Projects page of the dashboard by selecting Modify Users from the Actions column, as shown in Figure 9-2.

From this view, you can do a number of useful things, as well as a few dangerous ones.

The first column of this form, named All Users, includes a list of all the users in your cloud who are not already associated with this project. The second column shows all the users who are. These lists can be quite long, but they can be limited by typing a substring of the username you are looking for in the filter field at the top of the column.

From here, click the + icon to add users to the project. Click the - to remove them.

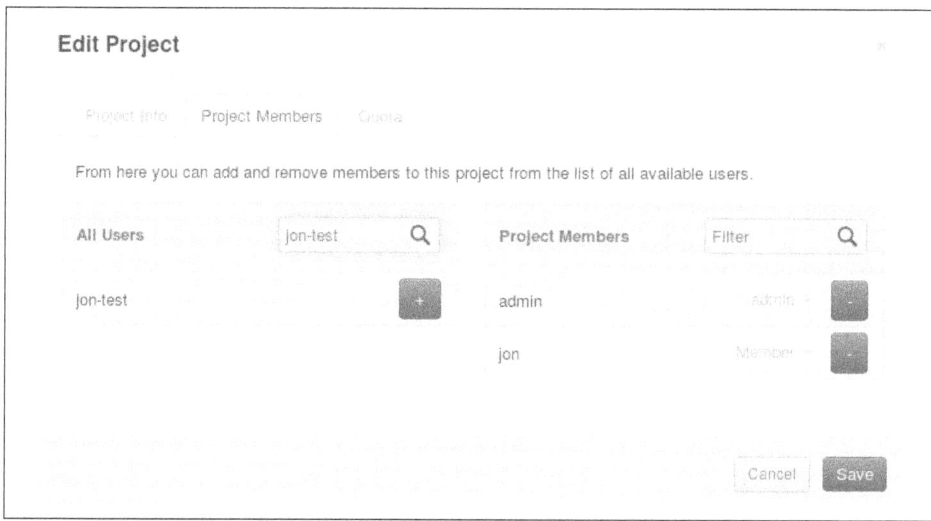

Figure 9-2. Edit Project Members tab

The dangerous possibility comes with the ability to change member roles. This is the dropdown list below the username in the Project Members list. In virtually all cases, this value should be set to Member. This example purposefully shows an administrative user where this value is admin.

The admin is global, not per project, so granting a user the admin role in any project gives the user administrative rights across the whole cloud.

Typical use is to only create administrative users in a single project, by convention the admin project, which is created by default during cloud setup. If your administrative users also use the cloud to launch and manage instances, it is strongly recommended that you use separate user accounts for administrative access and normal operations and that they be in distinct projects.

Customizing Authorization

The default authorization settings allow administrative users only to create resources on behalf of a different project. OpenStack handles two kinds of authorization policies:

Operation based
: Policies specify access criteria for specific operations, possibly with fine-grained control over specific attributes.

Resource based
: Whether access to a specific resource might be granted or not according to the permissions configured for the resource (currently available only for the network resource). The actual authorization policies enforced in an OpenStack service vary from deployment to deployment.

The policy engine reads entries from the `policy.json` file. The actual location of this file might vary from distribution to distribution: for nova, it is typically in `/etc/nova/policy.json`. You can update entries while the system is running, and you do not have to restart services. Currently, the only way to update such policies is to edit the policy file.

The OpenStack service's policy engine matches a policy directly. A rule indicates evaluation of the elements of such policies. For instance, in a `compute:create: [["rule:admin_or_owner"]]` statement, the policy is `compute:create`, and the rule is `admin_or_owner`.

Policies are triggered by an OpenStack policy engine whenever one of them matches an OpenStack API operation or a specific attribute being used in a given operation. For instance, the engine tests the `create:compute` policy every time a user sends a `POST /v2/{tenant_id}/servers` request to the OpenStack Compute API server. Policies can be also related to specific API extensions. For instance, if a user needs an extension like `compute_extension:rescue`, the attributes defined by the provider extensions trigger the rule test for that operation.

An authorization policy can be composed by one or more rules. If more rules are specified, evaluation policy is successful if any of the rules evaluates successfully; if an API operation matches multiple policies, then all the policies must evaluate successfully. Also, authorization rules are recursive. Once a rule is matched, the rule(s) can be resolved to another rule, until a terminal rule is reached. These are the rules defined:

Role-based rules
: Evaluate successfully if the user submitting the request has the specified role. For instance, `"role:admin"` is successful if the user submitting the request is an administrator.

Field-based rules
: Evaluate successfully if a field of the resource specified in the current request matches a specific value. For instance, `"field:networks:shared=True"` is successful if the attribute shared of the network resource is set to `true`.

Generic rules
: Compare an attribute in the resource with an attribute extracted from the user's security credentials and evaluates successfully if the comparison is successful. For instance, `"tenant_id:%(tenant_id)s"` is successful if the tenant identifier in the resource is equal to the tenant identifier of the user submitting the request.

Here are snippets of the default nova `policy.json` file:

```
{
        "context_is_admin":  [["role:admin"]],
        "admin_or_owner":  [["is_admin:True"], \
        ["project_id:%(project_id)s"]], ❶
        "default": [["rule:admin_or_owner"]], ❷
        "compute:create": [ ],
        "compute:create:attach_network": [ ],
        "compute:create:attach_volume": [ ],
        "compute:get_all": [ ],
    "admin_api": [["is_admin:True"]],
        "compute_extension:accounts": [["rule:admin_api"]],
        "compute_extension:admin_actions": [["rule:admin_api"]],
        "compute_extension:admin_actions:pause": [["rule:admin_or_owner"]],
        "compute_extension:admin_actions:unpause": [["rule:admin_or_owner"]],
        ...
        "compute_extension:admin_actions:migrate": [["rule:admin_api"]],
        "compute_extension:aggregates": [["rule:admin_api"]],
        "compute_extension:certificates": [ ],
        ...
        "compute_extension:flavorextraspecs": [ ],
        "compute_extension:flavormanage": [["rule:admin_api"]], ❸
        }
```

❶ Shows a rule that evaluates successfully if the current user is an administrator or the owner of the resource specified in the request (tenant identifier is equal).

❷ Shows the default policy, which is always evaluated if an API operation does not match any of the policies in `policy.json`.

❸ Shows a policy restricting the ability to manipulate flavors to administrators using the Admin API only.

In some cases, some operations should be restricted to administrators only. Therefore, as a further example, let us consider how this sample policy file could be modified in a scenario where we enable users to create their own flavors:

```
"compute_extension:flavormanage": [ ],
```

Users Who Disrupt Other Users

Users on your cloud can disrupt other users, sometimes intentionally and maliciously and other times by accident. Understanding the situation allows you to make a better decision on how to handle the disruption.

For example, a group of users have instances that are utilizing a large amount of compute resources for very compute-intensive tasks. This is driving the load up on compute nodes and affecting other users. In this situation, review your user use cases. You may find that high compute scenarios are common, and should then plan for proper segregation in your cloud, such as host aggregation or regions.

Another example is a user consuming a very large amount of bandwidth. Again, the key is to understand what the user is doing. If she naturally needs a high amount of bandwidth, you might have to limit her transmission rate as to not affect other users or move her to an area with more bandwidth available. On the other hand, maybe her instance has been hacked and is part of a botnet launching DDOS attacks. Resolution of this issue is the same as though any other server on your network has been hacked. Contact the user and give her time to respond. If she doesn't respond, shut down the instance.

A final example is if a user is hammering cloud resources repeatedly. Contact the user and learn what he is trying to do. Maybe he doesn't understand that what he's doing is inappropriate, or maybe there is an issue with the resource he is trying to access that is causing his requests to queue or lag.

Summary

One key element of systems administration that is often overlooked is that end users are the reason systems administrators exist. Don't go the BOFH route and terminate every user who causes an alert to go off. Work with users to understand what they're trying to accomplish and see how your environment can better assist them in achieving their goals. Meet your users needs by organizing your users into projects, applying policies, managing quotas, and working with them.

CHAPTER 10

User-Facing Operations

This guide is for OpenStack operators and does not seek to be an exhaustive reference for users, but as an operator, you should have a basic understanding of how to use the cloud facilities. This chapter looks at OpenStack from a basic user perspective, which helps you understand your users' needs and determine, when you get a trouble ticket, whether it is a user issue or a service issue. The main concepts covered are images, flavors, security groups, block storage, and instances.

Images

OpenStack images can often be thought of as "virtual machine templates." Images can also be standard installation media such as ISO images. Essentially, they contain bootable file systems that are used to launch instances.

Adding Images

Several premade images exist and can easily be imported into the Image Service. A common image to add is the CirrOS image, which is very small and used for testing purposes. To add this image, simply do:

```
$ wget http://download.cirros-cloud.net/0.3.1/cirros-0.3.1-x86_64-disk.img
$ glance image-create --name='cirros image' --is-public=true \
  --container-format=bare --disk-format=qcow2 < cirros-0.3.1-x86_64-disk.img
```

The `glance image-create` command provides a large set of options for working with your image. For example, the `min-disk` option is useful for images that require root disks of a certain size (for example, large Windows images). To view these options, do:

```
$ glance help image-create
```

The `location` option is important to note. It does not copy the entire image into the Image Service, but references an original location where the image can be found. Upon launching an instance of that image, the Image Service accesses the image from the location specified.

The `copy-from` option copies the image from the location specified into the `/var/lib/glance/images` directory. The same thing is done when using the STDIN redirection with <, as shown in the example.

Run the following command to view the properties of existing images:

```
$ glance details
```

Sharing Images Between Projects

In a multitenant cloud environment, users sometimes want to share their personal images or snapshots with other projects. This can be done on the command line with the `glance` tool by the owner of the image.

To share an image or snapshot with another project, do the following:

1. Obtain the UUID of the image:

    ```
    $ glance image-list
    ```

2. Obtain the UUID of the project with which you want to share your image. Unfortunately, nonadmin users are unable to use the `keystone` command to do this. The easiest solution is to obtain the UUID either from an administrator of the cloud or from a user located in the project.

3. Once you have both pieces of information, run the `glance` command:

    ```
    $ glance member-create <image-uuid> <project-uuid>
    ```

    For example:

    ```
    $ glance member-create 733d1c44-a2ea-414b-aca7-69decf20d810 \
        771ed149ef7e4b2b88665cc1c98f77ca
    ```

    Project 771ed149ef7e4b2b88665cc1c98f77ca will now have access to image 733d1c44-a2ea-414b-aca7-69decf20d810.

Deleting Images

To delete an image, just execute:

```
$ glance image-delete <image uuid>
```

Deleting an image does not affect instances or snapshots that were based on the image.

Other CLI Options

A full set of options can be found using:

```
$ glance help
```

or the OpenStack Image Service CLI Guide (*http://opsgui.de/NPH3Od*).

The Image Service and the Database

The only thing that the Image Service does not store in a database is the image itself. The Image Service database has two main tables:

- `images`
- `image_properties`

Working directly with the database and SQL queries can provide you with custom lists and reports of images. Technically, you can update properties about images through the database, although this is not generally recommended.

Example Image Service Database Queries

One interesting example is modifying the table of images and the owner of that image. This can be easily done if you simply display the unique ID of the owner. This example goes one step further and displays the readable name of the owner:

```
mysql> select glance.images.id,
              glance.images.name, keystone.tenant.name, is_public from
              glance.images inner join keystone.tenant on
              glance.images.owner=keystone.tenant.id;
```

Another example is displaying all properties for a certain image:

```
mysql> select name, value from
              image_properties where id = <image_id>
```

Flavors

Virtual hardware templates are called "flavors" in OpenStack, defining sizes for RAM, disk, number of cores, and so on. The default install provides five flavors.

These are configurable by admin users (the rights may also be delegated to other users by redefining the access controls for `compute_extension:flavormanage` in /etc/nova/policy.json on the nova-api server). To get the list of available flavors on your system, run:

```
$ nova flavor-list
+----+-----------+-----------+------+-----------+\+-------+-\+-------------+
| ID | Name      | Memory_MB | Disk | Ephemeral |/| VCPUs | /| extra_specs |
+----+-----------+-----------+------+-----------+\+-------+-\+-------------+
| 1  | m1.tiny   | 512       | 1    | 0         |/| 1     | /| {}          |
| 2  | m1.small  | 2048      | 10   | 20        |\| 1     | \| {}          |
| 3  | m1.medium | 4096      | 10   | 40        |/| 2     | /| {}          |
| 4  | m1.large  | 8192      | 10   | 80        |\| 4     | \| {}          |
| 5  | m1.xlarge | 16384     | 10   | 160       |/| 8     | /| {}          |
+----+-----------+-----------+------+-----------+\+-------+-\+-------------+
```

The nova flavor-create command allows authorized users to create new flavors. Additional flavor manipulation commands can be shown with the command:

```
$ nova help | grep flavor
```

Flavors define a number of parameters, resulting in the user having a choice of what type of virtual machine to run—just like they would have if they were purchasing a physical server. Table 10-1 lists the elements that can be set. Note in particular extra_specs, which can be used to define free-form characteristics, giving a lot of flexibility beyond just the size of RAM, CPU, and Disk.

Table 10-1. Flavor parameters

Column	Description
ID	A unique numeric ID.
Name	A descriptive name, such as xx.size_name, is conventional but not required, though some third-party tools may rely on it.
Memory_MB	Virtual machine memory in megabytes.
Disk	Virtual root disk size in gigabytes. This is an ephemeral disk the base image is copied into. You don't use it when you boot from a persistent volume. The "0" size is a special case that uses the native base image size as the size of the ephemeral root volume.
Ephemeral	Specifies the size of a secondary ephemeral data disk. This is an empty, unformatted disk and exists only for the life of the instance.
Swap	Optional swap space allocation for the instance.
VCPUs	Number of virtual CPUs presented to the instance.
RXTX_Factor	Optional property that allows created servers to have a different bandwidth cap from that defined in the network they are attached to. This factor is multiplied by the rxtx_base property of the network. Default value is 1.0 (that is, the same as the attached network).

Column	Description
Is_Public	Boolean value that indicates whether the flavor is available to all users or private. Private flavors do not get the current tenant assigned to them. Defaults to `True`.
extra_specs	Additional optional restrictions on which compute nodes the flavor can run on. This is implemented as key-value pairs that must match against the corresponding key-value pairs on compute nodes. Can be used to implement things like special resources (such as flavors that can run only on compute nodes with GPU hardware).

Private Flavors

A user might need a custom flavor that is uniquely tuned for a project she is working on. For example, the user might require 128 GB of memory. If you create a new flavor as described above, the user would have access to the custom flavor, but so would all other tenants in your cloud. Sometimes this sharing isn't desirable. In this scenario, allowing all users to have access to a flavor with 128 GB of memory might cause your cloud to reach full capacity very quickly. To prevent this, you can restrict access to the custom flavor using the `nova` command:

```
$ nova flavor-access-add <flavor-id> <project-id>
```

To view a flavor's access list, do the following:

```
$ nova flavor-access-list <flavor-id>
```

Best Practices

Once access to a flavor has been restricted, no other projects besides the ones granted explicit access will be able to see the flavor. This includes the admin project. Make sure to add the admin project in addition to the original project.

It's also helpful to allocate a specific numeric range for custom and private flavors. On UNIX-based systems, nonsystem accounts usually have a UID starting at 500. A similar approach can be taken with custom flavors. This helps you easily identify which flavors are custom, private, and public for the entire cloud.

How Do I Modify an Existing Flavor?

The OpenStack dashboard simulates the ability to modify a flavor by deleting an existing flavor and creating a new one with the same name.

Security Groups

A common new-user issue with OpenStack is failing to set an appropriate security group when launching an instance. As a result, the user is unable to contact the instance on the network.

Security groups are sets of IP filter rules that are applied to an instance's networking. They are project specific, and project members can edit the default rules for their group and add new rules sets. All projects have a "default" security group, which is applied to instances that have no other security group defined. Unless changed, this security group denies all incoming traffic.

General Security Groups Configuration

The `nova.conf` option `allow_same_net_traffic` (which defaults to `true`) globally controls whether the rules apply to hosts that share a network. When set to `true`, hosts on the same subnet are not filtered and are allowed to pass all types of traffic between them. On a flat network, this allows all instances from all projects unfiltered communication. With VLAN networking, this allows access between instances within the same project. If `allow_same_net_traffic` is set to `false`, security groups are enforced for all connections. In this case, it is possible for projects to simulate `allow_same_net_traffic` by configuring their default security group to allow all traffic from their subnet.

As noted in the previous chapter, the number of rules per security group is controlled by the `quota_security_group_rules`, and the number of allowed security groups per project is controlled by the `quota_security_groups` quota.

End-User Configuration of Security Groups

Security groups for the current project can be found on the OpenStack dashboard under Access & Security. To see details of an existing group, select the edit action for that security group. Obviously, modifying existing groups can be done from this edit interface. There is a Create Security Group button on the main Access & Security page for creating new groups. We discuss the terms used in these fields when we explain the command-line equivalents.

From the command line, you can get a list of security groups for the project you're acting in using the `nova` command:

```
$ nova secgroup-list
+---------+-------------+
| Name    | Description |
+---------+-------------+
| default | default     |
| open    | all ports   |
+---------+-------------+
```

To view the details of the "open" security group:

```
$ nova secgroup-list-rules open
+-------------+-----------+---------+-----------+--------------+
| IP Protocol | From Port | To Port | IP Range  | Source Group |
+-------------+-----------+---------+-----------+--------------+
| icmp        | -1        | 255     | 0.0.0.0/0 |              |
| tcp         | 1         | 65535   | 0.0.0.0/0 |              |
| udp         | 1         | 65535   | 0.0.0.0/0 |              |
+-------------+-----------+---------+-----------+--------------+
```

These rules are all "allow" type rules, as the default is deny. The first column is the IP protocol (one of icmp, tcp, or udp), and the second and third columns specify the affected port range. The fourth column specifies the IP range in CIDR format. This example shows the full port range for all protocols allowed from all IPs.

When adding a new security group, you should pick a descriptive but brief name. This name shows up in brief descriptions of the instances that use it where the longer description field often does not. Seeing that an instance is using security group `http` is much easier to understand than `bobs_group` or `secgrp1`.

As an example, let's create a security group that allows web traffic anywhere on the Internet. We'll call this group `global_http`, which is clear and reasonably concise, encapsulating what is allowed and from where. From the command line, do:

```
$ nova secgroup-create \
      global_http "allow web traffic from the Internet"
+-------------+-------------------------------------+
| Name        | Description                         |
+-------------+-------------------------------------+
| global_http | allow web traffic from the Internet |
+-------------+-------------------------------------+
```

This creates the empty security group. To make it do what we want, we need to add some rules:

```
$ nova secgroup-add-rule <secgroup> <ip-proto> <from-port> <to-port> <cidr>
$ nova secgroup-add-rule global_http tcp 80 80 0.0.0.0/0
+-------------+-----------+---------+-----------+--------------+
| IP Protocol | From Port | To Port | IP Range  | Source Group |
+-------------+-----------+---------+-----------+--------------+
| tcp         | 80        | 80      | 0.0.0.0/0 |              |
+-------------+-----------+---------+-----------+--------------+
```

Note that the arguments are positional, and the from-port and to-port arguments specify the allowed local port range connections. These arguments are not indicating source and destination ports of the connection. More complex rule sets can be built up through multiple invocations of nova secgroup-add-rule. For example, if you want to pass both http and https traffic, do this:

```
$ nova secgroup-add-rule global_http tcp 443 443 0.0.0.0/0
+-------------+-----------+---------+-----------+--------------+
| IP Protocol | From Port | To Port | IP Range  | Source Group |
+-------------+-----------+---------+-----------+--------------+
| tcp         | 443       | 443     | 0.0.0.0/0 |              |
+-------------+-----------+---------+-----------+--------------+
```

Despite only outputting the newly added rule, this operation is additive:

```
$ nova secgroup-list-rules global_http
+-------------+-----------+---------+-----------+--------------+
| IP Protocol | From Port | To Port | IP Range  | Source Group |
+-------------+-----------+---------+-----------+--------------+
| tcp         | 80        | 80      | 0.0.0.0/0 |              |
| tcp         | 443       | 443     | 0.0.0.0/0 |              |
+-------------+-----------+---------+-----------+--------------+
```

The inverse operation is called secgroup-delete-rule, using the same format. Whole security groups can be removed with secgroup-delete.

To create security group rules for a cluster of instances, you want to use SourceGroups.

SourceGroups are a special dynamic way of defining the CIDR of allowed sources. The user specifies a SourceGroup (security group name) and then all the users' other instances using the specified SourceGroup are selected dynamically. This dynamic selection alleviates the need for individual rules to allow each new member of the cluster.

The code is structured like this: nova secgroup-add-group-rule <secgroup> <source-group> <ip-proto> <from-port> <to-port>. An example usage is shown here:

```
$ nova secgroup-add-group-rule cluster global-http tcp 22 22
```

The "cluster" rule allows SSH access from any other instance that uses the global-http group.

Block Storage

OpenStack volumes are persistent block-storage devices that may be attached and detached from instances, but they can be attached to only one instance at a time. Similar to an external hard drive, they do not provide shared storage in the way a network file system or object store does. It is left to the operating system in the instance to put a file system on the block device and mount it, or not.

As with other removable disk technology, it is important that the operating system is not trying to make use of the disk before removing it. On Linux instances, this typically involves unmounting any file systems mounted from the volume. The OpenStack volume service cannot tell whether it is safe to remove volumes from an instance, so it does what it is told. If a user tells the volume service to detach a volume from an instance while it is being written to, you can expect some level of file system corruption as well as faults from whatever process within the instance was using the device.

There is nothing OpenStack-specific in being aware of the steps needed to access block devices from within the instance operating system, potentially formatting them for first use and being cautious when removing them. What is specific is how to create new volumes and attach and detach them from instances. These operations can all be done from the Volumes page of the dashboard or by using the `cinder` command-line client.

To add new volumes, you need only a name and a volume size in gigabytes. Either put these into the create volume web form or use the command line:

```
$ cinder create --display-name test-volume 10
```

This creates a 10 GB volume named `test-volume`. To list existing volumes and the instances they are connected to, if any:

```
$ cinder list
+------------+--------+------------------+------+-------------+-------------+
|     ID     | Status |   Display Name   | Size | Volume Type | Attached to |
+------------+--------+------------------+------+-------------+-------------+
| 0821...19f | active |   test-volume    |  10  |    None     |             |
+------------+--------+------------------+------+-------------+-------------+
```

OpenStack Block Storage also allows for creating snapshots of volumes. Remember that this is a block-level snapshot that is crash consistent, so it is best if the volume is not connected to an instance when the snapshot is taken and second best if the volume is not in use on the instance it is attached to. If the volume is under heavy use, the snapshot may have an inconsistent file system. In fact, by default, the volume service does not take a snapshot of a volume that is attached to an image, though it can be forced to. To take a volume snapshot, either select Create Snapshot from the actions column next to the volume name on the dashboard volume page, or run this from the command line:

```
usage: cinder snapshot-create [--force <True|False>]
[--display-name <display-name>]
[--display-description <display-description>]
<volume-id>
Add a new snapshot.
```

```
Positional arguments:  <volume-id>          ID of the volume to snapshot
Optional arguments:  --force <True|False>  Optional flag to indicate whether to
                                           snapshot a volume even if its
                                           attached to an instance.
                                           (Default=False)
--display-name <display-name>              Optional snapshot name.
                                           (Default=None)
--display-description <display-description>
Optional snapshot description. (Default=None)
```

Block Storage Creation Failures

If a user tries to create a volume and the volume immediately goes into an error state, the best way to troubleshoot is to grep the cinder log files for the volume's UUID. First try the log files on the cloud controller, and then try the storage node where the volume was attempted to be created:

```
# grep  903b85d0-bacc-4855-a261-10843fc2d65b /var/log/cinder/*.log
```

Instances

Instances are the running virtual machines within an OpenStack cloud. This section deals with how to work with them and their underlying images, their network properties, and how they are represented in the database.

Starting Instances

To launch an instance, you need to select an image, a flavor, and a name. The name needn't be unique, but your life will be simpler if it is because many tools will use the name in place of the UUID so long as the name is unique. You can start an instance from the dashboard from the Launch Instance button on the Instances page or by selecting the Launch action next to an image or snapshot on the Images & Snapshots page.

On the command line, do this:

```
$ nova boot --flavor <flavor> --image <image> <name>
```

There are a number of optional items that can be specified. You should read the rest of this section before trying to start an instance, but this is the base command that later details are layered upon.

To delete instances from the dashboard, select the Terminate instance action next to the instance on the Instances page. From the command line, do this:

```
$ nova delete <instance-uuid>
```

It is important to note that powering off an instance does not terminate it in the OpenStack sense.

Instance Boot Failures

If an instance fails to start and immediately moves to an error state, there are a few different ways to track down what has gone wrong. Some of these can be done with normal user access, while others require access to your log server or compute nodes.

The simplest reasons for nodes to fail to launch are quota violations or the scheduler being unable to find a suitable compute node on which to run the instance. In these cases, the error is apparent when you run a `nova show` on the faulted instance:

```
$ nova show test-instance
```

```
+------------------------+-----------------------------------------------------\
| Property               | Value                                               /
+------------------------+-----------------------------------------------------\
| OS-DCF:diskConfig      | MANUAL                                              /
| OS-EXT-STS:power_state | 0                                                   \
| OS-EXT-STS:task_state  | None                                                /
| OS-EXT-STS:vm_state    | error                                               \
| accessIPv4             |                                                     /
| accessIPv6             |                                                     \
| config_drive           |                                                     /
| created                | 2013-03-01T19:28:24Z                                \
| fault                  | {u'message': u'NoValidHost', u'code': 500, u'created/
| flavor                 | xxl.super (11)                                      \
| hostId                 |                                                     /
| id                     | 940f3b2f-bd74-45ad-bee7-eb0a7318aa84                \
| image                  | quantal-test (65b4f432-7375-42b6-a9b8-7f654a1e676e) /
| key_name               | None                                                \
| metadata               | {}                                                  /
| name                   | test-instance                                       \
| security_groups        | [{u'name': u'default'}]                             /
| status                 | ERROR                                               \
| tenant_id              | 98333a1a28e746fa8c629c83a818ad57                    /
| updated                | 2013-03-01T19:28:26Z                                \
| user_id                | a1ef823458d24a68955fec6f3d390019                    /
+------------------------+-----------------------------------------------------\
```

In this case, looking at the `fault` message shows `NoValidHost`, indicating that the scheduler was unable to match the instance requirements.

If `nova show` does not sufficiently explain the failure, searching for the instance UUID in the `nova-compute.log` on the compute node it was scheduled on or the `nova-scheduler.log` on your scheduler hosts is a good place to start looking for lower-level problems.

Using `nova show` as an admin user will show the compute node the instance was scheduled on as `hostId`. If the instance failed during scheduling, this field is blank.

Using Instance-Specific Data

There are two main types of instance-specific data: metadata and user data.

Instance metadata

For Compute, instance metadata is a collection of key-value pairs associated with an instance. Compute reads and writes to these key-value pairs any time during the instance lifetime, from inside and outside the instance, when the end user uses the Compute API to do so. However, you cannot query the instance-associated key-value pairs with the metadata service that is compatible with the Amazon EC2 metadata service.

For an example of instance metadata, users can generate and register SSH keys using the `nova` command:

```
$ nova keypair-add mykey > mykey.pem
```

This creates a key named **`mykey`**, which you can associate with instances. The file `mykey.pem` is the private key, which should be saved to a secure location because it allows root access to instances the **`mykey`** key is associated with.

Use this command to register an existing key with OpenStack:

```
$ nova keypair-add --pub-key mykey.pub mykey
```

You must have the matching private key to access instances associated with this key.

To associate a key with an instance on boot, add `--key_name mykey` to your command line. For example:

```
$ nova boot --image ubuntu-cloudimage --flavor 2 --key_name mykey myimage
```

When booting a server, you can also add arbitrary metadata so that you can more easily identify it among other running instances. Use the `--meta` option with a key-value pair, where you can make up the string for both the key and the value. For example, you could add a description and also the creator of the server:

```
$ nova boot --image=test-image --flavor=1 \
  --meta description='Small test image' smallimage
```

When viewing the server information, you can see the metadata included on the metadata line:

```
$ nova show smallimage
+------------------------+-------------------------------------+
|     Property           |                Value                |
+------------------------+-------------------------------------+
|   OS-DCF:diskConfig    |               MANUAL                |
| OS-EXT-STS:power_state |                 1                   |
| OS-EXT-STS:task_state  |                None                 |
|  OS-EXT-STS:vm_state   |               active                |
|    accessIPv4          |                                     |
|    accessIPv6          |                                     |
|      config_drive      |                                     |
|     created            |          2012-05-16T20:48:23Z       |
|      flavor            |            m1.small                 |
|      hostId            |           de0...487                 |
|        id              |           8ec...f915                |
|      image             |           natty-image               |
|     key_name           |                                     |
|     metadata           | {u'description': u'Small test image'} |
|       name             |           smallimage                |
|    private network     |          172.16.101.11              |
|     progress           |                0                    |
|     public network     |          10.4.113.11                |
|      status            |             ACTIVE                  |
|    tenant_id           |           e83...482                 |
|     updated            |          2012-05-16T20:48:35Z       |
|     user_id            |         de3...0a9                   |
+------------------------+-------------------------------------+
```

Instance user data

The `user-data` key is a special key in the metadata service that holds a file that cloud-aware applications within the guest instance can access. For example, cloudinit (*http://opsgui.de/1eLCtLs*) is an open source package from Ubuntu, but available in most distributions, that handles early initialization of a cloud instance that makes use of this user data.

This user data can be put in a file on your local system and then passed in at instance creation with the flag `--user-data <user-data-file>`. For example:

```
$ nova boot --image ubuntu-cloudimage --flavor 1 --user-data mydata.file
```

To understand the difference between user data and metadata, realize that user data is created before an instance is started. User data is accessible from within the instance when it is running. User data can be used to store configuration, a script, or anything the tenant wants.

File injection

Arbitrary local files can also be placed into the instance file system at creation time by using the `--file <dst-path=src-path>` option. You may store up to five files.

For example, let's say you have a special `authorized_keys` file named special_authorized_keysfile that for some reason you want to put on the instance instead of using the regular SSH key injection. In this case, you can use the following command:

```
$ nova boot --image ubuntu-cloudimage --flavor 1  \
  --file /root/.ssh/authorized_keys=special_authorized_keysfile
```

Associating Security Groups

Security groups, as discussed earlier, are typically required to allow network traffic to an instance, unless the default security group for a project has been modified to be more permissive.

Adding security groups is typically done on instance boot. When launching from the dashboard, you do this on the Access & Security tab of the Launch Instance dialog. When launching from the command line, append `--security-groups` with a comma-separated list of security groups.

It is also possible to add and remove security groups when an instance is running. Currently this is only available through the command-line tools. Here is an example:

```
$ nova add-secgroup <server> <securitygroup>
```

```
$ nova remove-secgroup <server> <securitygroup>
```

Floating IPs

Where floating IPs are configured in a deployment, each project will have a limited number of floating IPs controlled by a quota. However, these need to be allocated to the project from the central pool prior to their use—usually by the administrator of the project. To allocate a floating IP to a project, use the Allocate IP to Project button on the Access & Security page of the dashboard. The command line can also be used:

```
$ nova floating-ip-create
```

Once allocated, a floating IP can be assigned to running instances from the dashboard either by selecting Associate Floating IP from the actions drop-down next to the IP on the Access & Security page or by making this selection next to the instance you want to associate it with on the Instances page. The inverse action, Dissociate Floating IP, is available only from the Access & Security page and not from the Instances page.

To associate or disassociate a floating IP with a server from the command line, use the following commands:

```
$ nova add-floating-ip <server> <address>
```

```
$ nova remove-floating-ip <server> <address>
```

Attaching Block Storage

You can attach block storage to instances from the dashboard on the Volumes page. Click the Edit Attachments action next to the volume you want to attach.

To perform this action from command line, run the following command:

```
$ nova volume-attach <server> <volume> <device>
```

You can also specify block device mapping at instance boot time through the nova command-line client with this option set:

```
--block-device-mapping <dev-name=mapping>
```

The block device mapping format is `<dev-name>=<id>:<type>:<size(GB)>:<delete-on-terminate>`, where:

dev-name
: A device name where the volume is attached in the system at `/dev/`*`dev_name`*

id
: The ID of the volume to boot from, as shown in the output of `nova volume-list`

type
: Either `snap`, which means that the volume was created from a snapshot, or anything other than `snap` (a blank string is valid). In the preceding example, the volume was not created from a snapshot, so we leave this field blank in our following example.

size (GB)
: The size of the volume in gigabytes. It is safe to leave this blank and have the Compute Service infer the size.

delete-on-terminate
: A boolean to indicate whether the volume should be deleted when the instance is terminated. True can be specified as `True` or `1`. False can be specified as `False` or `0`.

The following command will boot a new instance and attach a volume at the same time. The volume of ID 13 will be attached as `/dev/vdc`. It is not a snapshot, does not specify a size, and will not be deleted when the instance is terminated:

```
$ nova boot --image 4042220e-4f5e-4398-9054-39fbd75a5dd7 \
           --flavor 2 --key-name mykey --block-device-mapping vdc=13:::0 \
           boot-with-vol-test
```

If you have previously prepared block storage with a bootable file system image, it is even possible to boot from persistent block storage. The following command boots an image from the specified volume. It is similar to the previous command, but the image is omitted and the volume is now attached as /dev/vda:

```
$ nova boot --flavor 2 --key-name mykey \
            --block-device-mapping vda=13:::0 boot-from-vol-test
```

Read more detailed instructions for launching an instance from a bootable volume in the OpenStack End User Guide (*http://opsgui.de/NPH30v*).

To boot normally from an image and attach block storage, map to a device other than vda. You can find instructions for launching an instance and attaching a volume to the instance and for copying the image to the attached volume in the OpenStack End User Guide (*http://opsgui.de/1eLCwHb*).

Taking Snapshots

The OpenStack snapshot mechanism allows you to create new images from running instances. This is very convenient for upgrading base images or for taking a published image and customizing it for local use. To snapshot a running instance to an image using the CLI, do this:

```
$ nova image-create <instance name or uuid> <name of new image>
```

The dashboard interface for snapshots can be confusing because the Images & Snapshots page splits content up into several areas:

- Images
- Instance snapshots
- Volume snapshots

However, an instance snapshot *is* an image. The only difference between an image that you upload directly to the Image Service and an image that you create by snapshot is that an image created by snapshot has additional properties in the glance database. These properties are found in the image_properties table and include:

Name	Value
image_type	snapshot
instance_uuid	<uuid of instance that was snapshotted>
base_image_ref	<uuid of original image of instance that was snapshotted>
image_location	snapshot

Live Snapshots

Live snapshots is a feature that allows users to snapshot the running virtual machines without pausing them. These snapshots are simply disk-only snapshots. Snapshotting an instance can now be performed with no downtime (assuming QEMU 1.3+ and libvirt 1.0+ are used).

Ensuring Snapshots Are Consistent

The following section is from Sébastien Han's "OpenStack: Perform Consistent Snapshots" blog entry (*http://opsgui.de/NPH5Wn*).

A snapshot captures the state of the file system, but not the state of the memory. Therefore, to ensure your snapshot contains the data that you want, before your snapshot you need to ensure that:

- Running programs have written their contents to disk
- The file system does not have any "dirty" buffers: where programs have issued the command to write to disk, but the operating system has not yet done the write

To ensure that important services have written their contents to disk (such as databases), we recommend that you read the documentation for those applications to determine what commands to issue to have them sync their contents to disk. If you are unsure how to do this, the safest approach is to simply stop these running services normally.

To deal with the "dirty" buffer issue, we recommend using the sync command before snapshotting:

```
# sync
```

Running `sync` writes dirty buffers (buffered blocks that have been modified but not written yet to the disk block) to disk.

Just running `sync` is not enough to ensure that the file system is consistent. We recommend that you use the `fsfreeze` tool, which halts new access to the file system, and create a stable image on disk that is suitable for snapshotting. The `fsfreeze` tool supports several file systems, including ext3, ext4, and XFS. If your virtual machine instance is running on Ubuntu, install the util-linux package to get `fsfreeze`:

```
# apt-get install util-linux
```

If your operating system doesn't have a version of `fsfreeze` available, you can use `xfs_freeze` instead, which is available on Ubuntu in the xfsprogs package. Despite the "xfs" in the name, xfs_freeze also works on ext3 and ext4 if you are using a Linux kernel version 2.6.29 or greater, since it works at the virtual file system (VFS) level starting at 2.6.29. The xfs_freeze version supports the same command-line arguments as `fsfreeze`.

Consider the example where you want to take a snapshot of a persistent block storage volume, detected by the guest operating system as `/dev/vdb` and mounted on `/mnt`. The fsfreeze command accepts two arguments:

-f
: Freeze the system

-u
: Thaw (unfreeze) the system

To freeze the volume in preparation for snapshotting, you would do the following, as root, inside the instance:

```
# fsfreeze -f /mnt
```

You *must mount the file system* before you run the `fsfreeze` command.

When the `fsfreeze -f` command is issued, all ongoing transactions in the file system are allowed to complete, new write system calls are halted, and other calls that modify the file system are halted. Most importantly, all dirty data, metadata, and log information are written to disk.

Once the volume has been frozen, do not attempt to read from or write to the volume, as these operations hang. The operating system stops every I/O operation and any I/O attempts are delayed until the file system has been unfrozen.

Once you have issued the `fsfreeze` command, it is safe to perform the snapshot. For example, if your instance was named `mon-instance` and you wanted to snapshot it to an image named `mon-snapshot`, you could now run the following:

```
$ nova image-create mon-instance mon-snapshot
```

When the snapshot is done, you can thaw the file system with the following command, as root, inside of the instance:

```
# fsfreeze -u /mnt
```

If you want to back up the root file system, you can't simply run the preceding command because it will freeze the prompt. Instead, run the following one-liner, as root, inside the instance:

```
# fsfreeze -f / && sleep 30 && fsfreeze -u /
```

Instances in the Database

While instance information is stored in a number of database tables, the table you most likely need to look at in relation to user instances is the instances table.

The instances table carries most of the information related to both running and deleted instances. It has a bewildering array of fields; for an exhaustive list, look at the database. These are the most useful fields for operators looking to form queries:

- The `deleted` field is set to `1` if the instance has been deleted and `NULL` if it has not been deleted. This field is important for excluding deleted instances from your queries.
- The `uuid` field is the UUID of the instance and is used throughout other tables in the database as a foreign key. This ID is also reported in logs, the dashboard, and command-line tools to uniquely identify an instance.
- A collection of foreign keys are available to find relations to the instance. The most useful of these—`user_id` and `project_id`—are the UUIDs of the user who launched the instance and the project it was launched in.
- The `host` field tells which compute node is hosting the instance.
- The `hostname` field holds the name of the instance when it is launched. The display-name is initially the same as hostname but can be reset using the nova rename command.

A number of time-related fields are useful for tracking when state changes happened on an instance:

- `created_at`
- `updated_at`
- `deleted_at`
- `scheduled_at`
- `launched_at`
- `terminated_at`

Good Luck!

This section was intended as a brief introduction to some of the most useful of many OpenStack commands. For an exhaustive list, please refer to the Admin User Guide (*http://opsgui.de/1eLBkDJ*), and for additional hints and tips, see the Cloud Admin Guide (*http://opsgui.de/1eLBL0N*). We hope your users remain happy and recognize your hard work! (For more hard work, turn the page to the next chapter, where we discuss the system-facing operations: maintenance, failures and debugging.)

CHAPTER 11

Maintenance, Failures, and Debugging

Downtime, whether planned or unscheduled, is a certainty when running a cloud. This chapter aims to provide useful information for dealing proactively, or reactively, with these occurrences.

Cloud Controller and Storage Proxy Failures and Maintenance

The cloud controller and storage proxy are very similar to each other when it comes to expected and unexpected downtime. One of each server type typically runs in the cloud, which makes them very noticeable when they are not running.

For the cloud controller, the good news is if your cloud is using the FlatDHCP multi-host HA network mode, existing instances and volumes continue to operate while the cloud controller is offline. For the storage proxy, however, no storage traffic is possible until it is back up and running.

Planned Maintenance

One way to plan for cloud controller or storage proxy maintenance is to simply do it off-hours, such as at 1 a.m. or 2 a.m. This strategy affects fewer users. If your cloud controller or storage proxy is too important to have unavailable at any point in time, you must look into high-availability options.

Rebooting a Cloud Controller or Storage Proxy

All in all, just issue the "reboot" command. The operating system cleanly shuts down services and then automatically reboots. If you want to be very thorough, run your backup jobs just before you reboot.

After a Cloud Controller or Storage Proxy Reboots

After a cloud controller reboots, ensure that all required services were successfully started. The following commands use `ps` and `grep` to determine if nova, glance, and keystone are currently running:

```
# ps aux | grep nova-
# ps aux | grep glance-
# ps aux | grep keystone
# ps aux | grep cinder
```

Also check that all services are functioning. The following set of commands sources the `openrc` file, then runs some basic glance, nova, and keystone commands. If the commands work as expected, you can be confident that those services are in working condition:

```
# source openrc
# glance index
# nova list
# keystone tenant-list
```

For the storage proxy, ensure that the Object Storage service has resumed:

```
# ps aux | grep swift
```

Also check that it is functioning:

```
# swift stat
```

Total Cloud Controller Failure

The cloud controller could completely fail if, for example, its motherboard goes bad. Users will immediately notice the loss of a cloud controller since it provides core functionality to your cloud environment. If your infrastructure monitoring does not alert you that your cloud controller has failed, your users definitely will. Unfortunately, this is a rough situation. The cloud controller is an integral part of your cloud. If you have only one controller, you will have many missing services if it goes down.

To avoid this situation, create a highly available cloud controller cluster. This is outside the scope of this document, but you can read more in the draft OpenStack High Availability Guide (*http://opsgui.de/NPGlAo*).

The next best approach is to use a configuration-management tool, such as Puppet, to automatically build a cloud controller. This should not take more than 15 minutes if you have a spare server available. After the controller rebuilds, restore any backups taken (see Chapter 14).

Also, in practice, the `nova-compute` services on the compute nodes do not always reconnect cleanly to rabbitmq hosted on the controller when it comes back up after a long reboot; a restart on the nova services on the compute nodes is required.

Compute Node Failures and Maintenance

Sometimes a compute node either crashes unexpectedly or requires a reboot for maintenance reasons.

Planned Maintenance

If you need to reboot a compute node due to planned maintenance (such as a software or hardware upgrade), first ensure that all hosted instances have been moved off the node. If your cloud is utilizing shared storage, use the `nova live-migration` command. First, get a list of instances that need to be moved:

```
# nova list --host c01.example.com --all-tenants
```

Next, migrate them one by one:

```
# nova live-migration <uuid> c02.example.com
```

If you are not using shared storage, you can use the `--block-migrate` option:

```
# nova live-migration --block-migrate <uuid> c02.example.com
```

After you have migrated all instances, ensure that the `nova-compute` service has stopped:

```
# stop nova-compute
```

If you use a configuration-management system, such as Puppet, that ensures the `nova-compute` service is always running, you can temporarily move the `init` files:

```
# mkdir /root/tmp
# mv /etc/init/nova-compute.conf /root/tmp
# mv /etc/init.d/nova-compute /root/tmp
```

Next, shut down your compute node, perform your maintenance, and turn the node back on. You can reenable the `nova-compute` service by undoing the previous commands:

```
# mv /root/tmp/nova-compute.conf /etc/init
# mv /root/tmp/nova-compute /etc/init.d/
```

Then start the `nova-compute` service:

```
# start nova-compute
```

You can now optionally migrate the instances back to their original compute node.

After a Compute Node Reboots

When you reboot a compute node, first verify that it booted successfully. This includes ensuring that the `nova-compute` service is running:

```
# ps aux | grep nova-compute
# status nova-compute
```

Also ensure that it has successfully connected to the AMQP server:

```
# grep AMQP /var/log/nova/nova-compute
2013-02-26 09:51:31 12427 INFO nova.openstack.common.rpc.common [-] Connected
to AMQP server on 199.116.232.36:5672
```

After the compute node is successfully running, you must deal with the instances that are hosted on that compute node because none of them are running. Depending on your SLA with your users or customers, you might have to start each instance and ensure that they start correctly.

Instances

You can create a list of instances that are hosted on the compute node by performing the following command:

```
# nova list --host c01.example.com --all-tenants
```

After you have the list, you can use the nova command to start each instance:

```
# nova reboot <uuid>
```

Any time an instance shuts down unexpectedly, it might have problems on boot. For example, the instance might require an `fsck` on the root partition. If this happens, the user can use the dashboard VNC console to fix this.

If an instance does not boot, meaning `virsh list` never shows the instance as even attempting to boot, do the following on the compute node:

```
# tail -f /var/log/nova/nova-compute.log
```

Try executing the `nova reboot` command again. You should see an error message about why the instance was not able to boot

In most cases, the error is the result of something in libvirt's XML file (`/etc/libvirt/qemu/instance-xxxxxxxx.xml`) that no longer exists. You can enforce re-creation of the XML file as well as rebooting the instance by running the following command:

```
# nova reboot --hard <uuid>
```

Inspecting and Recovering Data from Failed Instances

In some scenarios, instances are running but are inaccessible through SSH and do not respond to any command. The VNC console could be displaying a boot failure or kernel panic error messages. This could be an indication of file system corruption on the VM itself. If you need to recover files or inspect the content of the instance, qemu-nbd can be used to mount the disk.

If you access or view the user's content and data, get approval first!

To access the instance's disk (`/var/lib/nova/instances/instance-`*`xxxxxx`*`/disk`), use the following steps:

1. Suspend the instance using the `virsh` command.
2. Connect the qemu-nbd device to the disk.
3. Mount the qemu-nbd device.
4. Unmount the device after inspecting.
5. Disconnect the qemu-nbd device.
6. Resume the instance.

If you do not follow steps 4 through 6, OpenStack Compute cannot manage the instance any longer. It fails to respond to any command issued by OpenStack Compute, and it is marked as shut down.

Once you mount the disk file, you should be able to access it and treat it as a collection of normal directories with files and a directory structure. However, we do not recommend that you edit or touch any files because this could change the access control lists (ACLs) that are used to determine which accounts can perform what operations on files and directories. Changing ACLs can make the instance unbootable if it is not already.

1. Suspend the instance using the `virsh` command, taking note of the internal ID:

   ```
   # virsh list
   Id Name                 State
   ----------------------------------
   1 instance-00000981    running
   2 instance-000009f5    running
   30 instance-0000274a    running

   # virsh suspend 30
   Domain 30 suspended
   ```

2. Connect the qemu-nbd device to the disk:

```
# cd /var/lib/nova/instances/instance-0000274a
# ls -lh
total 33M
-rw-rw---- 1 libvirt-qemu kvm  6.3K Oct 15 11:31 console.log
-rw-r--r-- 1 libvirt-qemu kvm   33M Oct 15 22:06 disk
-rw-r--r-- 1 libvirt-qemu kvm  384K Oct 15 22:06 disk.local
-rw-rw-r-- 1 nova         nova 1.7K Oct 15 11:30 libvirt.xml
# qemu-nbd -c /dev/nbd0 `pwd`/disk
```

3. Mount the qemu-nbd device.

   The qemu-nbd device tries to export the instance disk's different partitions as separate devices. For example, if vda is the disk and vda1 is the root partition, qemu-nbd exports the device as `/dev/nbd0` and `/dev/nbd0p1`, respectively:

   ```
   # mount /dev/nbd0p1 /mnt/
   ```

   You can now access the contents of `/mnt`, which correspond to the first partition of the instance's disk.

   To examine the secondary or ephemeral disk, use an alternate mount point if you want both primary and secondary drives mounted at the same time:

   ```
   # umount /mnt
   # qemu-nbd -c /dev/nbd1 `pwd`/disk.local
   # mount /dev/nbd1 /mnt/
   ```

   ```
   # ls -lh /mnt/
   total 76K
   lrwxrwxrwx.  1 root root    7 Oct 15 00:44 bin -> usr/bin
   dr-xr-xr-x.  4 root root 4.0K Oct 15 01:07 boot
   drwxr-xr-x.  2 root root 4.0K Oct 15 00:42 dev
   drwxr-xr-x. 70 root root 4.0K Oct 15 11:31 etc
   drwxr-xr-x.  3 root root 4.0K Oct 15 01:07 home
   lrwxrwxrwx.  1 root root    7 Oct 15 00:44 lib -> usr/lib
   lrwxrwxrwx.  1 root root    9 Oct 15 00:44 lib64 -> usr/lib64
   drwx------.  2 root root  16K Oct 15 00:42 lost+found
   drwxr-xr-x.  2 root root 4.0K Feb  3  2012 media
   drwxr-xr-x.  2 root root 4.0K Feb  3  2012 mnt
   drwxr-xr-x.  2 root root 4.0K Feb  3  2012 opt
   drwxr-xr-x.  2 root root 4.0K Oct 15 00:42 proc
   dr-xr-x---.  3 root root 4.0K Oct 15 21:56 root
   drwxr-xr-x. 14 root root 4.0K Oct 15 01:07 run
   lrwxrwxrwx.  1 root root    8 Oct 15 00:44 sbin -> usr/sbin
   drwxr-xr-x.  2 root root 4.0K Feb  3  2012 srv
   drwxr-xr-x.  2 root root 4.0K Oct 15 00:42 sys
   drwxrwxrwt.  9 root root 4.0K Oct 15 16:29 tmp
   drwxr-xr-x. 13 root root 4.0K Oct 15 00:44 usr
   drwxr-xr-x. 17 root root 4.0K Oct 15 00:44 var
   ```

4. Once you have completed the inspection, unmount the mount point and release the qemu-nbd device:

```
# umount /mnt
# qemu-nbd -d /dev/nbd0
/dev/nbd0 disconnected
```

5. Resume the instance using `virsh`:

```
# virsh list
Id Name                 State
----------------------------------
1 instance-00000981    running
2 instance-000009f5    running
30 instance-0000274a    paused

# virsh resume 30
Domain 30 resumed
```

Volumes

If the affected instances also had attached volumes, first generate a list of instance and volume UUIDs:

```
mysql> select nova.instances.uuid as instance_uuid,
cinder.volumes.id as volume_uuid, cinder.volumes.status,
cinder.volumes.attach_status, cinder.volumes.mountpoint,
cinder.volumes.display_name from cinder.volumes
inner join nova.instances on cinder.volumes.instance_uuid=nova.instances.uuid
 where nova.instances.host = 'c01.example.com';
```

You should see a result similar to the following:

```
+-------------+-----------+-------+-------------+----------+-------------+
|instance_uuid |volume_uuid |status |attach_status |mountpoint | display_name |
+-------------+-----------+-------+-------------+----------+-------------+
|9b969a05      |1f0fbf36    |in-use |attached      |/dev/vdc   | test         |
+-------------+-----------+-------+-------------+----------+-------------+
1 row in set (0.00 sec)
```

Next, manually detach and reattach the volumes, where X is the proper mount point:

```
# nova volume-detach <instance_uuid> <volume_uuid>
# nova volume-attach <instance_uuid> <volume_uuid> /dev/vdX
```

Be sure that the instance has successfully booted and is at a login screen before doing the above.

Total Compute Node Failure

Compute nodes can fail the same way a cloud controller can fail. A motherboard failure or some other type of hardware failure can cause an entire compute node to go offline. When this happens, all instances running on that compute node will not be available. Just like with a cloud controller failure, if your infrastructure monitoring does not detect a failed compute node, your users will notify you because of their lost instances.

If a compute node fails and won't be fixed for a few hours (or at all), you can relaunch all instances that are hosted on the failed node if you use shared storage for `/var/lib/nova/instances`.

To do this, generate a list of instance UUIDs that are hosted on the failed node by running the following query on the nova database:

```
mysql> select uuid from instances where host = \
       'c01.example.com' and deleted = 0;
```

Next, update the nova database to indicate that all instances that used to be hosted on c01.example.com are now hosted on c02.example.com:

```
mysql> update instances set host = 'c02.example.com' where host = \
       'c01.example.com' and deleted = 0;
```

After that, use the `nova` command to reboot all instances that were on c01.example.com while regenerating their XML files at the same time:

```
# nova reboot --hard <uuid>
```

Finally, reattach volumes using the same method described in the section Volumes.

/var/lib/nova/instances

It's worth mentioning this directory in the context of failed compute nodes. This directory contains the libvirt KVM file-based disk images for the instances that are hosted on that compute node. If you are not running your cloud in a shared storage environment, this directory is unique across all compute nodes.

`/var/lib/nova/instances` contains two types of directories.

The first is the `_base` directory. This contains all the cached base images from glance for each unique image that has been launched on that compute node. Files ending in `_20` (or a different number) are the ephemeral base images.

The other directories are titled `instance-xxxxxxxx`. These directories correspond to instances running on that compute node. The files inside are related to one of the files in the `_base` directory. They're essentially differential-based files containing only the changes made from the original `_base` directory.

All files and directories in `/var/lib/nova/instances` are uniquely named. The files in _base are uniquely titled for the glance image that they are based on, and the directory names `instance-xxxxxxxx` are uniquely titled for that particular instance. For example, if you copy all data from `/var/lib/nova/instances` on one compute node to another, you do not overwrite any files or cause any damage to images that have the same unique name, because they are essentially the same file.

Although this method is not documented or supported, you can use it when your compute node is permanently offline but you have instances locally stored on it.

Storage Node Failures and Maintenance

Because of the high redundancy of Object Storage, dealing with object storage node issues is a lot easier than dealing with compute node issues.

Rebooting a Storage Node

If a storage node requires a reboot, simply reboot it. Requests for data hosted on that node are redirected to other copies while the server is rebooting.

Shutting Down a Storage Node

If you need to shut down a storage node for an extended period of time (one or more days), consider removing the node from the storage ring. For example:

```
# swift-ring-builder account.builder remove <ip address of storage node>
# swift-ring-builder container.builder remove <ip address of storage node>
# swift-ring-builder object.builder remove <ip address of storage node>
# swift-ring-builder account.builder rebalance
# swift-ring-builder container.builder rebalance
# swift-ring-builder object.builder rebalance
```

Next, redistribute the ring files to the other nodes:

```
# for i in s01.example.com s02.example.com s03.example.com
> do
> scp *.ring.gz $i:/etc/swift
> done
```

These actions effectively take the storage node out of the storage cluster.

When the node is able to rejoin the cluster, just add it back to the ring. The exact syntax you use to add a node to your swift cluster with `swift-ring-builder` heavily depends on the original options used when you originally created your cluster. Please refer back to those commands.

Replacing a Swift Disk

If a hard drive fails in an Object Storage node, replacing it is relatively easy. This assumes that your Object Storage environment is configured correctly, where the data that is stored on the failed drive is also replicated to other drives in the Object Storage environment.

This example assumes that `/dev/sdb` has failed.

First, unmount the disk:

```
# umount /dev/sdb
```

Next, physically remove the disk from the server and replace it with a working disk.

Ensure that the operating system has recognized the new disk:

```
# dmesg | tail
```

You should see a message about `/dev/sdb`.

Because it is recommended to not use partitions on a swift disk, simply format the disk as a whole:

```
# mkfs.xfs /dev/sdb
```

Finally, mount the disk:

```
# mount -a
```

Swift should notice the new disk and that no data exists. It then begins replicating the data to the disk from the other existing replicas.

Handling a Complete Failure

A common way of dealing with the recovery from a full system failure, such as a power outage of a data center, is to assign each service a priority, and restore in order. Table 11-1 shows an example.

Table 11-1. Example service restoration priority list

Priority	Services
1	Internal network connectivity
2	Backing storage services
3	Public network connectivity for user virtual machines
4	`nova-compute`, `nova-network`, cinder hosts
5	User virtual machines
10	Message queue and database services
15	Keystone services

Priority	Services
20	`cinder-scheduler`
21	Image Catalog and Delivery services
22	`nova-scheduler` services
98	`cinder-api`
99	`nova-api` services
100	Dashboard node

Use this example priority list to ensure that user-affected services are restored as soon as possible, but not before a stable environment is in place. Of course, despite being listed as a single-line item, each step requires significant work. For example, just after starting the database, you should check its integrity, or, after starting the nova services, you should verify that the hypervisor matches the database and fix any mismatches.

Configuration Management

Maintaining an OpenStack cloud requires that you manage multiple physical servers, and this number might grow over time. Because managing nodes manually is error prone, we strongly recommend that you use a configuration-management tool. These tools automate the process of ensuring that all your nodes are configured properly and encourage you to maintain your configuration information (such as packages and configuration options) in a version-controlled repository.

Several configuration-management tools are available, and this guide does not recommend a specific one. The two most popular ones in the OpenStack community are Puppet (*http://opsgui.de/1eLBsD7*), with available OpenStack Puppet modules (*http://opsgui.de/NPGmnU*); and Chef (*http://opsgui.de/1eLBtqO*), with available OpenStack Chef recipes (*http://opsgui.de/NPGnID*). Other newer configuration tools include Juju (*http://opsgui.de/1eLBxqm*), Ansible (*http://opsgui.de/NPGpQQ*), and Salt (*http://opsgui.de/1eLBACD*); and more mature configuration management tools include CFEngine (*http://opsgui.de/NPGoMP*) and Bcfg2 (*http://opsgui.de/1eLBB9M*).

Working with Hardware

As for your initial deployment, you should ensure that all hardware is appropriately burned in before adding it to production. Run software that uses the hardware to its limits—maxing out RAM, CPU, disk, and network. Many options are available, and normally double as benchmark software, so you also get a good idea of the performance of your system.

Adding a Compute Node

If you find that you have reached or are reaching the capacity limit of your computing resources, you should plan to add additional compute nodes. Adding more nodes is quite easy. The process for adding compute nodes is the same as when the initial compute nodes were deployed to your cloud: use an automated deployment system to bootstrap the bare-metal server with the operating system and then have a configuration-management system install and configure OpenStack Compute. Once the Compute Service has been installed and configured in the same way as the other compute nodes, it automatically attaches itself to the cloud. The cloud controller notices the new node(s) and begins scheduling instances to launch there.

If your OpenStack Block Storage nodes are separate from your compute nodes, the same procedure still applies because the same queuing and polling system is used in both services.

We recommend that you use the same hardware for new compute and block storage nodes. At the very least, ensure that the CPUs are similar in the compute nodes to not break live migration.

Adding an Object Storage Node

Adding a new object storage node is different from adding compute or block storage nodes. You still want to initially configure the server by using your automated deployment and configuration-management systems. After that is done, you need to add the local disks of the object storage node into the object storage ring. The exact command to do this is the same command that was used to add the initial disks to the ring. Simply rerun this command on the object storage proxy server for all disks on the new object storage node. Once this has been done, rebalance the ring and copy the resulting ring files to the other storage nodes.

If your new object storage node has a different number of disks than the original nodes have, the command to add the new node is different from the original commands. These parameters vary from environment to environment.

Replacing Components

Failures of hardware are common in large-scale deployments such as an infrastructure cloud. Consider your processes and balance time saving against availability. For example, an Object Storage cluster can easily live with dead disks in it for some period of time if it has sufficient capacity. Or, if your compute installation is not full, you could consider live migrating instances off a host with a RAM failure until you have time to deal with the problem.

Databases

Almost all OpenStack components have an underlying database to store persistent information. Usually this database is MySQL. Normal MySQL administration is applicable to these databases. OpenStack does not configure the databases out of the ordinary. Basic administration includes performance tweaking, high availability, backup, recovery, and repairing. For more information, see a standard MySQL administration guide.

You can perform a couple of tricks with the database to either more quickly retrieve information or fix a data inconsistency error—for example, an instance was terminated, but the status was not updated in the database. These tricks are discussed throughout this book.

Database Connectivity

Review the component's configuration file to see how each OpenStack component accesses its corresponding database. Look for either `sql_connection` or simply `connection`. The following command uses `grep` to display the SQL connection string for nova, glance, cinder, and keystone:

```
# grep -hE "connection ?=" /etc/nova/nova.conf /etc/glance/glance-*.conf
/etc/cinder/cinder.conf /etc/keystone/keystone.conf
sql_connection = mysql://nova:nova@cloud.alberta.sandbox.cybera.ca/nova
sql_connection = mysql://glance:password@cloud.example.com/glance
sql_connection = mysql://glance:password@cloud.example.com/glance
sql_connection = mysql://cinder:password@cloud.example.com/cinder
    connection = mysql://keystone_admin:password@cloud.example.com/keystone
```

The connection strings take this format:

```
mysql:// <username> : <password> @ <hostname> / <database name>
```

Performance and Optimizing

As your cloud grows, MySQL is utilized more and more. If you suspect that MySQL might be becoming a bottleneck, you should start researching MySQL optimization.

The MySQL manual has an entire section dedicated to this topic: Optimization Overview (*http://opsgui.de/NPGqUV*).

HDWMY

Here's a quick list of various to-do items for each hour, day, week, month, and year. Please note that these tasks are neither required nor definitive but helpful ideas:

Hourly

- Check your monitoring system for alerts and act on them.
- Check your ticket queue for new tickets.

Daily

- Check for instances in a failed or weird state and investigate why.
- Check for security patches and apply them as needed.

Weekly

- Check cloud usage:
  - User quotas
  - Disk space
  - Image usage
  - Large instances
  - Network usage (bandwidth and IP usage)
- Verify your alert mechanisms are still working.

Monthly

- Check usage and trends over the past month.
- Check for user accounts that should be removed.
- Check for operator accounts that should be removed.

Quarterly

- Review usage and trends over the past quarter.
- Prepare any quarterly reports on usage and statistics.
- Review and plan any necessary cloud additions.
- Review and plan any major OpenStack upgrades.

Semiannually

- Upgrade OpenStack.
- Clean up after an OpenStack upgrade (any unused or new services to be aware of?).

Determining Which Component Is Broken

OpenStack's collection of different components interact with each other strongly. For example, uploading an image requires interaction from `nova-api`, `glance-api`, `glance-registry`, keystone, and potentially `swift-proxy`. As a result, it is sometimes difficult to determine exactly where problems lie. Assisting in this is the purpose of this section.

Tailing Logs

The first place to look is the log file related to the command you are trying to run. For example, if `nova list` is failing, try tailing a nova log file and running the command again:

Terminal 1:

```
# tail -f /var/log/nova/nova-api.log
```

Terminal 2:

```
# nova list
```

Look for any errors or traces in the log file. For more information, see Chapter 13.

If the error indicates that the problem is with another component, switch to tailing that component's log file. For example, if nova cannot access glance, look at the `glance-api` log:

Terminal 1:

```
# tail -f /var/log/glance/api.log
```

Terminal 2:

```
# nova list
```

Wash, rinse, and repeat until you find the core cause of the problem.

Running Daemons on the CLI

Unfortunately, sometimes the error is not apparent from the log files. In this case, switch tactics and use a different command; maybe run the service directly on the command line. For example, if the `glance-api` service refuses to start and stay running, try launching the daemon from the command line:

```
# sudo -u glance -H glance-api
```

This might print the error and cause of the problem.

The `-H` flag is required when running the daemons with sudo because some daemons will write files relative to the user's home directory, and this write may fail if `-H` is left off.

Example of Complexity

One morning, a compute node failed to run any instances. The log files were a bit vague, claiming that a certain instance was unable to be started. This ended up being a red herring because the instance was simply the first instance in alphabetical order, so it was the first instance that `nova-compute` would touch.

Further troubleshooting showed that libvirt was not running at all. This made more sense. If libvirt wasn't running, then no instance could be virtualized through KVM. Upon trying to start libvirt, it would silently die immediately. The libvirt logs did not explain why.

Next, the `libvirtd` daemon was run on the command line. Finally a helpful error message: it could not connect to d-bus. As ridiculous as it sounds, libvirt, and thus `nova-compute`, relies on d-bus and somehow d-bus crashed. Simply starting d-bus set the entire chain back on track, and soon everything was back up and running.

Uninstalling

While we'd always recommend using your automated deployment system to reinstall systems from scratch, sometimes you do need to remove OpenStack from a system the hard way. Here's how:

- Remove all packages.
- Remove remaining files.
- Remove databases.

These steps depend on your underlying distribution, but in general you should be looking for "purge" commands in your package manager, like `aptitude purge ~c $package`. Following this, you can look for orphaned files in the directories referenced throughout this guide. To uninstall the database properly, refer to the manual appropriate for the product in use.

CHAPTER 12
Network Troubleshooting

Network troubleshooting can unfortunately be a very difficult and confusing procedure. A network issue can cause a problem at several points in the cloud. Using a logical troubleshooting procedure can help mitigate the confusion and more quickly isolate where exactly the network issue is. This chapter aims to give you the information you need to identify any issues for either `nova-network` or OpenStack Networking (neutron) with Linux Bridge or Open vSwitch.

Using "ip a" to Check Interface States

On compute nodes and nodes running `nova-network`, use the following command to see information about interfaces, including information about IPs, VLANs, and whether your interfaces are up:

```
# ip a
```

If you're encountering any sort of networking difficulty, one good initial sanity check is to make sure that your interfaces are up. For example:

```
$ ip a | grep state
1: lo: <LOOPBACK,UP,LOWER_UP> mtu 16436 qdisc noqueue state UNKNOWN
2: eth0: <BROADCAST,MULTICAST,UP,LOWER_UP> mtu 1500 qdisc pfifo_fast state UP
   qlen 1000
3: eth1: <BROADCAST,MULTICAST,UP,LOWER_UP> mtu 1500 qdisc pfifo_fast
   master br100 state UP qlen 1000
4: virbr0: <NO-CARRIER,BROADCAST,MULTICAST,UP> mtu 1500 qdisc noqueue state DOWN
5: br100: <BROADCAST,MULTICAST,UP,LOWER_UP> mtu 1500 qdisc noqueue state
   UP
```

You can safely ignore the state of `virbr0`, which is a default bridge created by libvirt and not used by OpenStack.

Visualizing nova-network Traffic in the Cloud

If you are logged in to an instance and ping an external host—for example, Google—the ping packet takes the route shown in Figure 12-1.

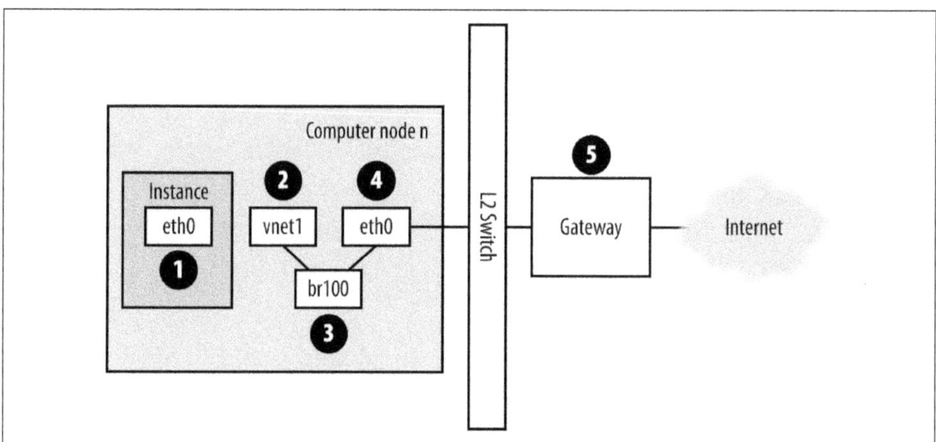

Figure 12-1. Traffic route for ping packet

1. The instance generates a packet and places it on the virtual Network Interface Card (NIC) inside the instance, such as `eth0`.
2. The packet transfers to the virtual NIC of the compute host, such as, `vnet1`. You can find out what vnet NIC is being used by looking at the `/etc/libvirt/qemu/instance-xxxxxxxx.xml` file.
3. From the vnet NIC, the packet transfers to a bridge on the compute node, such as `br100`.

   If you run FlatDHCPManager, one bridge is on the compute node. If you run VlanManager, one bridge exists for each VLAN.

   To see which bridge the packet will use, run the command:

   ```
   $ brctl show
   ```

   Look for the vnet NIC. You can also reference `nova.conf` and look for the `flat_interface_bridge` option.
4. The packet transfers to the main NIC of the compute node. You can also see this NIC in the `brctl` output, or you can find it by referencing the `flat_interface` option in `nova.conf`.
5. After the packet is on this NIC, it transfers to the compute node's default gateway. The packet is now most likely out of your control at this point. The diagram de-

picts an external gateway. However, in the default configuration with multi-host, the compute host is the gateway.

Reverse the direction to see the path of a ping reply. From this path, you can see that a single packet travels across four different NICs. If a problem occurs with any of these NICs, a network issue occurs.

Visualizing OpenStack Networking Service Traffic in the Cloud

The OpenStack Networking Service, neutron, has many more degrees of freedom than `nova-network` does because of its pluggable backend. It can be configured with open source or vendor proprietary plug-ins that control software defined networking (SDN) hardware or plug-ins that use Linux native facilities on your hosts, such as Open vSwitch or Linux Bridge.

The networking chapter of the OpenStack Cloud Administrator Guide (*http://opsgui.de/1eLBD1f*) shows a variety of networking scenarios and their connection paths. The purpose of this section is to give you the tools to troubleshoot the various components involved however they are plumbed together in your environment.

For this example, we will use the Open vSwitch (OVS) backend. Other backend plug-ins will have very different flow paths. OVS is the most popularly deployed network driver, according to the October 2013 OpenStack User Survey, with 50 percent more sites using it than the second place Linux Bridge driver. We'll describe each step in turn, with Figure 12-2 for reference.

1. The instance generates a packet and places it on the virtual NIC inside the instance, such as eth0.
2. The packet transfers to a Test Access Point (TAP) device on the compute host, such as tap690466bc-92. You can find out what TAP is being used by looking at the `/etc/libvirt/qemu/instance-xxxxxxxx.xml` file.

   The TAP device name is constructed using the first 11 characters of the port ID (10 hex digits plus an included '-'), so another means of finding the device name is to use the `neutron` command. This returns a pipe-delimited list, the first item of which is the port ID. For example, to get the port ID associated with IP address 10.0.0.10, do this:

   ```
   # neutron port-list |grep 10.0.0.10|cut -d \
   | -f 2 ff387e54-9e54-442b-94a3-aa4481764f1d
   ```

   Taking the first 11 characters, we can construct a device name of tapff387e54-9e from this output.

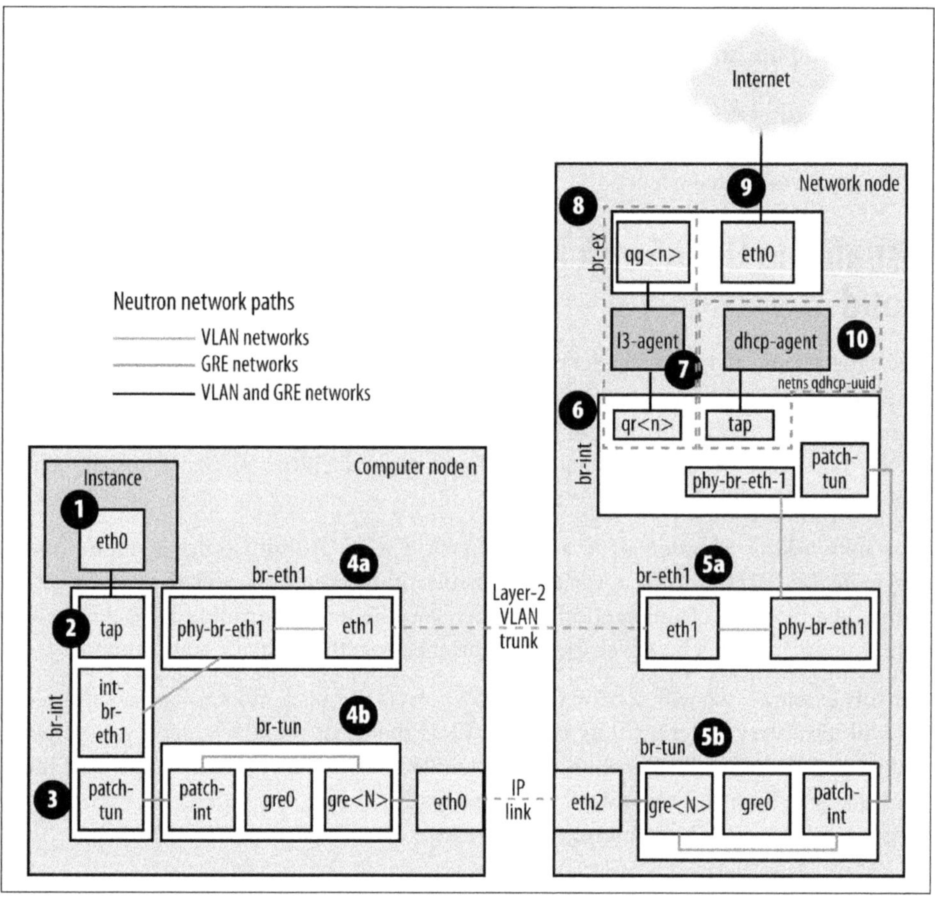

Figure 12-2. Neutron network paths

3. The TAP device is connected to the integration bridge, `br-int`. This bridge connects all the instance TAP devices and any other bridges on the system. In this example, we have `int-br-eth1` and `patch-tun`. `int-br-eth1` is one half of a veth pair connecting to the bridge `br-eth1`, which handles VLAN networks trunked over the physical Ethernet device `eth1`. `patch-tun` is an Open vSwitch internal port that connects to the `br-tun` bridge for GRE networks.

   The TAP devices and veth devices are normal Linux network devices and may be inspected with the usual tools, such as `ip` and `tcpdump`. Open vSwitch internal devices, such as `patch-tun`, are only visible within the Open vSwitch environment. If you try to run `tcpdump -i patch-tun`, it will raise an error, saying that the device does not exist.

It is possible to watch packets on internal interfaces, but it does take a little bit of networking gymnastics. First you need to create a dummy network device that normal Linux tools can see. Then you need to add it to the bridge containing the internal interface you want to snoop on. Finally, you need to tell Open vSwitch to mirror all traffic to or from the internal port onto this dummy port. After all this, you can then run `tcpdump` on the dummy interface and see the traffic on the internal port.

To capture packets from the `patch-tun` internal interface on integration bridge, `br-int`:

a. Create and bring up a dummy interface, `snooper0`:

```
# ip link add name snooper0 type dummy
```

```
# ip link set dev snooper0 up
```

b. Add device `snooper0` to bridge `br-int`:

```
# ovs-vsctl add-port br-int snooper0
```

c. Create mirror of `patch-tun` to `snooper0` (returns UUID of mirror port):

```
# ovs-vsctl -- set Bridge br-int mirrors=@m  -- --id=@snooper0 \
get Port snooper0  -- --id=@patch-tun get Port patch-tun  \
-- --id=@m create Mirror name=mymirror select-dst-port=@patch-tun \
select-src-port=@patch-tun output-port=@snooper0 \
90eb8cb9-8441-4f6d-8f67-0ea037f40e6c
```

d. Profit. You can now see traffic on `patch-tun` by running `tcpdump -i snooper0`.

e. Clean up by clearing all mirrors on `br-int` and deleting the dummy interface:

```
# ovs-vsctl clear Bridge br-int mirrors
```

```
# ip link delete dev snooper0
```

On the integration bridge, networks are distinguished using internal VLANs regardless of how the networking service defines them. This allows instances on the same host to communicate directly without transiting the rest of the virtual, or physical, network. These internal VLAN IDs are based on the order they are created on the node and may vary between nodes. These IDs are in no way related to the segmentation IDs used in the network definition and on the physical wire.

VLAN tags are translated between the external tag defined in the network settings, and internal tags in several places. On the `br-int`, incoming packets from the `int-br-eth1` are translated from external tags to internal tags. Other translations also happen on the other bridges and will be discussed in those sections.

To discover which internal VLAN tag is in use for a given external VLAN by using the `ovs-ofctl` command:

a. Find the external VLAN tag of the network you're interested in. This is the `provider:segmentation_id` as returned by the networking service:

```
# neutron net-show --fields provider:segmentation_id <network name>
+---------------------------+--------------------------------------+
| Field                     | Value                                |
+---------------------------+--------------------------------------+
| provider:network_type     | vlan                                 |
| provider:segmentation_id  | 2113                                 |
+---------------------------+--------------------------------------+
```

b. Grep for the `provider:segmentation_id`, 2113 in this case, in the output of `ovs-ofctl dump-flows br-int`:

```
# ovs-ofctl dump-flows br-int|grep vlan=2113
cookie=0x0, duration=173615.481s, table=0, n_packets=7676140, \
n_bytes=444818637, idle_age=0, hard_age=65534, priority=3, \
in_port=1,dl_vlan=2113 actions=mod_vlan_vid:7,NORMAL
```

Here you can see packets received on port ID 1 with the VLAN tag 2113 are modified to have the internal VLAN tag 7. Digging a little deeper, you can confirm that port 1 is in fact `int-br-eth1`:

```
# ovs-ofctl show br-int
OFPT_FEATURES_REPLY (xid=0x2): dpid:000022bc45e1914b
n_tables:254, n_buffers:256
capabilities: FLOW_STATS TABLE_STATS PORT_STATS QUEUE_STATS \
ARP_MATCH_IP
actions: OUTPUT SET_VLAN_VID SET_VLAN_PCP STRIP_VLAN SET_DL_SRC \
SET_DL_DST SET_NW_SRC SET_NW_DST SET_NW_TOS SET_TP_SRC \
SET_TP_DST ENQUEUE
 1(int-br-eth1): addr:c2:72:74:7f:86:08
     config:     0
     state:      0
     current:    10GB-FD COPPER
     speed: 10000 Mbps now, 0 Mbps max
 2(patch-tun): addr:fa:24:73:75:ad:cd
     config:     0
     state:      0
     speed: 0 Mbps now, 0 Mbps max
 3(tap9be586e6-79): addr:fe:16:3e:e6:98:56
     config:     0
     state:      0
     current:    10MB-FD COPPER
     speed: 10 Mbps now, 0 Mbps max
 LOCAL(br-int): addr:22:bc:45:e1:91:4b
     config:     0
     state:      0
     speed: 0 Mbps now, 0 Mbps max
OFPT_GET_CONFIG_REPLY (xid=0x4): frags=normal miss_send_len=0
```

4. The next step depends on whether the virtual network is configured to use 802.1q VLAN tags or GRE:

   a. VLAN-based networks exit the integration bridge via veth interface `int-br-eth1` and arrive on the bridge `br-eth1` on the other member of the veth pair `phy-br-eth1`. Packets on this interface arrive with internal VLAN tags and are translated to external tags in the reverse of the process described above:

      ```
      # ovs-ofctl dump-flows br-eth1|grep 2113
      cookie=0x0, duration=184168.225s, table=0, n_packets=0, n_bytes=0, \
      idle_age=65534, hard_age=65534, priority=4,in_port=1,dl_vlan=7 \
      actions=mod_vlan_vid:2113,NORMAL
      ```

      Packets, now tagged with the external VLAN tag, then exit onto the physical network via `eth1`. The Layer2 switch this interface is connected to must be configured to accept traffic with the VLAN ID used. The next hop for this packet must also be on the same layer-2 network.

   b. GRE-based networks are passed with `patch-tun` to the tunnel bridge `br-tun` on interface `patch-int`. This bridge also contains one port for each GRE tunnel peer, so one for each compute node and network node in your network. The ports are named sequentially from `gre-1` onward.

      Matching `gre-<n>` interfaces to tunnel endpoints is possible by looking at the Open vSwitch state:

      ```
      # ovs-vsctl show |grep -A 3 -e Port\ \"gre-
              Port "gre-1"
                  Interface "gre-1"
                      type: gre
                      options: {in_key=flow, local_ip="10.10.128.21", \
                      out_key=flow, remote_ip="10.10.128.16"}
      ```

      In this case, `gre-1` is a tunnel from IP 10.10.128.21, which should match a local interface on this node, to IP 10.10.128.16 on the remote side.

      These tunnels use the regular routing tables on the host to route the resulting GRE packet, so there is no requirement that GRE endpoints are all on the same layer-2 network, unlike VLAN encapsulation.

      All interfaces on the `br-tun` are internal to Open vSwitch. To monitor traffic on them, you need to set up a mirror port as described above for `patch-tun` in the `br-int` bridge.

      All translation of GRE tunnels to and from internal VLANs happens on this bridge.

To discover which internal VLAN tag is in use for a GRE tunnel by using the `ovs-ofctl` command:

   a. Find the `provider:segmentation_id` of the network you're interested in. This is the same field used for the VLAN ID in VLAN-based networks:

```
# neutron net-show --fields provider:segmentation_id <network name>
+--------------------------+-------+
| Field                    | Value |
+--------------------------+-------+
| provider:network_type    | gre   |
| provider:segmentation_id | 3     |
+--------------------------+-------+
```

b. Grep for 0x<provider:segmentation_id>, 0x3 in this case, in the output of `ovs-ofctl dump-flows br-int`:

```
# ovs-ofctl dump-flows br-int|grep 0x3
cookie=0x0, duration=380575.724s, table=2, n_packets=1800, \
n_bytes=286104, priority=1,tun_id=0x3 \
actions=mod_vlan_vid:1,resubmit(,10)
 cookie=0x0, duration=715.529s, table=20, n_packets=5, \
n_bytes=830, hard_timeout=300,priority=1, \
vlan_tci=0x0001/0x0fff,dl_dst=fa:16:3e:a6:48:24 \
actions=load:0->NXM_OF_VLAN_TCI[], \
load:0x3->NXM_NX_TUN_ID[],output:53
 cookie=0x0, duration=193729.242s, table=21, n_packets=58761, \
n_bytes=2618498, dl_vlan=1 actions=strip_vlan,set_tunnel:0x3, \
output:4,output:58,output:56,output:11,output:12,output:47, \
output:13,output:48,output:49,output:44,output:43,output:45, \
output:46,output:30,output:31,output:29,output:28,output:26, \
output:27,output:24,output:25,output:32,output:19,output:21, \
output:59,output:60,output:57,output:6,output:5,output:20, \
output:18,output:17,output:16,output:15,output:14,output:7, \
output:9,output:8,output:53,output:10,output:3,output:2, \
output:38,output:37,output:39,output:40,output:34,output:23, \
output:36,output:35,output:22,output:42,output:41,output:54, \
output:52,output:51,output:50,output:55,output:33
```

Here, you see three flows related to this GRE tunnel. The first is the translation from inbound packets with this tunnel ID to internal VLAN ID 1. The second shows a unicast flow to output port 53 for packets destined for MAC address fa:16:3e:a6:48:24. The third shows the translation from the internal VLAN representation to the GRE tunnel ID flooded to all output ports. For further details of the flow descriptions, see the man page for `ovs-ofctl`. As in the previous VLAN example, numeric port IDs can be matched with their named representations by examining the output of `ovs-ofctl show br-tun`.

5. The packet is then received on the network node. Note that any traffic to the l3-agent or dhcp-agent will be visible only within their network namespace. Watching any interfaces outside those namespaces, even those that carry the network traffic, will only show broadcast packets like Address Resolution Protocols (ARPs), but unicast traffic to the router or DHCP address will not be seen. See "Dealing with Network Namespaces" for detail on how to run commands within these namespaces.

Alternatively, it is possible to configure VLAN-based networks to use external routers rather than the l3-agent shown here, so long as the external router is on the same VLAN:

   a. VLAN-based networks are received as tagged packets on a physical network interface, `eth1` in this example. Just as on the compute node, this interface is a member of the `br-eth1` bridge.

   b. GRE-based networks will be passed to the tunnel bridge `br-tun`, which behaves just like the GRE interfaces on the compute node.

6. Next, the packets from either input go through the integration bridge, again just as on the compute node.

7. The packet then makes it to the l3-agent. This is actually another TAP device within the router's network namespace. Router namespaces are named in the form `qrouter-<router-uuid>`. Running `ip a` within the namespace will show the TAP device name, qr-e6256f7d-31 in this example:

```
# ip netns exec qrouter-e521f9d0-a1bd-4ff4-bc81-78a60dd88fe5 ip a|grep state
10: qr-e6256f7d-31: <BROADCAST,UP,LOWER_UP> mtu 1500 qdisc noqueue \
    state UNKNOWN
11: qg-35916e1f-36: <BROADCAST,MULTICAST,UP,LOWER_UP> mtu 1500 \
    qdisc pfifo_fast state UNKNOWN qlen 500
28: lo: <LOOPBACK,UP,LOWER_UP> mtu 16436 qdisc noqueue state UNKNOWN
```

8. The `qg-<n>` interface in the l3-agent router namespace sends the packet on to its next hop through device `eth0` on the external bridge `br-ex`. This bridge is constructed similarly to `br-eth1` and may be inspected in the same way.

9. This external bridge also includes a physical network interface, `eth0` in this example, which finally lands the packet on the external network destined for an external router or destination.

10. DHCP agents running on OpenStack networks run in namespaces similar to the l3-agents. DHCP namespaces are named `qdhcp-<uuid>` and have a TAP device on the integration bridge. Debugging of DHCP issues usually involves working inside this network namespace.

Finding a Failure in the Path

Use ping to quickly find where a failure exists in the network path. In an instance, first see whether you can ping an external host, such as google.com. If you can, then there shouldn't be a network problem at all.

If you can't, try pinging the IP address of the compute node where the instance is hosted. If you can ping this IP, then the problem is somewhere between the compute node and that compute node's gateway.

If you can't ping the IP address of the compute node, the problem is between the instance and the compute node. This includes the bridge connecting the compute node's main NIC with the vnet NIC of the instance.

One last test is to launch a second instance and see whether the two instances can ping each other. If they can, the issue might be related to the firewall on the compute node.

tcpdump

One great, although very in-depth, way of troubleshooting network issues is to use `tcpdump`. We recommended using `tcpdump` at several points along the network path to correlate where a problem might be. If you prefer working with a GUI, either live or by using a `tcpdump` capture, do also check out Wireshark (*http://opsgui.de/NPGrIm*).

For example, run the following command:

```
tcpdump -i any -n -v \ 'icmp[icmptype] = icmp-echoreply or icmp[icmptype] =
icmp-echo'
```

Run this on the command line of the following areas:

1. An external server outside of the cloud
2. A compute node
3. An instance running on that compute node

In this example, these locations have the following IP addresses:

```
Instance
                                        10.0.2.24
                                        203.0.113.30
                                        Compute Node
                                        10.0.0.42
                                        203.0.113.34
                                        External Server
                                        1.2.3.4
```

Next, open a new shell to the instance and then ping the external host where `tcpdump` is running. If the network path to the external server and back is fully functional, you see something like the following:

On the external server:

```
12:51:42.020227 IP (tos 0x0, ttl 61, id 0, offset 0, flags [DF], \
proto ICMP (1), length 84)
    203.0.113.30 > 1.2.3.4: ICMP echo request, id 24895, seq 1, length 64
12:51:42.020255 IP (tos 0x0, ttl 64, id 8137, offset 0, flags [none], \
proto ICMP (1), length 84)
```

```
    1.2.3.4 > 203.0.113.30: ICMP echo reply, id 24895, seq 1, \
    length 64
```

On the compute node:

```
12:51:42.019519 IP (tos 0x0, ttl 64, id 0, offset 0, flags [DF], \
proto ICMP (1), length 84)
    10.0.2.24 > 1.2.3.4: ICMP echo request, id 24895, seq 1, length 64
12:51:42.019519 IP (tos 0x0, ttl 64, id 0, offset 0, flags [DF], \
proto ICMP (1), length 84)
    10.0.2.24 > 1.2.3.4: ICMP echo request, id 24895, seq 1, length 64
12:51:42.019545 IP (tos 0x0, ttl 63, id 0, offset 0, flags [DF], \
proto ICMP (1), length 84)
    203.0.113.30 > 1.2.3.4: ICMP echo request, id 24895, seq 1, length 64
12:51:42.019780 IP (tos 0x0, ttl 62, id 8137, offset 0, flags [none], \
proto ICMP (1), length 84)
    1.2.3.4 > 203.0.113.30: ICMP echo reply, id 24895, seq 1, length 64
12:51:42.019801 IP (tos 0x0, ttl 61, id 8137, offset 0, flags [none], \
proto ICMP (1), length 84)
    1.2.3.4 > 10.0.2.24: ICMP echo reply, id 24895, seq 1, length 64
12:51:42.019807 IP (tos 0x0, ttl 61, id 8137, offset 0, flags [none], \
proto ICMP (1), length 84)
    1.2.3.4 > 10.0.2.24: ICMP echo reply, id 24895, seq 1, length 64
```

On the instance:

```
12:51:42.020974 IP (tos 0x0, ttl 61, id 8137, offset 0, flags [none], \
proto ICMP (1), length 84)
 1.2.3.4 > 10.0.2.24: ICMP echo reply, id 24895, seq 1, length 64
```

Here, the external server received the ping request and sent a ping reply. On the compute node, you can see that both the ping and ping reply successfully passed through. You might also see duplicate packets on the compute node, as seen above, because `tcpdump` captured the packet on both the bridge and outgoing interface.

iptables

Through `nova-network`, OpenStack Compute automatically manages iptables, including forwarding packets to and from instances on a compute node, forwarding floating IP traffic, and managing security group rules.

Run the following command to view the current iptables configuration:

```
# iptables-save
```

If you modify the configuration, it reverts the next time you restart `nova-network`. You must use OpenStack to manage iptables.

Network Configuration in the Database for nova-network

With `nova-network`, the nova database table contains a few tables with networking information:

`fixed_ips`
: Contains each possible IP address for the subnet(s) added to Compute. This table is related to the `instances` table by way of the `fixed_ips.instance_uuid` column.

`floating_ips`
: Contains each floating IP address that was added to Compute. This table is related to the `fixed_ips` table by way of the `floating_ips.fixed_ip_id` column.

`instances`
: Not entirely network specific, but it contains information about the instance that is utilizing the `fixed_ip` and optional `floating_ip`.

From these tables, you can see that a floating IP is technically never directly related to an instance; it must always go through a fixed IP.

Manually Deassociating a Floating IP

Sometimes an instance is terminated but the floating IP was not correctly deassociated from that instance. Because the database is in an inconsistent state, the usual tools to deassociate the IP no longer work. To fix this, you must manually update the database.

First, find the UUID of the instance in question:

```
mysql> select uuid from instances where hostname = 'hostname';
```

Next, find the fixed IP entry for that UUID:

```
mysql> select * from fixed_ips where instance_uuid = '<uuid>';
```

You can now get the related floating IP entry:

```
mysql> select * from floating_ips where fixed_ip_id = '<fixed_ip_id>';
```

And finally, you can deassociate the floating IP:

```
mysql> update floating_ips set fixed_ip_id = NULL, host = NULL where
       fixed_ip_id = '<fixed_ip_id>';
```

You can optionally also deallocate the IP from the user's pool:

```
mysql> update floating_ips set project_id = NULL where
       fixed_ip_id = '<fixed_ip_id>';
```

Debugging DHCP Issues with nova-network

One common networking problem is that an instance boots successfully but is not reachable because it failed to obtain an IP address from dnsmasq, which is the DHCP server that is launched by the `nova-network` service.

The simplest way to identify that this is the problem with your instance is to look at the console output of your instance. If DHCP failed, you can retrieve the console log by doing:

```
$ nova console-log <instance name or uuid>
```

If your instance failed to obtain an IP through DHCP, some messages should appear in the console. For example, for the Cirros image, you see output that looks like the following:

```
udhcpc (v1.17.2) started
Sending discover...
Sending discover...
Sending discover...
No lease, forking to background
starting DHCP forEthernet interface eth0 [ [1;32mOK[0;39m ]
cloud-setup: checking http://169.254.169.254/2009-04-04/meta-data/instance-id
wget: can't connect to remote host (169.254.169.254): Network is
unreachable
```

After you establish that the instance booted properly, the task is to figure out where the failure is.

A DHCP problem might be caused by a misbehaving dnsmasq process. First, debug by checking logs and then restart the dnsmasq processes only for that project (tenant). In VLAN mode, there is a dnsmasq process for each tenant. Once you have restarted targeted dnsmasq processes, the simplest way to rule out dnsmasq causes is to kill all of the dnsmasq processes on the machine and restart `nova-network`. As a last resort, do this as root:

```
# killall dnsmasq
# restart nova-network
```

> Use `openstack-nova-network` on RHEL/CentOS/Fedora but `nova-network` on Ubuntu/Debian.

Several minutes after `nova-network` is restarted, you should see new dnsmasq processes running:

```
# ps aux | grep dnsmasq
```

```
nobody 3735 0.0 0.0 27540 1044 ? S 15:40 0:00 /usr/sbin/dnsmasq --strict-order \
    --bind-interfaces --conf-file= \
    --domain=novalocal --pid-file=/var/lib/nova/networks/nova-br100.pid \
    --listen-address=192.168.100.1 --except-interface=lo \
    --dhcp-range=set:'novanetwork',192.168.100.2,static,120s \
    --dhcp-lease-max=256 \
    --dhcp-hostsfile=/var/lib/nova/networks/nova-br100.conf \
    --dhcp-script=/usr/bin/nova-dhcpbridge --leasefile-ro
root 3736 0.0 0.0 27512 444 ? S 15:40 0:00 /usr/sbin/dnsmasq --strict-order \
     --bind-interfaces --conf-file= \
     --domain=novalocal --pid-file=/var/lib/nova/networks/nova-br100.pid \
     --listen-address=192.168.100.1 --except-interface=lo \
     --dhcp-range=set:'novanetwork',192.168.100.2,static,120s \
     --dhcp-lease-max=256
     --dhcp-hostsfile=/var/lib/nova/networks/nova-br100.conf
     --dhcp-script=/usr/bin/nova-dhcpbridge --leasefile-ro
```

If your instances are still not able to obtain IP addresses, the next thing to check is whether dnsmasq is seeing the DHCP requests from the instance. On the machine that is running the dnsmasq process, which is the compute host if running in multi-host mode, look at `/var/log/syslog` to see the dnsmasq output. If dnsmasq is seeing the request properly and handing out an IP, the output looks like this:

```
Feb 27 22:01:36 mynode dnsmasq-dhcp[2438]: DHCPDISCOVER(br100) fa:16:3e:56:0b:6f
Feb 27 22:01:36 mynode dnsmasq-dhcp[2438]: DHCPOFFER(br100) 192.168.100.3
                                           fa:16:3e:56:0b:6f
Feb 27 22:01:36 mynode dnsmasq-dhcp[2438]: DHCPREQUEST(br100) 192.168.100.3
                                           fa:16:3e:56:0b:6f
Feb 27 22:01:36 mynode dnsmasq-dhcp[2438]: DHCPACK(br100) 192.168.100.3
fa:16:3e:56:0b:6f test
```

If you do not see the `DHCPDISCOVER`, a problem exists with the packet getting from the instance to the machine running dnsmasq. If you see all of the preceding output and your instances are still not able to obtain IP addresses, then the packet is able to get from the instance to the host running dnsmasq, but it is not able to make the return trip.

You might also see a message such as this:

```
Feb 27 22:01:36 mynode dnsmasq-dhcp[25435]: DHCPDISCOVER(br100)
            fa:16:3e:78:44:84 no address available
```

This may be a dnsmasq and/or `nova-network` related issue. (For the preceding example, the problem happened to be that dnsmasq did not have any more IP addresses to give away because there were no more fixed IPs available in the OpenStack Compute database.)

If there's a suspicious-looking dnsmasq log message, take a look at the command-line arguments to the dnsmasq processes to see if they look correct:

```
$ ps aux | grep dnsmasq
```

The output looks something like the following:

```
108 1695 0.0 0.0 25972 1000 ? S Feb26 0:00 /usr/sbin/dnsmasq
-u libvirt-dnsmasq \
--strict-order --bind-interfaces
 --pid-file=/var/run/libvirt/network/default.pid --conf-file=
 --except-interface lo --listen-address 192.168.122.1
 --dhcp-range 192.168.122.2,192.168.122.254
 --dhcp-leasefile=/var/lib/libvirt/dnsmasq/default.leases
 --dhcp-lease-max=253 --dhcp-no-override
nobody 2438 0.0 0.0 27540 1096 ? S Feb26 0:00 /usr/sbin/dnsmasq --strict-order
--bind-interfaces --conf-file=
 --domain=novalocal --pid-file=/var/lib/nova/networks/nova-br100.pid
 --listen-address=192.168.100.1
 --except-interface=lo \
 --dhcp-range=set:'novanetwork',192.168.100.2,static,120s
 --dhcp-lease-max=256
 --dhcp-hostsfile=/var/lib/nova/networks/nova-br100.conf
 --dhcp-script=/usr/bin/nova-dhcpbridge --leasefile-ro
  root 2439 0.0 0.0 27512 472 ? S Feb26 0:00 /usr/sbin/dnsmasq --strict-order
--bind-interfaces --conf-file=
 --domain=novalocal --pid-file=/var/lib/nova/networks/nova-br100.pid
 --listen-address=192.168.100.1
 --except-interface=lo
 --dhcp-range=set:'novanetwork',192.168.100.2,static,120s
 --dhcp-lease-max=256
 --dhcp-hostsfile=/var/lib/nova/networks/nova-br100.conf
 --dhcp-script=/usr/bin/nova-dhcpbridge --leasefile-ro
```

The output shows three different dnsmasq processes. The dnsmasq process that has the DHCP subnet range of 192.168.122.0 belongs to libvirt and can be ignored. The other two dnsmasq processes belong to `nova-network`. The two processes are actually related—one is simply the parent process of the other. The arguments of the dnsmasq processes should correspond to the details you configured `nova-network` with.

If the problem does not seem to be related to dnsmasq itself, at this point use `tcpdump` on the interfaces to determine where the packets are getting lost.

DHCP traffic uses UDP. The client sends from port 68 to port 67 on the server. Try to boot a new instance and then systematically listen on the NICs until you identify the one that isn't seeing the traffic. To use `tcpdump` to listen to ports 67 and 68 on br100, you would do:

```
# tcpdump -i br100 -n port 67 or port 68
```

You should be doing sanity checks on the interfaces using command such as `ip a` and `brctl show` to ensure that the interfaces are actually up and configured the way that you think that they are.

Debugging DNS Issues

If you are able to use SSH to log into an instance, but it takes a very long time (on the order of a minute) to get a prompt, then you might have a DNS issue. The reason a DNS issue can cause this problem is that the SSH server does a reverse DNS lookup on the IP address that you are connecting from. If DNS lookup isn't working on your instances, then you must wait for the DNS reverse lookup timeout to occur for the SSH login process to complete.

When debugging DNS issues, start by making sure that the host where the dnsmasq process for that instance runs is able to correctly resolve. If the host cannot resolve, then the instances won't be able to either.

A quick way to check whether DNS is working is to resolve a hostname inside your instance by using the `host` command. If DNS is working, you should see:

```
$ host openstack.org
openstack.org has address 174.143.194.225
openstack.org mail is handled by 10 mx1.emailsrvr.com.
openstack.org mail is handled by 20 mx2.emailsrvr.com.
```

If you're running the Cirros image, it doesn't have the "host" program installed, in which case you can use ping to try to access a machine by hostname to see whether it resolves. If DNS is working, the first line of ping would be:

```
$ ping openstack.org
PING openstack.org (174.143.194.225): 56 data bytes
```

If the instance fails to resolve the hostname, you have a DNS problem. For example:

```
$ ping openstack.org
ping: bad address 'openstack.org'
```

In an OpenStack cloud, the dnsmasq process acts as the DNS server for the instances in addition to acting as the DHCP server. A misbehaving dnsmasq process may be the source of DNS-related issues inside the instance. As mentioned in the previous section, the simplest way to rule out a misbehaving dnsmasq process is to kill all the dnsmasq processes on the machine and restart `nova-network`. However, be aware that this command affects everyone running instances on this node, including tenants that have not seen the issue. As a last resort, as root:

```
# killall dnsmasq
# restart nova-network
```

After the dnsmasq processes start again, check whether DNS is working.

If restarting the dnsmasq process doesn't fix the issue, you might need to use `tcpdump` to look at the packets to trace where the failure is. The DNS server listens on UDP port 53. You should see the DNS request on the bridge (such as, br100) of your compute node. Let's say you start listening with `tcpdump` on the compute node:

```
# tcpdump -i br100 -n -v udp port 53
tcpdump: listening on br100, link-type EN10MB (Ethernet), capture size 65535
bytes
```

Then, if you use SSH to log into your instance and try `ping openstack.org`, you should see something like:

```
16:36:18.807518 IP (tos 0x0, ttl 64, id 56057, offset 0, flags [DF],
proto UDP (17), length 59)
 192.168.100.4.54244 > 192.168.100.1.53: 2+ A? openstack.org. (31)
16:36:18.808285 IP (tos 0x0, ttl 64, id 0, offset 0, flags [DF],
proto UDP (17), length 75)
 192.168.100.1.53 > 192.168.100.4.54244: 2 1/0/0 openstack.org. A
 174.143.194.225 (47)
```

Troubleshooting Open vSwitch

Open vSwitch as used in the previous OpenStack Networking Service examples is a full-featured multilayer virtual switch licensed under the open source Apache 2.0 license. Full documentation can be found at the project's website (*http://opsgui.de/1eLBFGA*). In practice, given the preceding configuration, the most common issues are being sure that the required bridges (`br-int`, `br-tun`, `br-ex`, etc.) exist and have the proper ports connected to them.

The Open vSwitch driver should and usually does manage this automatically, but it is useful to know how to do this by hand with the `ovs-vsctl` command. This command has many more subcommands than we will use here; see the man page or use `ovs-vsctl --help` for the full listing.

To list the bridges on a system, use `ovs-vsctl list-br`. This example shows a compute node that has an internal bridge and a tunnel bridge. VLAN networks are trunked through the `eth1` network interface:

```
# ovs-vsctl list-br
br-int
br-tun
eth1-br
```

Working from the physical interface inwards, we can see the chain of ports and bridges. First, the bridge `eth1-br`, which contains the physical network interface `eth1` and the virtual interface `phy-eth1-br`:

```
# ovs-vsctl list-ports eth1-br
eth1
phy-eth1-br
```

Next, the internal bridge, `br-int`, contains `int-eth1-br`, which pairs with `phy-eth1-br` to connect to the physical network shown in the previous bridge, `patch-tun`, which is used to connect to the GRE tunnel bridge and the TAP devices that connect to the instances currently running on the system:

```
# ovs-vsctl list-ports br-int
int-eth1-br
patch-tun
tap2d782834-d1
tap690466bc-92
tap8a864970-2d
```

The tunnel bridge, `br-tun`, contains the `patch-int` interface and `gre-<N>` interfaces for each peer it connects to via GRE, one for each compute and network node in your cluster:

```
# ovs-vsctl list-ports br-tun
patch-int
gre-1
.
.
.
gre-<N>
```

If any of these links is missing or incorrect, it suggests a configuration error. Bridges can be added with `ovs-vsctl add-br`, and ports can be added to bridges with `ovs-vsctl add-port`. While running these by hand can be useful debugging, it is imperative that manual changes that you intend to keep be reflected back into your configuration files.

Dealing with Network Namespaces

Linux network namespaces are a kernel feature the networking service uses to support multiple isolated layer-2 networks with overlapping IP address ranges. The support may be disabled, but it is on by default. If it is enabled in your environment, your network nodes will run their dhcp-agents and l3-agents in isolated namespaces. Network interfaces and traffic on those interfaces will not be visible in the default namespace.

To see whether you are using namespaces, run `ip netns`:

```
# ip netns
qdhcp-e521f9d0-a1bd-4ff4-bc81-78a60dd88fe5
qdhcp-a4d00c60-f005-400e-a24c-1bf8b8308f98
qdhcp-fe178706-9942-4600-9224-b2ae7c61db71
qdhcp-0a1d0a27-cffa-4de3-92c5-9d3fd3f2e74d
qrouter-8a4ce760-ab55-4f2f-8ec5-a2e858ce0d39
```

L3-agent router namespaces are named qrouter-*<router_uuid>*, and dhcp-agent name spaces are named qdhcp-*<net_uuid>*. This output shows a network node with four networks running dhcp-agents, one of which is also running an l3-agent router. It's important to know which network you need to be working in. A list of existing networks and their UUIDs can be obtained buy running neutron net-list with administrative credentials.

Once you've determined which namespace you need to work in, you can use any of the debugging tools mention earlier by prefixing the command with ip netns exec <namespace>. For example, to see what network interfaces exist in the first qdhcp namespace returned above, do this:

```
# ip netns exec qdhcp-e521f9d0-a1bd-4ff4-bc81-78a60dd88fe5 ip a
10: tape6256f7d-31: <BROADCAST,UP,LOWER_UP> mtu 1500 qdisc noqueue state UNKNOWN
    link/ether fa:16:3e:aa:f7:a1 brd ff:ff:ff:ff:ff:ff
    inet 10.0.1.100/24 brd 10.0.1.255 scope global tape6256f7d-31
    inet 169.254.169.254/16 brd 169.254.255.255 scope global tape6256f7d-31
    inet6 fe80::f816:3eff:feaa:f7a1/64 scope link
       valid_lft forever preferred_lft forever
28: lo: <LOOPBACK,UP,LOWER_UP> mtu 16436 qdisc noqueue state UNKNOWN
    link/loopback 00:00:00:00:00:00 brd 00:00:00:00:00:00
    inet 127.0.0.1/8 scope host lo
    inet6 ::1/128 scope host
       valid_lft forever preferred_lft forever
```

From this you see that the DHCP server on that network is using the tape6256f7d-31 device and has an IP address of 10.0.1.100. Seeing the address 169.254.169.254, you can also see that the dhcp-agent is running a metadata-proxy service. Any of the commands mentioned previously in this chapter can be run in the same way. It is also possible to run a shell, such as bash, and have an interactive session within the namespace. In the latter case, exiting the shell returns you to the top-level default namespace.

Summary

The authors have spent too much time looking at packet dumps in order to distill this information for you. We trust that, following the methods outlined in this chapter, you will have an easier time! Aside from working with the tools and steps above, don't forget that sometimes an extra pair of eyes goes a long way to assist.

CHAPTER 13

Logging and Monitoring

As an OpenStack cloud is composed of so many different services, there are a large number of log files. This chapter aims to assist you in locating and working with them and describes other ways to track the status of your deployment.

Where Are the Logs?

Most services use the convention of writing their log files to subdirectories of the `/var/log directory`, as listed in Table 13-1.

Table 13-1. OpenStack log locations

Node type	Service	Log location
Cloud controller	`nova-*`	`/var/log/nova`
Cloud controller	`glance-*`	`/var/log/glance`
Cloud controller	`cinder-*`	`/var/log/cinder`
Cloud controller	`keystone-*`	`/var/log/keystone`
Cloud controller	`neutron-*`	`/var/log/neutron`
Cloud controller	horizon	`/var/log/apache2/`
All nodes	misc (swift, dnsmasq)	`/var/log/syslog`
Compute nodes	libvirt	`/var/log/libvirt/libvirtd.log`

Node type	Service	Log location
Compute nodes	Console (boot up messages) for VM instances:	/var/lib/nova/instances/instance-<instance id>/console.log
Block Storage nodes	cinder-volume	/var/log/cinder/cinder-volume.log

Reading the Logs

OpenStack services use the standard logging levels, at increasing severity: DEBUG, INFO, AUDIT, WARNING, ERROR, CRITICAL, and TRACE. That is, messages only appear in the logs if they are more "severe" than the particular log level, with DEBUG allowing all log statements through. For example, TRACE is logged only if the software has a stack trace, while INFO is logged for every message including those that are only for information.

To disable DEBUG-level logging, edit `/etc/nova/nova.conf` as follows:

```
debug=false
```

Keystone is handled a little differently. To modify the logging level, edit the `/etc/keystone/logging.conf` file and look at the `logger_root` and `handler_file` sections.

Logging for horizon is configured in `/etc/openstack_dashboard/local_settings.py`. Because horizon is a Django web application, it follows the Django Logging framework conventions (*http://opsgui.de/NPGgww*).

The first step in finding the source of an error is typically to search for a CRITICAL, TRACE, or ERROR message in the log starting at the bottom of the log file.

Here is an example of a CRITICAL log message, with the corresponding TRACE (Python traceback) immediately following:

```
2013-02-25 21:05:51 17409 CRITICAL cinder [-] Bad or unexpected response from
the storage volume backend API: volume group
 cinder-volumes doesn't exist
2013-02-25 21:05:51 17409 TRACE cinder Traceback (most recent call last):
2013-02-25 21:05:51 17409 TRACE cinder File "/usr/bin/cinder-volume", line 48,
in <module>
2013-02-25 21:05:51 17409 TRACE cinder service.wait()
2013-02-25 21:05:51 17409 TRACE cinder File "/usr/lib/python2.7/dist-packages/
cinder/service.py", line 422, in wait
2013-02-25 21:05:51 17409 TRACE cinder _launcher.wait()
2013-02-25 21:05:51 17409 TRACE cinder File "/usr/lib/python2.7/dist-packages/
cinder/service.py", line 127, in wait
2013-02-25 21:05:51 17409 TRACE cinder service.wait()
2013-02-25 21:05:51 17409 TRACE cinder File "/usr/lib/python2.7/dist-packages/
eventlet/greenthread.py", line 166, in wait
```

```
2013-02-25 21:05:51 17409 TRACE cinder return self._exit_event.wait()
2013-02-25 21:05:51 17409 TRACE cinder File "/usr/lib/python2.7/dist-packages/
eventlet/event.py", line 116, in wait
2013-02-25 21:05:51 17409 TRACE cinder return hubs.get_hub().switch()
2013-02-25 21:05:51 17409 TRACE cinder File "/usr/lib/python2.7/dist-packages/
eventlet/hubs/hub.py", line 177, in switch
2013-02-25 21:05:51 17409 TRACE cinder return self.greenlet.switch()
2013-02-25 21:05:51 17409 TRACE cinder File "/usr/lib/python2.7/dist-packages/
eventlet/greenthread.py", line 192, in main
2013-02-25 21:05:51 17409 TRACE cinder result = function(*args, **kwargs)
2013-02-25 21:05:51 17409 TRACE cinder File "/usr/lib/python2.7/dist-packages/
cinder/service.py", line 88, in run_server
2013-02-25 21:05:51 17409 TRACE cinder server.start()
2013-02-25 21:05:51 17409 TRACE cinder File "/usr/lib/python2.7/dist-packages/
cinder/service.py", line 159, in start
2013-02-25 21:05:51 17409 TRACE cinder self.manager.init_host()
2013-02-25 21:05:51 17409 TRACE cinder File "/usr/lib/python2.7/dist-packages/
cinder/volume/manager.py", line 95,
 in init_host
2013-02-25 21:05:51 17409 TRACE cinder self.driver.check_for_setup_error()
2013-02-25 21:05:51 17409 TRACE cinder File "/usr/lib/python2.7/dist-packages/
cinder/volume/driver.py", line 116,
 in check_for_setup_error
2013-02-25 21:05:51 17409 TRACE cinder raise exception.VolumeBackendAPIExcep
tion(data=exception_message)
2013-02-25 21:05:51 17409 TRACE cinder VolumeBackendAPIException: Bad or unexpec
ted response from the storage volume
 backend API: volume group cinder-volumes doesn't exist
2013-02-25 21:05:51 17409 TRACE cinder
```

In this example, `cinder-volumes` failed to start and has provided a stack trace, since its volume backend has been unable to set up the storage volume—probably because the LVM volume that is expected from the configuration does not exist.

Here is an example error log:

```
2013-02-25 20:26:33 6619 ERROR nova.openstack.common.rpc.common [-] AMQP server
on localhost:5672 is unreachable:
 [Errno 111] ECONNREFUSED. Trying again in 23 seconds.
```

In this error, a nova service has failed to connect to the RabbitMQ server because it got a connection refused error.

Tracing Instance Requests

When an instance fails to behave properly, you will often have to trace activity associated with that instance across the log files of various `nova-*` services and across both the cloud controller and compute nodes.

The typical way is to trace the UUID associated with an instance across the service logs.

Consider the following example:

```
$ nova list
+--------------------------------+--------+--------+-------------------------+
| ID                             | Name   | Status | Networks                |
+--------------------------------+--------+--------+-------------------------+
| fafed8-4a46-413b-b113-f1959ffe | cirros | ACTIVE | novanetwork=192.168.100.3|
+------------------------------------+--------+--------+--------------------+
```

Here, the ID associated with the instance is `faf7ded8-4a46-413b-b113-f19590746ffe`. If you search for this string on the cloud controller in the `/var/log/nova-*.log` files, it appears in `nova-api.log` and `nova-scheduler.log`. If you search for this on the compute nodes in `/var/log/nova-*.log`, it appears in `nova-network.log` and `nova-compute.log`. If no ERROR or CRITICAL messages appear, the most recent log entry that reports this may provide a hint about what has gone wrong.

Adding Custom Logging Statements

If there is not enough information in the existing logs, you may need to add your own custom logging statements to the `nova-*` services.

The source files are located in `/usr/lib/python2.7/dist-packages/nova`.

To add logging statements, the following line should be near the top of the file. For most files, these should already be there:

```
from nova.openstack.common import log as logging
LOG = logging.getLogger(__name__)
```

To add a DEBUG logging statement, you would do:

```
LOG.debug("This is a custom debugging statement")
```

You may notice that all the existing logging messages are preceded by an underscore and surrounded by parentheses, for example:

```
LOG.debug(_("Logging statement appears here"))
```

This formatting is used to support translation of logging messages into different languages using the gettext (*http://opsgui.de/1eLBlHT*) internationalization library. You don't need to do this for your own custom log messages. However, if you want to contribute the code back to the OpenStack project that includes logging statements, you must surround your log messages with underscores and parentheses.

RabbitMQ Web Management Interface or rabbitmqctl

Aside from connection failures, RabbitMQ log files are generally not useful for debugging OpenStack related issues. Instead, we recommend you use the RabbitMQ web management interface. Enable it on your cloud controller:

```
# /usr/lib/rabbitmq/bin/rabbitmq-plugins enable rabbitmq_management
```

```
# service rabbitmq-server restart
```

The RabbitMQ web management interface is accessible on your cloud controller at *http://localhost:55672*.

Ubuntu 12.04 installs RabbitMQ version 2.7.1, which uses port 55672. RabbitMQ versions 3.0 and above use port 15672 instead. You can check which version of RabbitMQ you have running on your local Ubuntu machine by doing:

```
$ dpkg -s rabbitmq-server | grep "Version:"
Version: 2.7.1-0ubuntu4
```

An alternative to enabling the RabbitMQ web management interface is to use the `rabbitmqctl` commands. For example, `rabbitmqctl list_queues| grep cinder` displays any messages left in the queue. If there are messages, it's a possible sign that cinder services didn't connect properly to rabbitmq and might have to be restarted.

Items to monitor for RabbitMQ include the number of items in each of the queues and the processing time statistics for the server.

Centrally Managing Logs

Because your cloud is most likely composed of many servers, you must check logs on each of those servers to properly piece an event together. A better solution is to send the logs of all servers to a central location so that they can all be accessed from the same area.

Ubuntu uses rsyslog as the default logging service. Since it is natively able to send logs to a remote location, you don't have to install anything extra to enable this feature, just modify the configuration file. In doing this, consider running your logging over a management network or using an encrypted VPN to avoid interception.

rsyslog Client Configuration

To begin, configure all OpenStack components to log to syslog in addition to their standard log file location. Also configure each component to log to a different syslog facility. This makes it easier to split the logs into individual components on the central server:

`nova.conf`:

```
use_syslog=True
syslog_log_facility=LOG_LOCAL0
```

`glance-api.conf` and `glance-registry.conf`:

```
use_syslog=True
syslog_log_facility=LOG_LOCAL1
```

`cinder.conf`:

```
use_syslog=True
syslog_log_facility=LOG_LOCAL2
```

`keystone.conf`:

```
use_syslog=True
syslog_log_facility=LOG_LOCAL3
```

By default, Object Storage logs to syslog.

Next, create `/etc/rsyslog.d/client.conf` with the following line:

```
*.* @192.168.1.10
```

This instructs rsyslog to send all logs to the IP listed. In this example, the IP points to the cloud controller.

rsyslog Server Configuration

Designate a server as the central logging server. The best practice is to choose a server that is solely dedicated to this purpose. Create a file called `/etc/rsyslog.d/server.conf` with the following contents:

```
# Enable UDP
$ModLoad imudp
# Listen on 192.168.1.10 only
$UDPServerAddress 192.168.1.10
# Port 514
$UDPServerRun 514

# Create logging templates for nova
$template NovaFile,"/var/log/rsyslog/%HOSTNAME%/nova.log"
$template NovaAll,"/var/log/rsyslog/nova.log"

# Log everything else to syslog.log
$template DynFile,"/var/log/rsyslog/%HOSTNAME%/syslog.log"
*.* ?DynFile

# Log various openstack components to their own individual file
local0.* ?NovaFile
local0.* ?NovaAll
& ~
```

This example configuration handles the nova service only. It first configures rsyslog to act as a server that runs on port 514. Next, it creates a series of logging templates. Logging templates control where received logs are stored. Using the last example, a nova log from c01.example.com goes to the following locations:

- /var/log/rsyslog/c01.example.com/nova.log
- /var/log/rsyslog/nova.log

This is useful, as logs from c02.example.com go to:

- /var/log/rsyslog/c02.example.com/nova.log
- /var/log/rsyslog/nova.log

You have an individual log file for each compute node as well as an aggregated log that contains nova logs from all nodes.

StackTach

StackTach is a tool created by Rackspace to collect and report the notifications sent by nova. Notifications are essentially the same as logs but can be much more detailed. A good overview of notifications can be found at System Usage Data (*http://opsgui.de/NPGh3H*).

To enable nova to send notifications, add the following to nova.conf:

```
notification_topics=monitor
notification_driver=nova.openstack.common.notifier.rabbit_notifier
```

Once nova is sending notifications, install and configure StackTach. Since StackTach is relatively new and constantly changing, installation instructions would quickly become outdated. Please refer to the StackTach GitHub repo (*http://opsgui.de/1eLBpqQ*) for instructions as well as a demo video.

Monitoring

There are two types of monitoring: watching for problems and watching usage trends. The former ensures that all services are up and running, creating a functional cloud. The latter involves monitoring resource usage over time in order to make informed decisions about potential bottlenecks and upgrades.

> ### Nagios
>
> Nagios is an open source monitoring service. It's capable of executing arbitrary commands to check the status of server and network services, remotely executing arbitrary commands directly on servers, and allowing servers to push notifications back in the form of passive monitoring. Nagios has been around since 1999. Although newer monitoring services are available, Nagios is a tried-and-true systems administration staple.

Process Monitoring

A basic type of alert monitoring is to simply check and see whether a required process is running. For example, ensure that the `nova-api` service is running on the cloud controller:

```
# ps aux | grep nova-api
nova 12786 0.0 0.0 37952 1312 ? Ss Feb11 0:00 su -s /bin/sh -c exec nova-api
--config-file=/etc/nova/nova.conf nova
nova 12787 0.0 0.1 135764 57400 ? S Feb11 0:01 /usr/bin/python
 /usr/bin/nova-api --config-file=/etc/nova/nova.conf
nova 12792 0.0 0.0 96052 22856 ? S Feb11 0:01 /usr/bin/python
/usr/bin/nova-api --config-file=/etc/nova/nova.conf
nova 12793 0.0 0.3 290688 115516 ? S Feb11 1:23 /usr/bin/python
/usr/bin/nova-api --config-file=/etc/nova/nova.conf
nova 12794 0.0 0.2 248636 77068 ? S Feb11 0:04 /usr/bin/python
/usr/bin/nova-api --config-file=/etc/nova/nova.conf
root 24121 0.0 0.0 11688 912 pts/5 S+ 13:07 0:00 grep nova-api
```

You can create automated alerts for critical processes by using Nagios and NRPE. For example, to ensure that the `nova-compute` process is running on compute nodes, create an alert on your Nagios server that looks like this:

```
define service {
    host_name c01.example.com
    check_command check_nrpe_1arg!check_nova-compute
    use generic-service
    notification_period 24x7
    contact_groups sysadmins
    service_description nova-compute
}
```

Then on the actual compute node, create the following NRPE configuration:

```
\command[check_nova-compute]=/usr/lib/nagios/plugins/check_procs -c 1: \
-a nova-compute
```

Nagios checks that at least one `nova-compute` service is running at all times.

Resource Alerting

Resource alerting provides notifications when one or more resources are critically low. While the monitoring thresholds should be tuned to your specific OpenStack environment, monitoring resource usage is not specific to OpenStack at all—any generic type of alert will work fine.

Some of the resources that you want to monitor include:

- Disk usage
- Server load
- Memory usage
- Network I/O
- Available vCPUs

For example, to monitor disk capacity on a compute node with Nagios, add the following to your Nagios configuration:

```
define service {
    host_name c01.example.com
    check_command check_nrpe!check_all_disks!20% 10%
    use generic-service
    contact_groups sysadmins
    service_description Disk
}
```

On the compute node, add the following to your NRPE configuration:

```
command[check_all_disks]=/usr/lib/nagios/plugins/check_disk -w $ARG1$ -c \
$ARG2$ -e
```

Nagios alerts you with a WARNING when any disk on the compute node is 80 percent full and CRITICAL when 90 percent is full.

Metering and Telemetry with Ceilometer

An integrated OpenStack project (code-named ceilometer) collects metering data and provides alerts for Compute, Storage, and Networking. Data collected by the metering system could be used for billing. Depending on deployment configuration, metered data may be accessible to users based on the deployment configuration. The Telemetry service provides a REST API documented at *http://api.openstack.org/api-ref-telemetry.html*. You can read more about the project at *http://docs.openstack.org/developer/ceilometer*.

OpenStack-Specific Resources

Resources such as memory, disk, and CPU are generic resources that all servers (even non-OpenStack servers) have and are important to the overall health of the server. When dealing with OpenStack specifically, these resources are important for a second reason: ensuring that enough are available to launch instances. There are a few ways you can see OpenStack resource usage. The first is through the nova command:

```
# nova usage-list
```

This command displays a list of how many instances a tenant has running and some light usage statistics about the combined instances. This command is useful for a quick overview of your cloud, but it doesn't really get into a lot of details.

Next, the nova database contains three tables that store usage information.

The nova.quotas and nova.quota_usages tables store quota information. If a tenant's quota is different from the default quota settings, its quota is stored in the nova.quotas table. For example:

```
mysql> select project_id, resource, hard_limit from quotas;
+----------------------------------+-----------------------------+------------+
| project_id                       | resource                    | hard_limit |
+----------------------------------+-----------------------------+------------+
| 628df59f091142399e0689a2696f5baa | metadata_items              | 128        |
| 628df59f091142399e0689a2696f5baa | injected_file_content_bytes | 10240      |
| 628df59f091142399e0689a2696f5baa | injected_files              | 5          |
| 628df59f091142399e0689a2696f5baa | gigabytes                   | 1000       |
| 628df59f091142399e0689a2696f5baa | ram                         | 51200      |
| 628df59f091142399e0689a2696f5baa | floating_ips                | 10         |
| 628df59f091142399e0689a2696f5baa | instances                   | 10         |
| 628df59f091142399e0689a2696f5baa | volumes                     | 10         |
| 628df59f091142399e0689a2696f5baa | cores                       | 20         |
+----------------------------------+-----------------------------+------------+
```

The nova.quota_usages table keeps track of how many resources the tenant currently has in use:

```
mysql> select project_id, resource, in_use from quota_usages where project_id
like '628%';
+----------------------------------+--------------+--------+
| project_id                       | resource     | in_use |
+----------------------------------+--------------+--------+
| 628df59f091142399e0689a2696f5baa | instances    | 1      |
| 628df59f091142399e0689a2696f5baa | ram          | 512    |
| 628df59f091142399e0689a2696f5baa | cores        | 1      |
| 628df59f091142399e0689a2696f5baa | floating_ips | 1      |
| 628df59f091142399e0689a2696f5baa | volumes      | 2      |
| 628df59f091142399e0689a2696f5baa | gigabytes    | 12     |
| 628df59f091142399e0689a2696f5baa | images       | 1      |
+----------------------------------+--------------+--------+
```

By comparing a tenant's hard limit with their current resource usage, you can see their usage percentage. For example, if this tenant is using 1 floating IP out of 10, then they are using 10 percent of their floating IP quota. Rather than doing the calculation manually, you can use SQL or the scripting language of your choice and create a formatted report:

```
+-----------------------------------+------------+------------+---------------+
| some_tenant                                                                 |
+-----------------------------------+------------+------------+---------------+
| Resource                          | Used       | Limit      |               |
+-----------------------------------+------------+------------+---------------+
| cores                             | 1          | 20         |           5 % |
| floating_ips                      | 1          | 10         |          10 % |
| gigabytes                         | 12         | 1000       |           1 % |
| images                            | 1          | 4          |          25 % |
| injected_file_content_bytes       | 0          | 10240      |           0 % |
| injected_file_path_bytes          | 0          | 255        |           0 % |
| injected_files                    | 0          | 5          |           0 % |
| instances                         | 1          | 10         |          10 % |
| key_pairs                         | 0          | 100        |           0 % |
| metadata_items                    | 0          | 128        |           0 % |
| ram                               | 512        | 51200      |           1 % |
| reservation_expire                | 0          | 86400      |           0 % |
| security_group_rules              | 0          | 20         |           0 % |
| security_groups                   | 0          | 10         |           0 % |
| volumes                           | 2          | 10         |          20 % |
+-----------------------------------+------------+------------+---------------+
```

The preceding information was generated by using a custom script that can be found on GitHub (*http://opsgui.de/NPGjbX*).

This script is specific to a certain OpenStack installation and must be modified to fit your environment. However, the logic should easily be transferable.

Intelligent Alerting

Intelligent alerting can be thought of as a form of continuous integration for operations. For example, you can easily check to see whether the Image Service is up and running by ensuring that the `glance-api` and `glance-registry` processes are running or by seeing whether `glace-api` is responding on port 9292.

But how can you tell whether images are being successfully uploaded to the Image Service? Maybe the disk that Image Service is storing the images on is full or the S3 backend is down. You could naturally check this by doing a quick image upload:

```
#!/bin/bash
#
# assumes that reasonable credentials have been stored at
# /root/auth


. /root/openrc
wget https://launchpad.net/cirros/trunk/0.3.0/+download/ \
     cirros-0.3.0-x86_64-disk.img
glance image-create --name='cirros image' --is-public=true
--container-format=bare --disk-format=qcow2 < cirros-0.3.0-x8
6_64-disk.img
```

By taking this script and rolling it into an alert for your monitoring system (such as Nagios), you now have an automated way of ensuring that image uploads to the Image Catalog are working.

You must remove the image after each test. Even better, test whether you can successfully delete an image from the Image Service.

Intelligent alerting takes considerably more time to plan and implement than the other alerts described in this chapter. A good outline to implement intelligent alerting is:

- Review common actions in your cloud.
- Create ways to automatically test these actions.
- Roll these tests into an alerting system.

Some other examples for Intelligent Alerting include:

- Can instances launch and be destroyed?
- Can users be created?
- Can objects be stored and deleted?
- Can volumes be created and destroyed?

Trending

Trending can give you great insight into how your cloud is performing day to day. You can learn, for example, if a busy day was simply a rare occurrence or if you should start adding new compute nodes.

Trending takes a slightly different approach than alerting. While alerting is interested in a binary result (whether a check succeeds or fails), trending records the current state of something at a certain point in time. Once enough points in time have been recorded, you can see how the value has changed over time.

All of the alert types mentioned earlier can also be used for trend reporting. Some other trend examples include:

- The number of instances on each compute node
- The types of flavors in use
- The number of volumes in use
- The number of Object Storage requests each hour
- The number of `nova-api` requests each hour
- The I/O statistics of your storage services

As an example, recording `nova-api` usage can allow you to track the need to scale your cloud controller. By keeping an eye on `nova-api` requests, you can determine whether you need to spawn more `nova-api` processes or go as far as introducing an entirely new server to run `nova-api`. To get an approximate count of the requests, look for standard INFO messages in `/var/log/nova/nova-api.log`:

```
# grep INFO /var/log/nova/nova-api.log | wc
```

You can obtain further statistics by looking for the number of successful requests:

```
# grep " 200 " /var/log/nova/nova-api.log | wc
```

By running this command periodically and keeping a record of the result, you can create a trending report over time that shows whether your `nova-api` usage is increasing, decreasing, or keeping steady.

A tool such as collectd can be used to store this information. While collectd is out of the scope of this book, a good starting point would be to use collectd to store the result as a COUNTER data type. More information can be found in collectd's documentation (*http://opsgui.de/1eLBriA*).

Summary

For stable operations, you want to detect failure promptly and determine causes efficiently. With a distributed system, it's even more important to track the right items to meet a service-level target. Learning where these logs are located in the file system or API gives you an advantage. This chapter also showed how to read, interpret, and manipulate information from OpenStack services so that you can monitor effectively.

CHAPTER 14
Backup and Recovery

Standard backup best practices apply when creating your OpenStack backup policy. For example, how often to back up your data is closely related to how quickly you need to recover from data loss.

If you cannot have any data loss at all, you should also focus on a highly available deployment. The *OpenStack High Availability Guide (http://opsgui.de/1eLAYwS)* offers suggestions for elimination of a single point of failure that could cause system downtime. While it is not a completely prescriptive document, it offers methods and techniques for avoiding downtime and data loss.

Other backup considerations include:

- How many backups to keep?
- Should backups be kept off-site?
- How often should backups be tested?

Just as important as a backup policy is a recovery policy (or at least recovery testing).

What to Back Up

While OpenStack is composed of many components and moving parts, backing up the critical data is quite simple.

This chapter describes only how to back up configuration files and databases that the various OpenStack components need to run. This chapter does not describe how to back up objects inside Object Storage or data contained inside Block Storage. Generally these areas are left for users to back up on their own.

Database Backups

The example OpenStack architecture designates the cloud controller as the MySQL server. This MySQL server hosts the databases for nova, glance, cinder, and keystone. With all of these databases in one place, it's very easy to create a database backup:

```
# mysqldump --opt --all-databases > openstack.sql
```

If you only want to backup a single database, you can instead run:

```
# mysqldump --opt nova > nova.sql
```

where `nova` is the database you want to back up.

You can easily automate this process by creating a cron job that runs the following script once per day:

```
#!/bin/bash
backup_dir="/var/lib/backups/mysql"
filename="${backup_dir}/mysql-`hostname`-`eval date +%Y%m%d`.sql.gz"
# Dump the entire MySQL database
/usr/bin/mysqldump --opt --all-databases | gzip > $filename
# Delete backups older than 7 days
find $backup_dir -ctime +7 -type f -delete
```

This script dumps the entire MySQL database and deletes any backups older than seven days.

File System Backups

This section discusses which files and directories should be backed up regularly, organized by service.

Compute

The `/etc/nova` directory on both the cloud controller and compute nodes should be regularly backed up.

`/var/log/nova` does not need to be backed up if you have all logs going to a central area. It is highly recommended to use a central logging server or back up the log directory.

`/var/lib/nova` is another important directory to back up. The exception to this is the `/var/lib/nova/instances` subdirectory on compute nodes. This subdirectory contains the KVM images of running instances. You would want to back up this directory only if you need to maintain backup copies of all instances. Under most circumstances, you do not need to do this, but this can vary from cloud to cloud and your service levels. Also be aware that making a backup of a live KVM instance can cause that instance to not boot properly if it is ever restored from a backup.

Image Catalog and Delivery

/etc/glance and /var/log/glance follow the same rules as their nova counterparts.

/var/lib/glance should also be backed up. Take special notice of /var/lib/glance/images. If you are using a file-based backend of glance, /var/lib/glance/images is where the images are stored and care should be taken.

There are two ways to ensure stability with this directory. The first is to make sure this directory is run on a RAID array. If a disk fails, the directory is available. The second way is to use a tool such as rsync to replicate the images to another server:

```
# rsync -az --progress /var/lib/glance/images \
backup-server:/var/lib/glance/images/
```

Identity

/etc/keystone and /var/log/keystone follow the same rules as other components.

/var/lib/keystone, although it should not contain any data being used, can also be backed up just in case.

Block Storage

/etc/cinder and /var/log/cinder follow the same rules as other components.

/var/lib/cinder should also be backed up.

Object Storage

/etc/swift is very important to have backed up. This directory contains the swift configuration files as well as the ring files and ring builder files, which if lost, render the data on your cluster inaccessible. A best practice is to copy the builder files to all storage nodes along with the ring files. Multiple backup copies are spread throughout your storage cluster.

Recovering Backups

Recovering backups is a fairly simple process. To begin, first ensure that the service you are recovering is not running. For example, to do a full recovery of nova on the cloud controller, first stop all nova services:

```
# stop nova-api
# stop nova-cert
# stop nova-consoleauth
# stop nova-novncproxy
# stop nova-objectstore
# stop nova-scheduler
```

Now you can import a previously backed-up database:

```
# mysql nova < nova.sql
```

You can also restore backed-up nova directories:

```
# mv /etc/nova{,.orig}
# cp -a /path/to/backup/nova /etc/
```

Once the files are restored, start everything back up:

```
# start mysql
# for i in nova-api nova-cert nova-consoleauth nova-novncproxy
nova-objectstore nova-scheduler
> do
> start $i
> done
```

Other services follow the same process, with their respective directories and databases.

Summary

Backup and subsequent recovery is one of the first tasks system administrators learn. However, each system has different items that need attention. By taking care of your database, image service, and appropriate file system locations, you can be assured that you can handle any event requiring recovery.

CHAPTER 15

Customization

OpenStack might not do everything you need it to do out of the box. To add a new feature, you can follow different paths.

To take the first path, you can modify the OpenStack code directly. Learn how to contribute (*http://opsgui.de/NPG68B*), follow the code review workflow (*http://opsgui.de/1eLB2ww*), make your changes, and contribute them back to the upstream OpenStack project. This path is recommended if the feature you need requires deep integration with an existing project. The community is always open to contributions and welcomes new functionality that follows the feature-development guidelines. This path still requires you to use DevStack for testing your feature additions, so this chapter walks you through the DevStack environment.

For the second path, you can write new features and plug them in using changes to a configuration file. If the project where your feature would need to reside uses the Python Paste framework, you can create middleware for it and plug it in through configuration. There may also be specific ways of customizing a project, such as creating a new scheduler driver for Compute or a custom tab for the dashboard.

This chapter focuses on the second path for customizing OpenStack by providing two examples for writing new features. The first example shows how to modify Object Storage (swift) middleware to add a new feature, and the second example provides a new scheduler feature for OpenStack Compute (nova). To customize OpenStack this way you need a development environment. The best way to get an environment up and running quickly is to run DevStack within your cloud.

Create an OpenStack Development Environment

To create a development environment, you can use DevStack. DevStack is essentially a collection of shell scripts and configuration files that builds an OpenStack development environment for you. You use it to create such an environment for developing a new feature.

You can find all of the documentation at the DevStack (*http://opsgui.de/NPG9kK*) website.

To run DevStack for the stable Havana branch on an instance in your OpenStack cloud:

1. Boot an instance from the dashboard or the nova command-line interface (CLI) with the following parameters:

   - Name: devstack-havana
   - Image: Ubuntu 12.04 LTS
   - Memory Size: 4 GB RAM
   - Disk Size: minimum 5 GB

   If you are using the `nova` client, specify `--flavor 3` for the `nova boot` command to get adequate memory and disk sizes.

2. Log in and set up DevStack. Here's an example of the commands you can use to set up DevStack on a virtual machine:

   a. Log in to the instance:

   ```
   $ ssh username@my.instance.ip.address
   ```

   b. Update the virtual machine's operating system:

   ```
   # apt-get -y update
   ```

   c. Install git:

   ```
   # apt-get -y install git
   ```

   d. Clone the stable/havana branch of the `devstack` repository:

   ```
   $ git clone https://github.com/openstack-dev/devstack.git -b
   stable/havana devstack/
   ```

   e. Change to the `devstack` repository:

   ```
   $ cd devstack
   ```

3. (Optional) If you've logged in to your instance as the root user, you must create a "stack" user; otherwise you'll run into permission issues. If you've logged in as a user other than root, you can skip these steps:

   a. Run the DevStack script to create the stack user:

   ```
   # tools/create-stack-user.sh
   ```

   b. Give ownership of the `devstack` directory to the stack user:

   ```
   # chown -R stack:stack /root/devstack
   ```

c. Set some permissions you can use to view the DevStack screen later:

```
# chmod o+rwx /dev/pts/0
```

d. Switch to the stack user:

```
$ su stack
```

4. Edit the `localrc` configuration file that controls what DevStack will deploy. Copy the example `localrc` file at the end of this section (Example 15-1):

```
$ vim localrc
```

5. Run the stack script that will install OpenStack:

```
$ ./stack.sh
```

6. When the stack script is done, you can open the screen session it started to view all of the running OpenStack services:

```
$ screen -r stack
```

7. Press Ctrl+A followed by 0 to go to the first `screen` window.

- The `stack.sh` script takes a while to run. Perhaps you can take this opportunity to join the OpenStack Foundation (*http://opsgui.de/1eLB5bJ*).
- `Screen` is a useful program for viewing many related services at once. For more information, see the GNU screen quick reference (*http://opsgui.de/NPG9Bi*).

Now that you have an OpenStack development environment, you're free to hack around without worrying about damaging your production deployment. Example 15-1 provides a working environment for running OpenStack Identity, Compute, Block Storage, Image Service, the OpenStack dashboard, and Object Storage with the stable/havana branches as the starting point.

Example 15-1. localrc

```
# Credentials
ADMIN_PASSWORD=devstack
MYSQL_PASSWORD=devstack
RABBIT_PASSWORD=devstack
SERVICE_PASSWORD=devstack
SERVICE_TOKEN=devstack

# OpenStack Identity Service branch
KEYSTONE_BRANCH=stable/havana
```

```
# OpenStack Compute branch
NOVA_BRANCH=stable/havana

# OpenStack Block Storage branch
CINDER_BRANCH=stable/havana

# OpenStack Image Service branch
GLANCE_BRANCH=stable/havana

# OpenStack Dashboard branch
HORIZON_BRANCH=stable/havana

# OpenStack Object Storage branch
SWIFT_BRANCH=stable/havana

enable_service swift

# Object Storage Settings
SWIFT_HASH=66a3d6b56c1f479c8b4e70ab5c2000f5
SWIFT_REPLICAS=1

# Block Storage Setting
VOLUME_BACKING_FILE_SIZE=20480M

# Output
LOGFILE=/opt/stack/logs/stack.sh.log
VERBOSE=True
LOG_COLOR=False
SCREEN_LOGDIR=/opt/stack/logs
```

Customizing Object Storage (Swift) Middleware

OpenStack Object Storage, known as swift when reading the code, is based on the Python Paste (*http://opsgui.de/1eLB8Ew*) framework. The best introduction to its architecture is A Do-It-Yourself Framework (*http://opsgui.de/NPG8xl*). Because of the swift project's use of this framework, you are able to add features to a project by placing some custom code in a project's pipeline without having to change any of the core code.

Imagine a scenario where you have public access to one of your containers, but what you really want is to restrict access to that to a set of IPs based on a whitelist. In this example, we'll create a piece of middleware for swift that allows access to a container from only a set of IP addresses, as determined by the container's metadata items. Only those IP addresses that you explicitly whitelist using the container's metadata will be able to access the container.

This example is for illustrative purposes only. It should not be used as a container IP whitelist solution without further development and extensive security testing.

When you join the screen session that `stack.sh` starts with `screen -r stack`, you see a screen for each service running, which can be a few or several, depending on how many services you configured DevStack to run.

The asterisk * indicates which screen window you are viewing. This example shows we are viewing the key (for keystone) screen window:

```
0$ shell  1$ key*  2$ horizon  3$ s-proxy  4$ s-object  5$ s-container  6$ s-
account
```

The purpose of the screen windows are as follows:

`shell`
: A shell where you can get some work done

`key*`
: The keystone service

`horizon`
: The horizon dashboard web application

`s-{name}`
: The swift services

To create the middleware and plug it in through Paste configuration:

1. Change to the directory where Object Storage is installed:

   ```
   $ cd /opt/stack/swift
   ```

2. Create the `ip_whitelist.py` Python source code file:

   ```
   $ vim swift/common/middleware/ip_whitelist.py
   ```

3. Copy the code in Example 15-2 into `ip_whitelist.py`. The following code is a middleware example that restricts access to a container based on IP address as explained at the beginning of the section. Middleware passes the request on to another application. This example uses the swift "swob" library to wrap Web Server Gateway Interface (WSGI) requests and responses into objects for swift to interact with. When you're done, save and close the file.

   Example 15-2. ip_whitelist.py

   ```
   # vim: tabstop=4 shiftwidth=4 softtabstop=4
   # Copyright (c) 2014 OpenStack Foundation
   ```

```
# All Rights Reserved.
#
#    Licensed under the Apache License, Version 2.0 (the "License"); you may
#    not use this file except in compliance with the License. You may obtain
#    a copy of the License at
#
#         http://www.apache.org/licenses/LICENSE-2.0
#
#    Unless required by applicable law or agreed to in writing, software
#    distributed under the License is distributed on an "AS IS" BASIS, WITHOUT
#    WARRANTIES OR CONDITIONS OF ANY KIND, either express or implied. See the
#    License for the specific language governing permissions and limitations
#    under the License.

import socket

from swift.common.utils import get_logger
from swift.proxy.controllers.base import get_container_info
from swift.common.swob import Request, Response

class IPWhitelistMiddleware(object):
    """
    IP Whitelist Middleware

    Middleware that allows access to a container from only a set of IP
    addresses as determined by the container's metadata items that start
    with the prefix 'allow'. E.G. allow-dev=192.168.0.20
    """

    def __init__(self, app, conf, logger=None):
        self.app = app

        if logger:
            self.logger = logger
        else:
            self.logger = get_logger(conf, log_route='ip_whitelist')

        self.deny_message = conf.get('deny_message', "IP Denied")
        self.local_ip = socket.gethostbyname(socket.gethostname())

    def __call__(self, env, start_response):
        """
        WSGI entry point.
        Wraps env in swob.Request object and passes it down.

        :param env: WSGI environment dictionary
        :param start_response: WSGI callable
        """
        req = Request(env)

        try:
            version, account, container, obj = req.split_path(1, 4, True)
```

```
        except ValueError:
            return self.app(env, start_response)

        container_info = get_container_info(
            req.environ, self.app, swift_source='IPWhitelistMiddleware')

        remote_ip = env['REMOTE_ADDR']
        self.logger.debug("Remote IP: %(remote_ip)s",
                          {'remote_ip': remote_ip})

        meta = container_info['meta']
        allow = {k:v for k,v in meta.iteritems() if k.startswith('allow')}
        allow_ips = set(allow.values())
        allow_ips.add(self.local_ip)
        self.logger.debug("Allow IPs: %(allow_ips)s",
                          {'allow_ips': allow_ips})

        if remote_ip in allow_ips:
            return self.app(env, start_response)
        else:
            self.logger.debug(
                "IP %(remote_ip)s denied access to Account=%(account)s "
                "Container=%(container)s. Not in %(allow_ips)s", locals())
            return Response(
                status=403,
                body=self.deny_message,
                request=req)(env, start_response)


def filter_factory(global_conf, **local_conf):
    """
    paste.deploy app factory for creating WSGI proxy apps.
    """
    conf = global_conf.copy()
    conf.update(local_conf)

    def ip_whitelist(app):
        return IPWhitelistMiddleware(app, conf)
    return ip_whitelist
```

There is a lot of useful information in `env` and `conf` that you can use to decide what to do with the request. To find out more about what properties are available, you can insert the following log statement into the `__init__` method:

```
self.logger.debug("conf = %(conf)s", locals())
```

and the following log statement into the `__call__` method:

```
self.logger.debug("env = %(env)s", locals())
```

4. To plug this middleware into the swift Paste pipeline, you edit one configuration file, `/etc/swift/proxy-server.conf`:

```
$ vim /etc/swift/proxy-server.conf
```

5. Find the `[filter:ratelimit]` section in `/etc/swift/proxy-server.conf`, and copy in the following configuration section after it:

   ```
   [filter:ip_whitelist]
   paste.filter_factory = swift.common.middleware.ip_whitelist:filter_factory
   # You can override the default log routing for this filter here:
   # set log_name = ratelimit
   # set log_facility = LOG_LOCAL0
   # set log_level = INFO
   # set log_headers = False
   # set log_address = /dev/log
   deny_message = You shall not pass!
   ```

6. Find the `[pipeline:main]` section in `/etc/swift/proxy-server.conf`, and add `ip_whitelist` after ratelimit to the list like so. When you're done, save and close the file:

   ```
   [pipeline:main]
   pipeline = catch_errors healthcheck proxy-logging cache bulk slo ratelimit
   ip_whitelist ...
   ```

7. Restart the `swift proxy` service to make swift use your middleware. Start by switching to the `swift-proxy` screen:

   a. Press Ctrl+A followed by 3.

   b. Press Ctrl+C to kill the service.

   c. Press Up Arrow to bring up the last command.

   d. Press Enter to run it.

8. Test your middleware with the `swift` CLI. Start by switching to the shell screen and finish by switching back to the `swift-proxy` screen to check the log output:

   a. Press Ctrl+A followed by 0.

   b. Make sure you're in the `devstack` directory:

      ```
      $ cd /root/devstack
      ```

   c. Source openrc to set up your environment variables for the CLI:

      ```
      $ source openrc
      ```

   d. Create a container called `middleware-test`:

      ```
      $ swift post middleware-test
      ```

   e. Press Ctrl+A followed by 3 to check the log output.

9. Among the log statements you'll see the lines:

   ```
   proxy-server Remote IP: my.instance.ip.address (txn: ...)
   proxy-server Allow IPs: set(['my.instance.ip.address']) (txn: ...)
   ```

These two statements are produced by our middleware and show that the request was sent from our DevStack instance and was allowed.

10. Test the middleware from outside DevStack on a remote machine that has access to your DevStack instance:

    a. Install the keystone and swift clients on your local machine:

    ```
    # pip install python-keystoneclient python-swiftclient
    ```

    b. Attempt to list the objects in the middleware-test container:

    ```
    $ swift --os-auth-url=http://my.instance.ip.address:5000/v2.0/ \
    --os-region-name=RegionOne --os-username=demo:demo \
    --os-password=devstack list middleware-test
    Container GET failed: http://my.instance.ip.address:8080/v1/AUTH_.../
        middleware-test?format=json 403 Forbidden   You shall not pass!
    ```

11. Press Ctrl+A followed by 3 to check the log output. Look at the swift log statements again, and among the log statements, you'll see the lines:

    ```
    proxy-server  Authorizing  from  an  overriding  middleware  (i.e:  tempurl)
    (txn: ...)
    proxy-server ... IPWhitelistMiddleware
    proxy-server Remote IP: my.local.ip.address (txn: ...)
    proxy-server Allow IPs: set(['my.instance.ip.address']) (txn: ...)
    proxy-server IP my.local.ip.address denied access to Account=AUTH_... \
       Container=None. Not in set(['my.instance.ip.address']) (txn: ...)
    ```

    Here we can see that the request was denied because the remote IP address wasn't in the set of allowed IPs.

12. Back in your DevStack instance on the shell screen, add some metadata to your container to allow the request from the remote machine:

    a. Press Ctrl+A followed by 0.

    b. Add metadata to the container to allow the IP:

    ```
    $ swift post --meta allow-dev:my.local.ip.address middleware-test
    ```

    c. Now try the command from Step 10 again and it succeeds. There are no objects in the container, so there is nothing to list; however, there is also no error to report.

Functional testing like this is not a replacement for proper unit and integration testing, but it serves to get you started.

You can follow a similar pattern in other projects that use the Python Paste framework. Simply create a middleware module and plug it in through configuration. The middleware runs in sequence as part of that project's pipeline and can call out to other services as necessary. No project core code is touched. Look for a `pipeline` value in the project's `conf` or `ini` configuration files in */etc/<project>* to identify projects that use Paste.

When your middleware is done, we encourage you to open source it and let the community know on the OpenStack mailing list. Perhaps others need the same functionality. They can use your code, provide feedback, and possibly contribute. If enough support exists for it, perhaps you can propose that it be added to the official swift middleware (*http://opsgui.de/1eLB87p*).

Customizing the OpenStack Compute (nova) Scheduler

Many OpenStack projects allow for customization of specific features using a driver architecture. You can write a driver that conforms to a particular interface and plug it in through configuration. For example, you can easily plug in a new scheduler for Compute. The existing schedulers for Compute are feature full and well documented at Scheduling (*http://opsgui.de/NPGaFk*). However, depending on your user's use cases, the existing schedulers might not meet your requirements. You might need to create a new scheduler.

To create a scheduler, you must inherit from the class `nova.scheduler.driver.Scheduler`. Of the five methods that you can override, you *must* override the two methods marked with an asterisk (*) below:

- `update_service_capabilities`
- `hosts_up`
- `group_hosts`
- * `schedule_run_instance`
- * `select_destinations`

To demonstrate customizing OpenStack, we'll create an example of a Compute scheduler that randomly places an instance on a subset of hosts, depending on the originating IP address of the request and the prefix of the hostname. Such an example could be useful when you have a group of users on a subnet and you want all of their instances to start within some subset of your hosts.

This example is for illustrative purposes only. It should not be used as a scheduler for Compute without further development and testing.

When you join the screen session that `stack.sh` starts with `screen -r stack`, you are greeted with many screen windows:

```
0$ shell*  1$ key  2$ horizon  ...  9$ n-api  ...  14$ n-sch ...
```

`shell`
: A shell where you can get some work done

`key`
: The keystone service

`horizon`
: The horizon dashboard web application

`n-{name}`
: The nova services

`n-sch`
: The nova scheduler service

To create the scheduler and plug it in through configuration:

1. The code for OpenStack lives in `/opt/stack`, so go to the nova directory and edit your scheduler module. Change to the directory where nova is installed:

   ```
   $ cd /opt/stack/nova
   ```

2. Create the `ip_scheduler.py` Python source code file:

   ```
   $ vim nova/scheduler/ip_scheduler.py
   ```

3. The code in Example 15-3 is a driver that will schedule servers to hosts based on IP address as explained at the beginning of the section. Copy the code into `ip_scheduler.py`. When you're done, save and close the file.

   Example 15-3. ip_scheduler.py

   ```
   # vim: tabstop=4 shiftwidth=4 softtabstop=4
   # Copyright (c) 2014 OpenStack Foundation
   # All Rights Reserved.
   #
   #    Licensed under the Apache License, Version 2.0 (the "License"); you may
   #    not use this file except in compliance with the License. You may obtain
   #    a copy of the License at
   #
   #         http://www.apache.org/licenses/LICENSE-2.0
   #
   #    Unless required by applicable law or agreed to in writing, software
   #    distributed under the License is distributed on an "AS IS" BASIS, WITHOUT
   #    WARRANTIES OR CONDITIONS OF ANY KIND, either express or implied. See the
   #    License for the specific language governing permissions and limitations
   #    under the License.
   ```

```
"""
IP Scheduler implementation
"""

import random

from oslo.config import cfg

from nova.compute import rpcapi as compute_rpcapi
from nova import exception
from nova.openstack.common import log as logging
from nova.openstack.common.gettextutils import _
from nova.scheduler import driver

CONF = cfg.CONF
CONF.import_opt('compute_topic', 'nova.compute.rpcapi')
LOG = logging.getLogger(__name__)

class IPScheduler(driver.Scheduler):
    """
    Implements Scheduler as a random node selector based on
    IP address and hostname prefix.
    """

    def __init__(self, *args, **kwargs):
        super(IPScheduler, self).__init__(*args, **kwargs)
        self.compute_rpcapi = compute_rpcapi.ComputeAPI()

    def _filter_hosts(self, request_spec, hosts, filter_properties,
        hostname_prefix):
        """Filter a list of hosts based on hostname prefix."""

        hosts = [host for host in hosts if host.startswith(hostname_prefix)]
        return hosts

    def _schedule(self, context, topic, request_spec, filter_properties):
        """Picks a host that is up at random."""

        elevated = context.elevated()
        hosts = self.hosts_up(elevated, topic)
        if not hosts:
            msg = _("Is the appropriate service running?")
            raise exception.NoValidHost(reason=msg)

        remote_ip = context.remote_address

        if remote_ip.startswith('10.1'):
            hostname_prefix = 'doc'
        elif remote_ip.startswith('10.2'):
            hostname_prefix = 'ops'
        else:
```

```
        hostname_prefix = 'dev'

    hosts = self._filter_hosts(request_spec, hosts, filter_properties,
        hostname_prefix)
    if not hosts:
        msg = _("Could not find another compute")
        raise exception.NoValidHost(reason=msg)

    host = random.choice(hosts)
    LOG.debug("Request from %(remote_ip)s scheduled to %(host)s" % locals())

    return host

def select_destinations(self, context, request_spec, filter_properties):
    """Selects random destinations."""
    num_instances = request_spec['num_instances']
    # NOTE(timello): Returns a list of dicts with 'host', 'nodename' and
    # 'limits' as keys for compatibility with filter_scheduler.
    dests = []
    for i in range(num_instances):
        host = self._schedule(context, CONF.compute_topic,
                request_spec, filter_properties)
        host_state = dict(host=host, nodename=None, limits=None)
        dests.append(host_state)

    if len(dests) < num_instances:
        raise exception.NoValidHost(reason='')
    return dests

def schedule_run_instance(self, context, request_spec,
                          admin_password, injected_files,
                          requested_networks, is_first_time,
                          filter_properties, legacy_bdm_in_spec):
    """Create and run an instance or instances."""
    instance_uuids = request_spec.get('instance_uuids')
    for num, instance_uuid in enumerate(instance_uuids):
        request_spec['instance_properties']['launch_index'] = num
        try:
            host = self._schedule(context, CONF.compute_topic,
                                  request_spec, filter_properties)
            updated_instance = driver.instance_update_db(context,
                    instance_uuid)
            self.compute_rpcapi.run_instance(context,
                    instance=updated_instance, host=host,
                    requested_networks=requested_networks,
                    injected_files=injected_files,
                    admin_password=admin_password,
                    is_first_time=is_first_time,
                    request_spec=request_spec,
                    filter_properties=filter_properties,
                    legacy_bdm_in_spec=legacy_bdm_in_spec)
        except Exception as ex:
```

```
# NOTE(vish): we don't reraise the exception here to make sure
#             that all instances in the request get set to
#             error properly
driver.handle_schedule_error(context, ex, instance_uuid,
                             request_spec)
```

There is a lot of useful information in `context`, `request_spec`, and `filter_properties` that you can use to decide where to schedule the instance. To find out more about what properties are available, you can insert the following log statements into the `schedule_run_instance` method of the scheduler above:

```
LOG.debug("context = %(context)s" % {'context': context.__dict__})
LOG.debug("request_spec = %(request_spec)s" % locals())
LOG.debug("filter_properties = %(filter_properties)s" % locals())
```

4. To plug this scheduler into nova, edit one configuration file, `/etc/nova/nova.conf`:

   ```
   $ vim /etc/nova/nova.conf
   ```

5. Find the `scheduler_driver` config and change it like so:

   ```
   scheduler_driver=nova.scheduler.ip_scheduler.IPScheduler
   ```

6. Restart the nova scheduler service to make nova use your scheduler. Start by switching to the `n-sch` screen:

   a. Press Ctrl+A followed by 9.

   b. Press Ctrl+A followed by N until you reach the `n-sch` screen.

   c. Press Ctrl+C to kill the service.

   d. Press Up Arrow to bring up the last command.

   e. Press Enter to run it.

7. Test your scheduler with the nova CLI. Start by switching to the `shell` screen and finish by switching back to the `n-sch` screen to check the log output:

   a. Press Ctrl+A followed by 0.

   b. Make sure you're in the `devstack` directory:

      ```
      $ cd /root/devstack
      ```

   c. Source `openrc` to set up your environment variables for the CLI:

      ```
      $ source openrc
      ```

   d. Put the image ID for the only installed image into an environment variable:

      ```
      $ IMAGE_ID=`nova image-list | egrep cirros | egrep -v "kernel|ramdisk" |
      awk '{print $2}'`
      ```

   e. Boot a test server:

      ```
      $ nova boot --flavor 1 --image $IMAGE_ID scheduler-test
      ```

8. Switch back to the n-sch screen. Among the log statements, you'll see the line:

```
2014-01-23 19:57:47.262 DEBUG nova.scheduler.ip_scheduler \
[req-... demo demo] Request from 162.242.221.84 \
scheduled to devstack-havana \
_schedule /opt/stack/nova/nova/scheduler/ip_scheduler.py:76
```

Functional testing like this is not a replacement for proper unit and integration testing, but it serves to get you started.

A similar pattern can be followed in other projects that use the driver architecture. Simply create a module and class that conform to the driver interface and plug it in through configuration. Your code runs when that feature is used and can call out to other services as necessary. No project core code is touched. Look for a "driver" value in the project's `.conf` configuration files in `/etc/<project>` to identify projects that use a driver architecture.

When your scheduler is done, we encourage you to open source it and let the community know on the OpenStack mailing list. Perhaps others need the same functionality. They can use your code, provide feedback, and possibly contribute. If enough support exists for it, perhaps you can propose that it be added to the official Compute schedulers (*http://opsgui.de/1eLBbA1*).

Customizing the Dashboard (Horizon)

The dashboard is based on the Python Django (*http://opsgui.de/NPGbZX*) web application framework. The best guide to customizing it has already been written and can be found at Building on Horizon (*http://opsgui.de/1eLBcnE*).

Conclusion

When operating an OpenStack cloud, you may discover that your users can be quite demanding. If OpenStack doesn't do what your users need, it may be up to you to fulfill those requirements. This chapter provided you with some options for customization and gave you the tools you need to get started.

CHAPTER 16

Upstream OpenStack

OpenStack is founded on a thriving community that is a source of help and welcomes your contributions. This chapter details some of the ways you can interact with the others involved.

Getting Help

There are several avenues available for seeking assistance. The quickest way is to help the community help you. Search the Q&A sites, mailing list archives, and bug lists for issues similar to yours. If you can't find anything, follow the directions for reporting bugs or use one of the channels for support, which are listed below.

Your first port of call should be the official OpenStack documentation, found on *http://docs.openstack.org*. You can get questions answered on *http://ask.openstack.org*.

Mailing lists (*http://opsgui.de/NPGELC*) are also a great place to get help. The wiki page has more information about the various lists. As an operator, the main lists you should be aware of are:

General list (http://opsgui.de/1eLBZoy)
: *openstack@lists.openstack.org*. The scope of this list is the current state of OpenStack. This is a very high-traffic mailing list, with many, many emails per day.

Operators list (http://opsgui.de/NPGF2c)
: *openstack-operators@lists.openstack.org.* This list is intended for discussion among existing OpenStack cloud operators, such as yourself. Currently, this list is relatively low traffic, on the order of one email a day.

Development list (http://opsgui.de/1eLC2Rk)
: *openstack-dev@lists.openstack.org*. The scope of this list is the future state of OpenStack. This is a high-traffic mailing list, with multiple emails per day.

We recommend that you subscribe to the general list and the operator list, although you must set up filters to manage the volume for the general list. You'll also find links to the mailing list archives on the mailing list wiki page, where you can search through the discussions.

Multiple IRC channels (*http://opsgui.de/NPGIuU*) are available for general questions and developer discussions. The general discussion channel is #openstack on *irc.freenode.net*.

Reporting Bugs

As an operator, you are in a very good position to report unexpected behavior with your cloud. Since OpenStack is flexible, you may be the only individual to report a particular issue. Every issue is important to fix, so it is essential to learn how to easily submit a bug report.

All OpenStack projects use Launchpad (*http://opsgui.de/1eLC2ku*) for bug tracking. You'll need to create an account on Launchpad before you can submit a bug report.

Once you have a Launchpad account, reporting a bug is as simple as identifying the project or projects that are causing the issue. Sometimes this is more difficult than expected, but those working on the bug triage are happy to help relocate issues if they are not in the right place initially:

- Report a bug in nova (*http://opsgui.de/NPGLa0*).
- Report a bug in python-novaclient (*http://opsgui.de/1eLC3Vv*).
- Report a bug in swift (*http://opsgui.de/NPGMea*).
- Report a bug in python-swiftclient (*http://opsgui.de/1eLC4Zu*).
- Report a bug in glance (*http://opsgui.de/NPGOmf*).
- Report a bug in python-glanceclient (*http://opsgui.de/1eLC8bQ*).
- Report a bug in keystone (*http://opsgui.de/NPGRhX*).
- Report a bug in python-keystoneclient (*http://opsgui.de/1eLC8Z6*).
- Report a bug in neutron (*http://opsgui.de/NPGSm2*).
- Report a bug in python-neutronclient (*http://opsgui.de/1eLC9ME*).
- Report a bug in cinder (*http://opsgui.de/NPGTGy*).
- Report a bug in python-cinderclient (*http://opsgui.de/1eLCcs7*).
- Report a bug in horizon (*http://opsgui.de/NPGUdz*).
- Report a bug with the documentation (*http://opsgui.de/1eLCcZ8*).
- Report a bug with the API documentation (*http://opsgui.de/NPGUKx*).

To write a good bug report, the following process is essential. First, search for the bug to make sure there is no bug already filed for the same issue. If you find one, be sure to click on "This bug affects X people. Does this bug affect you?" If you can't find the issue, then enter the details of your report. It should at least include:

- The release, or milestone, or commit ID corresponding to the software that you are running
- The operating system and version where you've identified the bug
- Steps to reproduce the bug, including what went wrong
- Description of the expected results instead of what you saw
- Portions of your log files so that you include only relevant excerpts

When you do this, the bug is created with:

- Status: *New*

In the bug comments, you can contribute instructions on how to fix a given bug, and set it to *Triaged*. Or you can directly fix it: assign the bug to yourself, set it to *In progress*, branch the code, implement the fix, and propose your change for merging. But let's not get ahead of ourselves; there are bug triaging tasks as well.

Confirming and Prioritizing

This stage is about checking that a bug is real and assessing its impact. Some of these steps require bug supervisor rights (usually limited to core teams). If the bug lacks information to properly reproduce or assess the importance of the bug, the bug is set to:

- Status: *Incomplete*

Once you have reproduced the issue (or are 100 percent confident that this is indeed a valid bug) and have permissions to do so, set:

- Status: *Confirmed*

Core developers also prioritize the bug, based on its impact:

- Importance: <Bug impact>

The bug impacts are categorized as follows:

1. *Critical* if the bug prevents a key feature from working properly (regression) for all users (or without a simple workaround) or results in data loss
2. *High* if the bug prevents a key feature from working properly for some users (or with a workaround)
3. *Medium* if the bug prevents a secondary feature from working properly
4. *Low* if the bug is mostly cosmetic
5. *Wishlist* if the bug is not really a bug but rather a welcome change in behavior

If the bug contains the solution, or a patch, set the bug status to *Triaged*.

Bug Fixing

At this stage, a developer works on a fix. During that time, to avoid duplicating the work, the developer should set:

- Status: *In Progress*
- Assignee: <yourself>

When the fix is ready, the developer proposes a change and gets the change reviewed.

After the Change Is Accepted

After the change is reviewed, accepted, and lands in master, it automatically moves to:

- Status: *Fix Committed*

When the fix makes it into a milestone or release branch, it automatically moves to:

- Milestone: Milestone the bug was fixed in
- Status: *Fix Released*

Join the OpenStack Community

Since you've made it this far in the book, you should consider becoming an official individual member of the community and join the OpenStack Foundation (*http://opsgui.de/1eLCejs*). The OpenStack Foundation is an independent body providing shared resources to help achieve the OpenStack mission by protecting, empowering, and promoting OpenStack software and the community around it, including users, developers, and the entire ecosystem. We all share the responsibility to make this community the best it can possibly be, and signing up to be a member is the first step to participating. Like the software, individual membership within the OpenStack Foundation is free and accessible to anyone.

How to Contribute to the Documentation

OpenStack documentation efforts encompass operator and administrator docs, API docs, and user docs.

The genesis of this book was an in-person event, but now that the book is in your hands, we want you to contribute to it. OpenStack documentation follows the coding principles of iterative work, with bug logging, investigating, and fixing.

Just like the code, *http://docs.openstack.org* is updated constantly using the Gerrit review system, with source stored in GitHub in the openstack-manuals repository (*http://opsgui.de/1eLCf75*) and the api-site repository (*http://opsgui.de/NPGYda*), in DocBook format.

To review the documentation before it's published, go to the OpenStack Gerrit server at *http://review.openstack.org* and search for project:openstack/openstack-manuals (*http://opsgui.de/NPGXpV*) or project:openstack/api-site (*http://opsgui.de/1eLClM1*).

See the How To Contribute page on the wiki (*http://opsgui.de/NPG68B*) for more information on the steps you need to take to submit your first documentation review or change.

Security Information

As a community, we take security very seriously and follow a specific process for reporting potential issues. We vigilantly pursue fixes and regularly eliminate exposures. You can report security issues you discover through this specific process. The OpenStack Vulnerability Management Team is a very small group of experts in vulnerability management drawn from the OpenStack community. The team's job is facilitating the reporting of vulnerabilities, coordinating security fixes and handling progressive disclosure of the vulnerability information. Specifically, the team is responsible for the following functions:

Vulnerability management
: All vulnerabilities discovered by community members (or users) can be reported to the team.

Vulnerability tracking
: The team will curate a set of vulnerability related issues in the issue tracker. Some of these issues are private to the team and the affected product leads, but once remediation is in place, all vulnerabilities are public.

Responsible disclosure
: As part of our commitment to work with the security community, the team ensures that proper credit is given to security researchers who responsibly report issues in OpenStack.

We provide two ways to report issues to the OpenStack Vulnerability Management Team, depending on how sensitive the issue is:

- Open a bug in Launchpad and mark it as a "security bug." This makes the bug private and accessible to only the Vulnerability Management Team.
- If the issue is extremely sensitive, send an encrypted email to one of the team's members. Find their GPG keys at OpenStack Security (*http://opsgui.de/1eLCkaQ*).

You can find the full list of security-oriented teams you can join at Security Teams (*http://opsgui.de/NPGZxO*). The vulnerability management process is fully documented at Vulnerability Management (*http://opsgui.de/1eLCkYk*).

Finding Additional Information

In addition to this book, there are many other sources of information about OpenStack. The OpenStack website (*http://opsgui.de/NPGZOt*) is a good starting point, with OpenStack Docs (*http://opsgui.de/NPFTC8*) and OpenStack API Docs (*http://opsgui.de/1eLAlDq*) providing technical documentation about OpenStack. The OpenStack wiki (*http://opsgui.de/1eLCrDo*) contains a lot of general information that cuts across the OpenStack projects, including a list of recommended tools (*http://opsgui.de/NPH3hd*). Finally, there are a number of blogs aggregated at Planet OpenStack (*http://opsgui.de/1eLCsXY*).

CHAPTER 17

Advanced Configuration

OpenStack is intended to work well across a variety of installation flavors, from very small private clouds to large public clouds. To achieve this, the developers add configuration options to their code that allow the behavior of the various components to be tweaked depending on your needs. Unfortunately, it is not possible to cover all possible deployments with the default configuration values.

At the time of writing, OpenStack has more than 1,500 configuration options. You can see them documented at the OpenStack configuration reference guide (*http://opsgui.de/1eLATt4*). This chapter cannot hope to document all of these, but we do try to introduce the important concepts so that you know where to go digging for more information.

Differences Between Various Drivers

Many OpenStack projects implement a driver layer, and each of these drivers will implement its own configuration options. For example, in OpenStack Compute (nova), there are various hypervisor drivers implemented—libvirt, xenserver, hyper-v, and vmware, for example. Not all of these hypervisor drivers have the same features, and each has different tuning requirements.

The currently implemented hypervisors are listed on the OpenStack documentation website (*http://opsgui.de/1eLAwP2*). You can see a matrix of the various features in OpenStack Compute (nova) hypervisor drivers on the OpenStack wiki at the Hypervisor support matrix page (*http://opsgui.de/NPFQ9w*).

The point we are trying to make here is that just because an option exists doesn't mean that option is relevant to your driver choices. Normally, the documentation notes which drivers the configuration applies to.

Implementing Periodic Tasks

Another common concept across various OpenStack projects is that of periodic tasks. Periodic tasks are much like cron jobs on traditional Unix systems, but they are run inside an OpenStack process. For example, when OpenStack Compute (nova) needs to work out what images it can remove from its local cache, it runs a periodic task to do this.

Periodic tasks are important to understand because of limitations in the threading model that OpenStack uses. OpenStack uses cooperative threading in Python, which means that if something long and complicated is running, it will block other tasks inside that process from running unless it voluntarily yields execution to another cooperative thread.

A tangible example of this is the `nova-compute` process. In order to manage the image cache with libvirt, `nova-compute` has a periodic process that scans the contents of the image cache. Part of this scan is calculating a checksum for each of the images and making sure that checksum matches what `nova-compute` expects it to be. However, images can be very large, and these checksums can take a long time to generate. At one point, before it was reported as a bug and fixed, `nova-compute` would block on this task and stop responding to RPC requests. This was visible to users as failure of operations such as spawning or deleting instances.

The take away from this is if you observe an OpenStack process that appears to "stop" for a while and then continue to process normally, you should check that periodic tasks aren't the problem. One way to do this is to disable the periodic tasks by setting their interval to zero. Additionally, you can configure how often these periodic tasks run—in some cases, it might make sense to run them at a different frequency from the default.

The frequency is defined separately for each periodic task. Therefore, to disable every periodic task in OpenStack Compute (nova), you would need to set a number of configuration options to zero. The current list of configuration options you would need to set to zero are:

- `bandwidth_poll_interval`
- `sync_power_state_interval`
- `heal_instance_info_cache_interval`
- `host_state_interval`

- `image_cache_manager_interval`
- `reclaim_instance_interval`
- `volume_usage_poll_interval`
- `shelved_poll_interval`
- `shelved_offload_time`
- `instance_delete_interval`

To set a configuration option to zero, include a line such as `image_cache_manager_interval=0` in your `nova.conf` file.

This list will change between releases, so please refer to your configuration guide for up-to-date information.

Specific Configuration Topics

This section covers specific examples of configuration options you might consider tuning. It is by no means an exhaustive list.

Security Configuration for Compute, Networking, and Storage

The *OpenStack Security Guide (http://opsgui.de/NPG4NW)* provides a deep dive into securing an OpenStack cloud, including SSL/TLS, key management, PKI and certificate management, data transport and privacy concerns, and compliance.

High Availability

The *OpenStack High Availability Guide (http://opsgui.de/1eLAYwS)* offers suggestions for elimination of a single point of failure that could cause system downtime. While it is not a completely prescriptive document, it offers methods and techniques for avoiding downtime and data loss.

Enabling IPv6 Support

The Havana release with OpenStack Networking (neutron) does not offer complete support of IPv6. Better support is planned for the Icehouse release. You can follow along the progress being made by watching the neutron IPv6 Subteam at work (*http://opsgui.de/NPG5kQ*).

By modifying your configuration setup, you can set up IPv6 when using `nova-network` for networking, and a tested setup is documented for FlatDHCP and a multi-host configuration. The key is to make `nova-network` think a `radvd` command ran successfully. The entire configuration is detailed in a Cybera blog post, "An IPv6 enabled cloud" (*http://opsgui.de/1eLB0F2*).

Periodic Task Frequency for Compute

Before the Grizzly release, the frequency of periodic tasks was specified in seconds between runs. This meant that if the periodic task took 30 minutes to run and the frequency was set to hourly, then the periodic task actually ran every 90 minutes, because the task would wait an hour after running before running again. This changed in Grizzly, and we now time the frequency of periodic tasks from the start of the work the task does. So, our 30 minute periodic task will run every hour, with a 30 minute wait between the end of the first run and the start of the next.

Geographical Considerations for Object Storage

Enhanced support for global clustering of object storage servers continues to be added since the Grizzly (1.8.0) release, when regions were introduced. You would implement these global clusters to ensure replication across geographic areas in case of a natural disaster and also to ensure that users can write or access their objects more quickly based on the closest data center. You configure a default region with one zone for each cluster, but be sure your network (WAN) can handle the additional request and response load between zones as you add more zones and build a ring that handles more zones. Refer to Geographically Distributed Clusters (*http://opsgui.de/NPG6FJ*) in the documentation for additional information.

CHAPTER 18
Upgrades

With the exception of Object Storage, upgrading from one version of OpenStack to another can take a great deal of effort. Until the situation improves, this chapter provides some guidance on the operational aspects that you should consider for performing an upgrade based on detailed steps for a basic architecture.

Pre-Upgrade Testing Environment

Probably the most important step of all is the pre-upgrade testing. Especially if you are upgrading immediately after release of a new version, undiscovered bugs might hinder your progress. Some deployers prefer to wait until the first point release is announced. However, if you have a significant deployment, you might follow the development and testing of the release, thereby ensuring that bugs for your use cases are fixed.

Each OpenStack cloud is different, and as a result, even with what may seem a near-identical architecture to this guide, you must still test upgrades between versions in your environment. For this, you need an approximate clone of your environment.

However, that is not to say that it needs to be the same size or use identical hardware as the production environment—few of us have that luxury. It is important to consider the hardware and scale of the cloud you are upgrading, but here are some tips to avoid that incredible cost:

Use your own cloud
: The simplest place to start testing the next version of OpenStack is by setting up a new environment inside your own cloud. This may seem odd—especially the double virtualization used in running compute nodes—but it's a sure way to very quickly test your configuration.

Use a public cloud
: Especially because your own cloud is unlikely to have sufficient space to scale test to the level of the entire cloud, consider using a public cloud to test the scalability limits of your cloud controller configuration. Most public clouds bill by the hour, which means it can be inexpensive to perform even a test with many nodes.

Make another storage endpoint on the same system
: If you use an external storage plug-in or shared file system with your cloud, in many cases, it's possible to test that it works by creating a second share or endpoint. This will enable you to test the system before entrusting the new version onto your storage.

Watch the network
: Even at smaller-scale testing, it should be possible to determine whether something is going horribly wrong in intercomponent communication if you look at the network packets and see too many.

To actually set up the test environment, there are several methods. Some prefer to do a full manual install using the *OpenStack Installation Guides (http://opsgui.de/NPFTC8)* and then see what the final configuration files look like and which packages were installed. Others prefer to create a clone of their automated configuration infrastructure with changed package repository URLs and then alter the configuration until it starts working. Either approach is valid, and which you use depends on experience.

An upgrade pre-testing system is excellent for getting the configuration to work; however, it is important to note that the historical use of the system and differences in user interaction can affect the success of upgrades, too. We've seen experiences where database migrations encountered a bug (later fixed!) because of slight table differences between fresh Grizzly installs and those that migrated from Folsom to Grizzly.

Artificial scale testing can go only so far. Once your cloud is upgraded, you'll also need to pay careful attention to the performance aspects of your cloud.

Preparing for a Rollback

Like all major system upgrades, your upgrade could fail for one or more difficult-to-determine reasons. You should prepare for this situation by leaving the ability to roll back your environment to the previous release, including databases, configuration files, and packages. We provide an example process for rolling back your environment in "Rolling Back a Failed Upgrade".

Upgrades

The upgrade process generally follows these steps:

1. Perform some "cleaning" of the environment prior to starting the upgrade process to ensure a consistent state. For example, instances not fully purged from the system after deletion may cause indeterminate behavior.
2. Read the release notes and documentation.
3. Find incompatibilities between your versions.
4. Develop an upgrade procedure and assess it thoroughly using a test environment similar to your production environment.
5. Run the upgrade procedure on the production environment.

You can perform an upgrade with operational instances, but this strategy can be dangerous. You might consider using live migration to temporarily relocate instances to other compute nodes while performing upgrades. However, you must ensure database consistency throughout the process; otherwise your environment may become unstable. Also, don't forget to provide sufficient notice to your users, including giving them plenty of time to perform their own backups.

The following order for service upgrades seems the most successful:

1. Upgrade the OpenStack Identity Service (keystone).
2. Upgrade the OpenStack Image Service (glance).
3. Upgrade OpenStack Compute (nova), including networking components.
4. Upgrade OpenStack Block Storage (cinder).
5. Upgrade the OpenStack dashboard.

The general upgrade process includes the following steps:

1. Create a backup of configuration files and databases.
2. Update the configuration files according to the release notes.
3. Upgrade the packages using your distribution's package manager.
4. Stop services, update database schemas, and restart services.
5. Verify proper operation of your environment.

How to Perform an Upgrade from Grizzly to Havana—Ubuntu

For this section, we assume that you are starting with the architecture provided in the OpenStack Installation Guide (*http://opsgui.de/NPGunp*) and upgrading to the same architecture for Havana. All nodes should run Ubuntu 12.04 LTS. This section primarily addresses upgrading core OpenStack services, such as the Identity Service (keystone); Image Service (glance); Compute (nova), including networking; Block Storage (cinder); and the dashboard.

Impact on Users

The upgrade process will interrupt management of your environment, including the dashboard. If you properly prepare for this upgrade, tenant instances will continue to operate normally.

Upgrade Considerations

Always review the release notes (*http://opsgui.de/1eLzHFY*) before performing an upgrade to learn about newly available features that you may want to enable and deprecated features that you should disable.

Perform a Backup

Save the configuration files on all nodes, as shown here:

```
# for i in keystone glance nova cinder openstack-dashboard
> do mkdir $i-grizzly
> done
# for i in keystone glance nova cinder openstack-dashboard
> do cp -r /etc/$i/* $i-grizzly/
> done
```

You can modify this example script on each node to handle different services.

Back up all databases on the controller:

```
# mysqldump -u root -p --opt --add-drop-database \
--all-databases > grizzly-db-backup.sql
```

Manage Repositories

On all nodes, remove the repository for Grizzly packages and add the repository for Havana packages:

```
# apt-add-repository -r cloud-archive:grizzly
# apt-add-repository cloud-archive:havana
```

Make sure any automatic updates are disabled.

Update Configuration Files

Update the glance configuration on the controller node for compatibility with Havana.

If not currently present and configured as follows, add or modify the following keys in /etc/glance/glance-api.conf and /etc/glance/glance-registry.conf:

```
[keystone_authtoken]
auth_uri = http://controller:5000
auth_host = controller
admin_tenant_name = service
admin_user = glance
admin_password = GLANCE_PASS

[paste_deploy]
flavor = keystone
```

If currently present, remove the following key from the [filter:authtoken] section in /etc/glance/glance-api-paste.ini and /etc/glance/glance-registry-paste.ini:

```
[filter:authtoken]
flavor = keystone
```

Update the nova configuration on all nodes for compatibility with Havana.

Add the new [database] section and associated key to /etc/nova/nova.conf:

```
[database]
connection = mysql://nova:NOVA_DBPASS@controller/nova
```

Remove defunct configuration from the [DEFAULT] section in /etc/nova/nova.conf:

```
[DEFAULT]
sql_connection = mysql://nova:NOVA_DBPASS@controller/nova
```

If not already present and configured as follows, add or modify the following keys in /etc/nova/nova.conf:

```
[keystone_authtoken]
auth_uri = http://controller:5000/v2.0
auth_host = controller
auth_port = 35357
auth_protocol = http
admin_tenant_name = service
admin_user = nova
admin_password = NOVA_PASS
```

On all compute nodes, increase the DHCP lease time (measured in seconds) in /etc/nova/nova.conf to enable currently active instances to continue leasing their IP addresses during the upgrade process:

```
[DEFAULT]
dhcp_lease_time = 86400
```

Setting this value too high may cause more dynamic environments to run out of available IP addresses. Use an appropriate value for your environment.

You must restart dnsmasq and the networking component of Compute to enable the new DHCP lease time:

```
# pkill -9 dnsmasq
# service nova-network restart
```

Update the Cinder configuration on the controller and storage nodes for compatibility with Havana.

Add the new [database] section and associated key to /etc/cinder/cinder.conf:

```
[database]
connection = mysql://cinder:CINDER_DBPASS@controller/cinder
```

Remove defunct configuration from the [DEFAULT] section in /etc/cinder/cinder.conf:

```
[DEFAULT]
sql_connection = mysql://cinder:CINDER_DBPASS@controller/cinder
```

If not currently present and configured as follows, add or modify the following key in /etc/cinder/cinder.conf:

```
[keystone_authtoken]
auth_uri = http://controller:5000
```

Update the dashboard configuration on the controller node for compatibility with Havana.

The dashboard installation procedure and configuration file changed substantially between Grizzly and Havana. Particularly, if you are running Django 1.5 or later, you must ensure that `/etc/openstack-dashboard/local_settings` contains a correctly configured `ALLOWED_HOSTS` key that contains a list of hostnames recognized by the dashboard.

If users will access your dashboard using *http://dashboard.example.com*, you would set:

```
ALLOWED_HOSTS=['dashboard.example.com']
```

If users will access your dashboard on the local system, you would set:

```
ALLOWED_HOSTS=['localhost']
```

If users will access your dashboard using an IP address in addition to a hostname, you would set:

```
ALLOWED_HOSTS=['dashboard.example.com', '192.168.122.200']
```

Upgrade Packages on the Controller Node

Upgrade packages on the controller node to Havana, as shown below:

```
# apt-get update
# apt-get dist-upgrade
```

Depending on your specific configuration, performing a `dist-upgrade` may restart services supplemental to your OpenStack environment. For example, if you use Open-iSCSI for Block Storage volumes and the upgrade includes a new `open-scsi` package, the package manager will restart Open-iSCSI services, which may cause the volumes for your users to be disconnected.

The package manager will ask you about updating various configuration files. We recommend denying these changes. The package manager will append `.dpkg-dist` to the end of newer versions of existing configuration files. You should consider adopting conventions associated with the newer configuration files and merging them with your existing configuration files after completing the upgrade process.

Stop Services, Update Database Schemas, and Restart Services on the Controller Node

Stop each service, run the database synchronization command if necessary to update the associated database schema, and restart each service to apply the new configuration. Some services require additional commands:

OpenStack Identity

```
# service keystone stop
# keystone-manage token_flush
# keystone-manage db_sync
# service keystone start
```

OpenStack Image Service

```
# service glance-api stop
# service glance-registry stop
# glance-manage db_sync
# service glance-api start
# service glance-registry start
```

OpenStack Compute

```
# service nova-api stop
# service nova-scheduler stop
# service nova-conductor stop
# service nova-cert stop
# service nova-consoleauth stop
# service nova-novncproxy stop
# nova-manage db sync
# service nova-api start
# service nova-scheduler start
# service nova-conductor start
# service nova-cert start
# service nova-consoleauth start
# service nova-novncproxy start
```

OpenStack Block Storage

```
# service cinder-api stop
# service cinder-scheduler stop
# cinder-manage db sync
# service cinder-api start
# service cinder-scheduler start
```

The controller node update is complete. Now you can upgrade the compute nodes.

Upgrade Packages and Restart Services on the Compute Nodes

Upgrade packages on the compute nodes to Havana:

```
# apt-get update
# apt-get dist-upgrade
```

Make sure you have removed the repository for Grizzly packages and added the repository for Havana packages.

Due to a packaging issue, this command may fail with the following error:

```
Errors were encountered while processing:
    /var/cache/apt/archives/
      qemu-utils_1.5.0+dfsg-3ubuntu5~cloud0_amd64.deb
    /var/cache/apt/archives/
      qemu-system-common_1.5.0+dfsg-3ubuntu5~cloud0_
        amd64.deb
    E: Sub-process /usr/bin/dpkg
    returned an error code (1)
```

You can fix this issue by using the following command:

```
# apt-get -f install
```

The packaging system will ask about updating the `/etc/nova/api-paste.ini` file. As with the controller upgrade, we recommend denying these changes and reviewing the `.dpkg-dist` file after completing the upgrade process.

To restart compute services:

```
# service nova-compute restart
# service nova-network restart
# service nova-api-metadata restart
```

Upgrade Packages and Restart Services on the Block Storage Nodes

Upgrade packages on the storage nodes to Havana:

```
# apt-get update
# apt-get dist-upgrade
```

Make sure you have removed the repository for Grizzly packages and added the repository for Havana packages.

The packaging system will ask about updating the `/etc/cinder/api-paste.ini` file. Like the controller upgrade, we recommend denying these changes and reviewing the `.dpkg-dist` file after completing the upgrade process.

To restart Block Storage services:

```
# service cinder-volume restart
```

How to Perform an Upgrade from Grizzly to Havana—Red Hat Enterprise Linux and Derivatives

For this section, we assume that you are starting with the architecture provided in the OpenStack Installation Guide (*http://opsgui.de/NPGvrs*) and upgrading to the same architecture for Havana. All nodes should run Red Hat Enterprise Linux 6.4 or compatible derivatives. Newer minor releases should also work. This section primarily addresses upgrading core OpenStack services, such as the Identity Service (keystone); Image Service (glance); Compute (nova), including networking; Block Storage (cinder); and the dashboard.

Impact on Users

The upgrade process will interrupt management of your environment, including the dashboard. If you properly prepare for this upgrade, tenant instances will continue to operate normally.

Upgrade Considerations

Always review the release notes (*http://opsgui.de/1eLzHFY*) before performing an upgrade to learn about newly available features that you may want to enable and deprecated features that you should disable.

Perform a Backup

First, save the configuration files on all nodes:

```
# for i in keystone glance nova cinder openstack-dashboard
> do mkdir $i-grizzly
> done
# for i in keystone glance nova cinder openstack-dashboard
> do cp -r /etc/$i/* $i-grizzly/
> done
```

You can modify this example script on each node to handle different services.

Next, back up all databases on the controller:

```
# mysqldump -u root -p --opt --add-drop-database \
  --all-databases > grizzly-db-backup.sql
```

Manage Repositories

On all nodes, remove the repository for Grizzly packages and add the repository for Havana packages:

```
# yum erase rdo-release-grizzly
# yum install http://repos.fedorapeople.org/repos/openstack/openstack-havana/  \
rdo-release-havana-7.noarch.rpm
```

Make sure any automatic updates are disabled.

Consider checking for newer versions of the Havana repository (*http://opsgui.de/1eLBXNB*).

Update Configuration Files

Update the glance configuration on the controller node for compatibility with Havana.

If not currently present and configured as follows, add or modify the following keys in /etc/glance/glance-api.conf and /etc/glance/glance-registry.conf:

```
# openstack-config --set /etc/glance/glance-api.conf keystone_authtoken \
  auth_uri http://controller:5000
# openstack-config --set /etc/glance/glance-api.conf keystone_authtoken \
  auth_host controller
# openstack-config --set /etc/glance/glance-api.conf keystone_authtoken \
  admin_tenant_name service
# openstack-config --set /etc/glance/glance-api.conf keystone_authtoken \
  admin_user glance
# openstack-config --set /etc/glance/glance-api.conf keystone_authtoken \
  admin_password GLANCE_PASS
# openstack-config --set /etc/glance/glance-api.conf paste_deploy \
  flavor keystone

# openstack-config --set /etc/glance/glance-registry.conf keystone_authtoken \
  auth_uri http://controller:5000
# openstack-config --set /etc/glance/glance-registry.conf keystone_authtoken \
  auth_host controller
# openstack-config --set /etc/glance/glance-registry.conf keystone_authtoken \
  admin_tenant_name service
```

```
# openstack-config --set /etc/glance/glance-registry.conf keystone_authtoken \
  admin_user glance
# openstack-config --set /etc/glance/glance-registry.conf keystone_authtoken \
  admin_password GLANCE_PASS
# openstack-config --set /etc/glance/glance-registry.conf paste_deploy \
  flavor keystone
```

If currently present, remove the following key from the [filter:authtoken] section in `/etc/glance/glance-api-paste.ini` and `/etc/glance/glance-registry-paste.ini`:

```
[filter:authtoken]
flavor = keystone
```

Update the nova configuration on all nodes for compatibility with Havana.

Add the new `[database]` section and associated key to `/etc/nova/nova.conf`:

```
# openstack-config --set /etc/nova/nova.conf database \
  connection mysql://nova:NOVA_DBPASS@controller/nova
```

Remove defunct database configuration from `/etc/nova/nova.conf`:

```
# openstack-config --del /etc/nova/nova.conf DEFAULT sql_connection
```

If not already present and configured as follows, add or modify the following keys in `/etc/nova/nova.conf`:

```
# openstack-config --set /etc/nova/nova.conf keystone_authtoken \
  auth_uri http://controller:5000/v2.0
# openstack-config --set /etc/nova/nova.conf keystone_authtoken \
  auth_host controller
# openstack-config --set /etc/nova/nova.conf keystone_authtoken \
  admin_tenant_name service
# openstack-config --set /etc/nova/nova.conf keystone_authtoken \
  admin_user nova
# openstack-config --set /etc/nova/nova.conf keystone_authtoken \
  admin_password NOVA_PASS
```

On all compute nodes, increase the DHCP lease time (measured in seconds) in `/etc/nova/nova.conf` to enable currently active instances to continue leasing their IP addresses during the upgrade process, as shown here:

```
# openstack-config --set /etc/nova/nova.conf DEFAULT \
  dhcp_lease_time 86400
```

Setting this value too high may cause more dynamic environments to run out of available IP addresses. Use an appropriate value for your environment.

You must restart dnsmasq and the nova networking service to enable the new DHCP lease time:

```
# pkill -9 dnsmasq
# service openstack-nova-network restart
```

Update the cinder configuration on the controller and storage nodes for compatibility with Havana.

Add the new [database] section and associated key to `/etc/cinder/cinder.conf`:

```
# openstack-config --set /etc/cinder/cinder.conf database \
  connection mysql://cinder:CINDER_DBPASS@controller/cinder
```

Remove defunct database configuration from `/etc/cinder/cinder.conf`:

```
# openstack-config --del /etc/cinder/cinder.conf DEFAULT sql_connection
```

If not currently present and configured as follows, add or modify the following key in `/etc/cinder/cinder.conf`:

```
# openstack-config --set /etc/cinder/cinder.conf keystone_authtoken \
  auth_uri http://controller:5000
```

Update the dashboard configuration on the controller node for compatibility with Havana.

The dashboard installation procedure and configuration file changed substantially between Grizzly and Havana. Particularly, if you are running Django 1.5 or later, you must ensure that `/etc/openstack-dashboard/local_settings` contains a correctly configured `ALLOWED_HOSTS` key that contains a list of hostnames recognized by the dashboard.

If users will access your dashboard using *http://dashboard.example.com*, you would set:

```
ALLOWED_HOSTS=['dashboard.example.com']
```

If users will access your dashboard on the local system, you would set:

```
ALLOWED_HOSTS=['localhost']
```

If users will access your dashboard using an IP address in addition to a hostname, you would set:

```
ALLOWED_HOSTS=['dashboard.example.com', '192.168.122.200']
```

Upgrade Packages on the Controller Node

Upgrade packages on the controller node to Havana:

```
# yum upgrade
```

Some services may terminate with an error during the package upgrade process. If this may cause a problem with your environment, consider stopping all services before upgrading them to Havana.

Install the OpenStack SELinux package on the controller node:

```
# yum install openstack-selinux
```

The package manager will append `.rpmnew` to the end of newer versions of existing configuration files. You should consider adopting conventions associated with the newer configuration files and merging them with your existing configuration files after completing the upgrade process.

Stop Services, Update Database Schemas, and Restart Services on the Controller Node

Stop each service, run the database synchronization command if necessary to update the associated database schema, and restart each service to apply the new configuration. Some services require additional commands:

OpenStack Identity

```
# service openstack-keystone stop
# keystone-manage token_flush
# keystone-manage db_sync
# service openstack-keystone start
```

OpenStack Image Service

```
# service openstack-glance-api stop
# service openstack-glance-registry stop
# glance-manage db_sync
# service openstack-glance-api start
# service openstack-glance-registry start
```

OpenStack Compute

```
# service openstack-nova-api stop
# service openstack-nova-scheduler stop
# service openstack-nova-conductor stop
# service openstack-nova-cert stop
# service openstack-nova-consoleauth stop
# service openstack-nova-novncproxy stop
# nova-manage db sync
# service openstack-nova-api start
# service openstack-nova-scheduler start
# service openstack-nova-conductor start
# service openstack-nova-cert start
# service openstack-nova-consoleauth start
# service openstack-nova-novncproxy start
```

OpenStack Block Storage

```
# service openstack-cinder-api stop
# service openstack-cinder-scheduler stop
# cinder-manage db sync
# service openstack-cinder-api start
# service openstack-cinder-scheduler start
```

The controller node update is complete. Now you can upgrade the compute nodes.

Upgrade Packages and Restart Services on the Compute Nodes

Upgrade packages on the compute nodes to Havana:

```
# yum upgrade
```

Make sure you have removed the repository for Grizzly packages and added the repository for Havana packages.

Install the OpenStack SELinux package on the compute nodes:

```
# yum install openstack-selinux
```

Restart compute services:

```
# service openstack-nova-compute restart
# service openstack-nova-network restart
# service openstack-nova-metadata-api restart
```

Upgrade Packages and Restart Services on the Block Storage Nodes

Upgrade packages on the storage nodes to Havana:

```
# yum upgrade
```

Make sure you have removed the repository for Grizzly packages and added the repository for Havana packages.

Install the OpenStack SELinux package on the storage nodes:

```
# yum install openstack-selinux
```

Restart Block Storage services:

```
# service openstack-cinder-volume restart
```

Cleaning Up and Final Configuration File Updates

On all distributions, you need to perform some final tasks to complete the upgrade process.

Decrease DHCP timeouts by modifying `/etc/nova/nova.conf` on the compute nodes back to the original value for your environment.

Update all of the `.ini` files to match passwords and pipelines as required for Havana in your environment.

After a migration, your users will see different results from `nova image-list` and `glance image-list` unless you match up policies for access to private images. To do so, edit `/etc/glance/policy.json` and `/etc/nova/policy.json` to contain `"context_is_admin": "role:admin"`, which limits access to private images for projects.

Thoroughly test the environment, and then let your users know that their cloud is running normally again.

Rolling Back a Failed Upgrade

While we do not wish this fate upon anyone, upgrades involve complex operations and can fail. This section provides guidance for rolling back to a previous release of OpenStack. Although only tested on Ubuntu, other distributions follow a similar procedure.

In this section, we consider only the most immediate case: you have taken down production management services in preparation for an upgrade, completed part of the upgrade process, discovered one or more problems not encountered during testing, and need to roll back your environment to the original "known good" state. We specifically assume that you did not make any state changes after attempting the upgrade process: no new instances, networks, storage volumes, etc.

Within this scope, you need to accomplish three main steps to successfully roll back your environment:

- Roll back configuration files
- Roll back databases
- Roll back packages

The upgrade instructions provided in earlier sections ensure that you have proper backups of your databases and configuration files. You should read through this section carefully and verify that you have the requisite backups to restore. Rolling back upgrades is a tricky process because distributions tend to put much more effort into testing upgrades than downgrades. Broken downgrades often take significantly more effort to troubleshoot and, hopefully, resolve than broken upgrades. Only you can weigh the risks of trying to push a failed upgrade forward versus rolling it back. Generally, we consider rolling back the very last option.

The following steps described for Ubuntu have worked on at least one production environment, but they may not work for all environments.

Perform the rollback from Havana to Grizzly

1. Stop all OpenStack services.
2. Copy contents of configuration backup directories `/etc/<service>.grizzly` that you created during the upgrade process back to `/etc/<service>`:
3. Restore databases from the backup file `grizzly-db-backup.sql` that you created with `mysqldump` during the upgrade process:

   ```
   # mysql -u root -p < grizzly-db-backup.sql
   ```

   If you created this backup using the `--add-drop-database` flag as instructed, you can proceed to the next step. If you omitted this flag, MySQL will revert all of the tables that existed in Grizzly, but not drop any tables created during the database migration for Havana. In this case, you need to manually determine which tables should not exist and drop them to prevent issues with your next upgrade attempt.
4. Downgrade OpenStack packages.

We consider downgrading packages by far the most complicated step; it is highly dependent on the distribution as well as overall administration of the system.

   a. Determine the OpenStack packages installed on your system. This is done using `dpkg --get-selections`, filtering for OpenStack packages, filtering again to omit packages explicitly marked in the `deinstall` state, and saving the final output to a file. For example, the following command covers a controller node with keystone, glance, nova, neutron, and cinder:

   ```
   # dpkg --get-selections | grep -e keystone -e glance -e nova -e neutron \
   -e cinder | grep -v deinstall | tee openstack-selections
   cinder-api                                      install
   cinder-common                                   install
   cinder-scheduler                                install
   cinder-volume                                   install
   glance                                          install
   glance-api                                      install
   glance-common                                   install
   glance-registry                                 install
   ```

```
neutron-common                                  install
neutron-dhcp-agent                              install
neutron-l3-agent                                install
neutron-lbaas-agent                             install
neutron-metadata-agent                          install
neutron-plugin-openvswitch                      install
neutron-plugin-openvswitch-agent                install
neutron-server                                  install
nova-api                                        install
nova-cert                                       install
nova-common                                     install
nova-conductor                                  install
nova-consoleauth                                install
nova-novncproxy                                 install
nova-objectstore                                install
nova-scheduler                                  install
python-cinder                                   install
python-cinderclient                             install
python-glance                                   install
python-glanceclient                             install
python-keystone                                 install
python-keystoneclient                           install
python-neutron                                  install
python-neutronclient                            install
python-nova                                     install
python-novaclient                               install
```

Depending on the type of server, the contents and order of your package list may vary from this example.

b. You can determine the package versions available for reversion by using `apt-cache policy`. If you removed the Grizzly repositories, you must first reinstall them and run `apt-get update`:

```
# apt-cache policy nova-common
nova-common:
  Installed: 1:2013.2-0ubuntu1~cloud0
  Candidate: 1:2013.2-0ubuntu1~cloud0
  Version table:
 *** 1:2013.2-0ubuntu1~cloud0 0
        500 http://ubuntu-cloud.archive.canonical.com/ubuntu/
            precise-updates/havana/main amd64 Packages
        100 /var/lib/dpkg/status
     1:2013.1.4-0ubuntu1~cloud0 0
        500 http://ubuntu-cloud.archive.canonical.com/ubuntu/
            precise-updates/grizzly/main amd64 Packages
     2012.1.3+stable-20130423-e52e6912-0ubuntu1.2 0
        500 http://us.archive.ubuntu.com/ubuntu/
```

```
        precise-updates/main amd64 Packages
    500 http://security.ubuntu.com/ubuntu/
        precise-security/main amd64 Packages
2012.1-0ubuntu2 0
    500 http://us.archive.ubuntu.com/ubuntu/
        precise/main amd64 Packages
```

This tells us the currently installed version of the package, newest candidate version, and all versions along with the repository that contains each version. Look for the appropriate Grizzly version—`1:2013.1.4-0ubuntu1~cloud0` in this case. The process of manually picking through this list of packages is rather tedious and prone to errors. You should consider using the following script to help with this process:

```
# for i in `cut -f 1 openstack-selections | sed 's/neutron/quantum/;'`;
  do echo -n $i ;apt-cache policy $i | grep -B 1 grizzly |
  grep -v Packages | awk '{print "="$1}';done | tr '\n' ' ' |
  tee openstack-grizzly-versions
cinder-api=1:2013.1.4-0ubuntu1~cloud0
cinder-common=1:2013.1.4-0ubuntu1~cloud0
cinder-scheduler=1:2013.1.4-0ubuntu1~cloud0
cinder-volume=1:2013.1.4-0ubuntu1~cloud0
glance=1:2013.1.4-0ubuntu1~cloud0
glance-api=1:2013.1.4-0ubuntu1~cloud0
glance-common=1:2013.1.4-0ubuntu1~cloud0
glance-registry=1:2013.1.4-0ubuntu1~cloud0
quantum-common=1:2013.1.4-0ubuntu1~cloud0
quantum-dhcp-agent=1:2013.1.4-0ubuntu1~cloud0
quantum-l3-agent=1:2013.1.4-0ubuntu1~cloud0
quantum-lbaas-agent=1:2013.1.4-0ubuntu1~cloud0
quantum-metadata-agent=1:2013.1.4-0ubuntu1~cloud0
quantum-plugin-openvswitch=1:2013.1.4-0ubuntu1~cloud0
quantum-plugin-openvswitch-agent=1:2013.1.4-0ubuntu1~cloud0
quantum-server=1:2013.1.4-0ubuntu1~cloud0
nova-api=1:2013.1.4-0ubuntu1~cloud0
nova-cert=1:2013.1.4-0ubuntu1~cloud0
nova-common=1:2013.1.4-0ubuntu1~cloud0
nova-conductor=1:2013.1.4-0ubuntu1~cloud0
nova-consoleauth=1:2013.1.4-0ubuntu1~cloud0
nova-novncproxy=1:2013.1.4-0ubuntu1~cloud0
nova-objectstore=1:2013.1.4-0ubuntu1~cloud0
nova-scheduler=1:2013.1.4-0ubuntu1~cloud0
python-cinder=1:2013.1.4-0ubuntu1~cloud0
python-cinderclient=1:1.0.3-0ubuntu1~cloud0
python-glance=1:2013.1.4-0ubuntu1~cloud0
python-glanceclient=1:0.9.0-0ubuntu1.2~cloud0
python-quantum=1:2013.1.4-0ubuntu1~cloud0
python-quantumclient=1:2.2.0-0ubuntu1~cloud0
python-nova=1:2013.1.4-0ubuntu1~cloud0
python-novaclient=1:2.13.0-0ubuntu1~cloud0
```

If you decide to continue this step manually, don't forget to change `neutron` to `quantum` where applicable.

c. Use `apt-get install` to install specific versions of each package by specifying `<package-name>=<version>`. The script in the previous step conveniently created a list of `package=version` pairs for you:

   ```
   # apt-get install `cat openstack-grizzly-versions`
   ```

   This completes the rollback procedure. You should remove the Havana repository and run `apt-get update` to prevent accidental upgrades until you solve whatever issue caused you to roll back your environment.

APPENDIX A

Use Cases

This appendix contains a small selection of use cases from the community, with more technical detail than usual. Further examples can be found on the OpenStack website (*http://opsgui.de/1eLAdUw*).

NeCTAR

Who uses it: researchers from the Australian publicly funded research sector. Use is across a wide variety of disciplines, with the purpose of instances ranging from running simple web servers to using hundreds of cores for high-throughput computing.

Deployment

Using OpenStack Compute cells, the NeCTAR Research Cloud spans eight sites with approximately 4,000 cores per site.

Each site runs a different configuration, as resource cells in an OpenStack Compute cells setup. Some sites span multiple data centers, some use off compute node storage with a shared file system, and some use on compute node storage with a nonshared file system. Each site deploys the Image Service with an Object Storage backend. A central Identity Service, dashboard, and Compute API service are used. A login to the dashboard triggers a SAML login with Shibboleth, which creates an account in the Identity Service with an SQL backend.

Compute nodes have 24 to 48 cores, with at least 4 GB of RAM per core and approximately 40 GB of ephemeral storage per core.

All sites are based on Ubuntu 12.04, with KVM as the hypervisor. The OpenStack version in use is typically the current stable version, with 5 to 10 percent back-ported code from trunk and modifications. Migration to Ubuntu 14.04 is planned as part of the Havana to Icehouse upgrade.

Resources

- OpenStack.org case study (*http://opsgui.de/NPFCiF*)
- NeCTAR-RC GitHub (*http://opsgui.de/1eLAhnd*)
- NeCTAR website (*http://opsgui.de/NPFEHm*)

MIT CSAIL

Who uses it: researchers from the MIT Computer Science and Artificial Intelligence Lab.

Deployment

The CSAIL cloud is currently 64 physical nodes with a total of 768 physical cores and 3,456 GB of RAM. Persistent data storage is largely outside the cloud on NFS, with cloud resources focused on compute resources. There are more than 130 users in more than 40 projects, typically running 2,000–2,500 vCPUs in 300 to 400 instances.

We initially deployed on Ubuntu 12.04 with the Essex release of OpenStack using FlatDHCP multi-host networking.

The software stack is still Ubuntu 12.04 LTS, but now with OpenStack Havana from the Ubuntu Cloud Archive. KVM is the hypervisor, deployed using FAI (*http://opsgui.de/1eLAhUr*) and Puppet for configuration management. The FAI and Puppet combination is used lab-wide, not only for OpenStack. There is a single cloud controller node, which also acts as network controller, with the remainder of the server hardware dedicated to compute nodes.

Host aggregates and instance-type extra specs are used to provide two different resource allocation ratios. The default resource allocation ratios we use are 4:1 CPU and 1.5:1 RAM. Compute-intensive workloads use instance types that require non-oversubscribed hosts where `cpu_ratio` and `ram_ratio` are both set to 1.0. Since we have hyperthreading enabled on our compute nodes, this provides one vCPU per CPU thread, or two vCPUs per physical core.

With our upgrade to Grizzly in August 2013, we moved to OpenStack Networking Service, neutron (quantum at the time). Compute nodes have two-gigabit network interfaces and a separate management card for IPMI management. One network interface is used for node-to-node communications. The other is used as a trunk port for OpenStack managed VLANs. The controller node uses two bonded 10g network interfaces for its public IP communications. Big pipes are used here because images are served over this port, and it is also used to connect to iSCSI storage, backending the image storage and database. The controller node also has a gigabit interface that is used in trunk mode for OpenStack managed VLAN traffic. This port handles traffic to the dhcp-agent and metadata-proxy.

We approximate the older `nova-network` multi-host HA setup by using "provider vlan networks" that connect instances directly to existing publicly addressable networks and use existing physical routers as their default gateway. This means that if our network controller goes down, running instances still have their network available, and no single Linux host becomes a traffic bottleneck. We are able to do this because we have a sufficient supply of IPv4 addresses to cover all of our instances and thus don't need NAT and don't use floating IP addresses. We provide a single generic public network to all projects and additional existing VLANs on a project-by-project basis as needed. Individual projects are also allowed to create their own private GRE based networks.

Resources

- CSAIL homepage (*http://opsgui.de/NPFFez*)

DAIR

Who uses it: DAIR is an integrated virtual environment that leverages the CANARIE network to develop and test new information communication technology (ICT) and other digital technologies. It combines such digital infrastructure as advanced networking and cloud computing and storage to create an environment for developing and testing innovative ICT applications, protocols, and services; performing at-scale experimentation for deployment; and facilitating a faster time to market.

Deployment

DAIR is hosted at two different data centers across Canada: one in Alberta and the other in Quebec. It consists of a cloud controller at each location, although, one is designated the "master" controller that is in charge of central authentication and quotas. This is done through custom scripts and light modifications to OpenStack. DAIR is currently running Grizzly.

For Object Storage, each region has a swift environment.

A NetApp appliance is used in each region for both block storage and instance storage. There are future plans to move the instances off the NetApp appliance and onto a distributed file system such as Ceph or GlusterFS.

VlanManager is used extensively for network management. All servers have two bonded 10GbE NICs that are connected to two redundant switches. DAIR is set up to use single-node networking where the cloud controller is the gateway for all instances on all compute nodes. Internal OpenStack traffic (for example, storage traffic) does not go through the cloud controller.

Resources

- DAIR homepage (*http://opsgui.de/NPFgIP*)

CERN

Who uses it: researchers at CERN (European Organization for Nuclear Research) conducting high-energy physics research.

Deployment

The environment is largely based on Scientific Linux 6, which is Red Hat compatible. We use KVM as our primary hypervisor, although tests are ongoing with Hyper-V on Windows Server 2008.

We use the Puppet Labs OpenStack modules to configure Compute, Image Service, Identity, and dashboard. Puppet is used widely for instance configuration, and Foreman is used as a GUI for reporting and instance provisioning.

Users and groups are managed through Active Directory and imported into the Identity Service using LDAP. CLIs are available for nova and Euca2ools to do this.

There are three clouds currently running at CERN, totaling about 3,400 compute nodes, with approximately 60,000 cores. The CERN IT cloud aims to expand to 300,000 cores by 2015.

Resources

- "OpenStack in Production: A tale of 3 OpenStack Clouds" (*http://opsgui.de/NPFGiu*)
- "Review of CERN Data Centre Infrastructure" (*http://opsgui.de/1eLAkPR*)
- "CERN Cloud Infrastructure User Guide" (*http://opsgui.de/NPFGPD*)

APPENDIX B

Tales From the Cryp^H^H^H^H Cloud

Herein lies a selection of tales from OpenStack cloud operators. Read and learn from their wisdom.

Double VLAN

I was on-site in Kelowna, British Columbia, Canada, setting up a new OpenStack cloud. The deployment was fully automated: Cobbler deployed the OS on the bare metal, bootstrapped it, and Puppet took over from there. I had run the deployment scenario so many times in practice and took for granted that everything was working.

On my last day in Kelowna, I was in a conference call from my hotel. In the background, I was fooling around on the new cloud. I launched an instance and logged in. Everything looked fine. Out of boredom, I ran `ps aux`, and all of the sudden the instance locked up.

Thinking it was just a one-off issue, I terminated the instance and launched a new one. By then, the conference call ended, and I was off to the data center.

At the data center, I was finishing up some tasks and remembered the lockup. I logged in to the new instance and ran `ps aux` again. It worked. Phew. I decided to run it one more time. It locked up. WTF.

After reproducing the problem several times, I came to the unfortunate conclusion that this cloud did indeed have a problem. Even worse, my time was up in Kelowna, and I had to return to Calgary.

Where do you even begin troubleshooting something like this? An instance just randomly locks when a command is issued. Is it the image? Nope—it happens on all images. Is it the compute node? Nope—all nodes. Is the instance locked up? No! New SSH connections work just fine!

We reached out for help. A networking engineer suggested it was an MTU issue. Great! MTU! Something to go on! What's MTU, and why would it cause a problem?

MTU is *maximum transmission unit*. It specifies the maximum number of bytes that the interface accepts for each packet. If two interfaces have two different MTUs, bytes might get chopped off and weird things happen—such as random session lockups.

Not all packets have a size of 1,500. Running the `ls` command over SSH might create only a single packet, less than 1,500 bytes. However, running a command with heavy output, such as `ps aux`, requires several packets of 1,500 bytes.

OK, so where is the MTU issue coming from? Why haven't we seen this in any other deployment? What's new in this situation? Well, new data center, new uplink, new switches, new model of switches, new servers, first time using this model of servers… so, basically, everything was new. Wonderful. We toyed around with raising the MTU at various areas: the switches, the NICs on the compute nodes, the virtual NICs in the instances; we even had the data center raise the MTU for our uplink interface. Some changes worked; some didn't. This line of troubleshooting didn't feel right, though. We shouldn't have to be changing the MTU in these areas.

As a last resort, our network admin (Alvaro) and I sat down with four terminal windows, a pencil, and a piece of paper. In one window, we ran `ping`. In the second window, we ran `tcpdump` on the cloud controller. In the third, `tcpdump` on the compute node. And the fourth had `tcpdump` on the instance. For background, this cloud was a multinode, non-multi-host setup.

One cloud controller acted as a gateway to all compute nodes. VlanManager was used for the network config. This means that the cloud controller and all compute nodes had a different VLAN for each OpenStack project. We used the -s option of `ping` to change the packet size. We watched as sometimes packets would fully return, sometimes only make it out and never back in, and sometimes stop at a random point. We changed `tcpdump` to start displaying the hex dump of the packet. We pinged between every combination of outside, controller, compute, and instance.

Finally, Alvaro noticed something. When a packet from the outside hits the cloud controller, it should not be configured with a VLAN. We verified this as true. When the packet went from the cloud controller to the compute node, it should have a VLAN only if it was destined for an instance. This was still true. When the ping reply was sent from the instance, it should be in a VLAN. True. When it came back to the cloud controller and on its way out to the public Internet, it should no longer have a VLAN. False. Uh oh. It looked as though the VLAN part of the packet was not being removed.

That made no sense.

While bouncing this idea around in our heads, I was randomly typing commands on the compute node:

```
$ ip a
...
10: vlan100@vlan20: <BROADCAST,MULTICAST,UP,LOWER_UP> mtu 1500 qdisc noqueue
master br100 state UP
...
```

"Hey Alvaro, can you run a VLAN on top of a VLAN?"

"If you did, you'd add an extra four bytes to the packet."

Then it all made sense:

```
$ grep vlan_interface /etc/nova/nova.conf
vlan_interface=vlan20
```

In `nova.conf`, `vlan_interface` specifies what interface OpenStack should attach all VLANs to. The correct setting should have been: `vlan_interface=bond0`.

This would be the server's bonded NIC.

The vlan20 setting is the VLAN that the data center gave us for outgoing public Internet access. It's a correct VLAN and is also attached to bond0.

By mistake, I configured OpenStack to attach all tenant VLANs to vlan20 instead of bond0, thereby stacking one VLAN on top of another. This then added an extra four bytes to each packet, which caused a packet of 1,504 bytes to be sent out, which would cause problems when it arrived at an interface that accepted 1,500!

As soon as this setting was fixed, everything worked.

The Issue

At the end of August 2012, a post-secondary school in Alberta, Canada, migrated its infrastructure to an OpenStack cloud. As luck would have it, within the first day or two of it running, one of its servers just disappeared from the network. Blip. Gone.

After restarting the instance, everything was back up and running. We reviewed the logs and saw that at some point, network communication stopped and then everything went idle. We chalked this up to a random occurrence.

A few nights later, it happened again.

We reviewed both sets of logs. The one thing that stood out the most was DHCP. At the time, OpenStack, by default, set DHCP leases for one minute (it's now two minutes). This means that every instance contacts the cloud controller (DHCP server) to renew its fixed IP. For some reason, this instance could not renew its IP. We correlated the instance's logs with the logs on the cloud controller and put together a conversation:

1. Instance tries to renew IP.
2. Cloud controller receives the renewal request and sends a response.
3. Instance "ignores" the response and resends the renewal request.
4. Cloud controller receives the second request and sends a new response.
5. Instance begins sending a renewal request to `255.255.255.255`, since it hasn't heard back from the cloud controller.
6. The cloud controller receives the `255.255.255.255` request and sends a third response.
7. The instance finally gives up.

With this information in hand, we were sure that the problem had to do with DHCP. We thought that, for some reason, the instance wasn't getting a new IP address, and with no IP, it shut itself off from the network.

A quick Google search turned up this: DHCP lease errors in VLAN mode (*http://opsgui.de/NPFfEJ*), which further supported our DHCP theory.

An initial idea was to just increase the lease time. If the instance renewed only once every week, the chances of this problem happening would be tremendously smaller than every minute. This didn't solve the problem, though. It was just covering the problem up.

We decided to have `tcpdump` run on this instance and see whether we could catch it in action again. Sure enough, we did.

The `tcpdump` looked very, very weird. In short, it looked as though network communication stopped before the instance tried to renew its IP. Since there is so much DHCP chatter from a one-minute lease, it's very hard to confirm it, but even with only milliseconds difference between packets, if one packet arrives first, it arrives first, and if that packet reported network issues, then it had to have happened before DHCP.

Additionally, the instance in question was responsible for a very, very large backup job each night. While "the Issue" (as we were now calling it) didn't happen exactly when the backup happened, it was close enough (a few hours) that we couldn't ignore it.

More days go by and we catch the Issue in action more and more. We find that dhclient is not running after the Issue happens. Now we're back to thinking it's a DHCP problem. Running `/etc/init.d/networking restart` brings everything back up and running.

Ever have one of those days where all of the sudden you get the Google results you were looking for? Well, that's what happened here. I was looking for information on dhclient and why it dies when it can't renew its lease, and all of the sudden I found a bunch of OpenStack and dnsmasq discussions that were identical to the problem we were seeing:

- "Problem with Heavy Network IO and Dnsmasq" (*http://opsgui.de/1eLzAKE*)
- "Instances losing IP address while running, due to No DHCPOFFER" (*http://opsgui.de/NPFgbL*)

Seriously, Google.

This bug report was the key to everything: "KVM images lose connectivity with bridged network" (*http://opsgui.de/1eLzBy8*).

It was funny to read the report. It was full of people who had some strange network problem but didn't quite explain it in the same way.

So it was a QEMU/KVM bug.

At the same time I found the bug report, a coworker was able to successfully reproduce the Issue! How? He used `iperf` to spew a ton of bandwidth at an instance. Within 30 minutes, the instance just disappeared from the network.

Armed with a patched QEMU and a way to reproduce, we set out to see if we had finally solved the Issue. After 48 straight hours of hammering the instance with bandwidth, we were confident. The rest is history. You can search the bug report for "joe" to find my comments and actual tests.

Disappearing Images

At the end of 2012, Cybera (a nonprofit with a mandate to oversee the development of cyberinfrastructure in Alberta, Canada) deployed an updated OpenStack cloud for its DAIR project (*http://opsgui.de/NPFgIP*). A few days into production, a compute node locked up. Upon rebooting the node, I checked to see what instances were hosted on that node so I could boot them on behalf of the customer. Luckily, only one instance.

The `nova reboot` command wasn't working, so I used `virsh`, but it immediately came back with an error saying it was unable to find the backing disk. In this case, the backing disk is the glance image that is copied to `/var/lib/nova/instances/_base` when the image is used for the first time. Why couldn't it find it? I checked the directory, and sure enough, it was gone.

I reviewed the nova database and saw the instance's entry in the nova.instances table. The image that the instance was using matched what virsh was reporting, so no inconsistency there.

I checked glance and noticed that this image was a snapshot that the user created. At least that was good news—this user would have been the only user affected.

Finally, I checked StackTach and reviewed the user's events. He had created and deleted several snapshots—most likely experimenting. Although the timestamps didn't match up, my conclusion was that he launched his instance and then deleted the snapshot and it was somehow removed from /var/lib/nova/instances/_base. None of that made sense, but it was the best I could come up with.

It turns out the reason that this compute node locked up was a hardware issue. We removed it from the DAIR cloud and called Dell to have it serviced. Dell arrived and began working. Somehow or another (or a fat finger), a different compute node was bumped and rebooted. Great.

When this node fully booted, I ran through the same scenario of seeing what instances were running so that I could turn them back on. There were a total of four. Three booted and one gave an error. It was the same error as before: unable to find the backing disk. Seriously, what?

Again, it turns out that the image was a snapshot. The three other instances that successfully started were standard cloud images. Was it a problem with snapshots? That didn't make sense.

A note about DAIR's architecture: /var/lib/nova/instances is a shared NFS mount. This means that all compute nodes have access to it, which includes the _base directory. Another centralized area is /var/log/rsyslog on the cloud controller. This directory collects all OpenStack logs from all compute nodes. I wondered if there were any entries for the file that virsh is reporting:

```
dair-ua-c03/nova.log:Dec 19 12:10:59 dair-ua-c03
2012-12-19 12:10:59 INFO nova.virt.libvirt.imagecache
[-] Removing base file:
/var/lib/nova/instances/_base/7b4783508212f5d242cbf9ff56fb8d33b4ce6166_10
```

Aha! So OpenStack was deleting it. But why?

A feature was introduced in Essex to periodically check and see whether there were any _base files not in use. If there were, nova would delete them. This idea sounds innocent enough and has some good qualities to it. But how did this feature end up turned on? It was disabled by default in Essex, as it should be, but it was decided to enable it in Folsom (*http://opsgui.de/1eLzAuj*). I cannot emphasize enough that:

Actions that delete things should not be enabled by default.

Disk space is cheap these days. Data recovery is not.

Secondly, DAIR's shared `/var/lib/nova/instances` directory contributed to the problem. Since all compute nodes have access to this directory, all compute nodes periodically review the `_base` directory. If there is only one instance using an image, and the node that the instance is on is down for a few minutes, it won't be able to mark the image as still in use. Therefore, the image seems like it's not in use and is deleted. When the compute node comes back online, the instance hosted on that node is unable to start.

The Valentine's Day Compute Node Massacre

Although the title of this story is much more dramatic than the actual event, I don't think, or hope, that I'll have the opportunity to use "Valentine's Day Massacre" again in a title.

This past Valentine's Day, I received an alert that a compute node was no longer available in the cloud—meaning:

```
$nova-manage service list
```

showed this particular node with a status of `XXX`.

I logged in to the cloud controller and was able to both `ping` and SSH into the problematic compute node, which seemed very odd. Usually when I receive this type of alert, the compute node has totally locked up and would be inaccessible.

After a few minutes of troubleshooting, I saw the following details:

- A user recently tried launching a CentOS instance on that node.
- This user was the only user on the node (new node).
- The load shot up to 8 right before I received the alert.
- The bonded 10gb network device (bond0) was in a DOWN state.
- The 1gb NIC was still alive and active.

I looked at the status of both NICs in the bonded pair and saw that neither was able to communicate with the switch port. Seeing as how each NIC in the bond is connected to a separate switch, I thought that the chance of a switch port dying on each switch at the same time was quite improbable. I concluded that the 10gb dual port NIC had died and needed to be replaced. I created a ticket for the hardware support department at the data center where the node was hosted. I felt lucky that this was a new node and no one else was hosted on it yet.

An hour later I received the same alert, but for another compute node. Crap. OK, now there's definitely a problem going on. Just as with the original node, I was able to log in by SSH. The bond0 NIC was DOWN, but the 1gb NIC was active.

And the best part: the same user had just tried creating a CentOS instance. What?

I was totally confused at this point, so I texted our network admin to see if he was available to help. He logged in to both switches and immediately saw the problem: the switches detected spanning tree packets coming from the two compute nodes and immediately shut the ports down to prevent spanning tree loops:

```
Feb 15 01:40:18 SW-1 Stp: %SPANTREE-4-BLOCK_BPDUGUARD: Received BPDU packet on
Port-Channel35 with BPDU guard enabled. Disabling interface.
(source mac fa:16:3e:24:e7:22)
Feb 15 01:40:18 SW-1 Ebra: %ETH-4-ERRDISABLE: bpduguard error detected
on Port-Channel35.
Feb 15 01:40:18 SW-1 Mlag: %MLAG-4-INTF_INACTIVE_LOCAL: Local interface
Port-Channel35 is link down. MLAG 35 is inactive.
Feb 15 01:40:18 SW-1 Ebra: %LINEPROTO-5-UPDOWN: Line protocol on Interface
Port-Channel35 (Server35), changed state to down
Feb 15 01:40:19 SW-1 Stp: %SPANTREE-6-INTERFACE_DEL: Interface Port-Channel35
has been removed from instance MST0
Feb 15 01:40:19 SW-1 Ebra: %LINEPROTO-5-UPDOWN: Line protocol on Interface
Ethernet35 (Server35), changed state to down
```

He reenabled the switch ports, and the two compute nodes immediately came back to life.

Unfortunately, this story has an open ending—we're still looking into why the CentOS image was sending out spanning tree packets. Further, we're researching a proper way to mitigate how often this happens. It's a bigger issue than one might think. While it's extremely important for switches to prevent spanning tree loops, it's very problematic to have an entire compute node be cut from the network when this occurs. If a compute node is hosting 100 instances and one of them sends a spanning tree packet, that instance has effectively DDOS'd the other 99 instances.

This is an ongoing and hot topic in networking circles—especially with the rise of virtualization and virtual switches.

Down the Rabbit Hole

Users being able to retrieve console logs from running instances is a boon for support—many times they can figure out what's going on inside their instance and fix what's going on without bothering you. Unfortunately, sometimes overzealous logging of failures can cause problems of its own.

A report came in: VMs were launching slowly, or not at all. Cue the standard checks—nothing on the Nagios, but there was a spike in network toward the current master of our RabbitMQ cluster. Investigation started, but soon the other parts of the queue cluster were leaking memory like a sieve. Then the alert came in: the master rabbit server went down. Connections failed over to the slave.

At that time, our control services were hosted by another team. We didn't have much debugging information to determine what was going on with the master, and couldn't reboot it. That team noted that the master failed without alert, but they managed to reboot it. After an hour, the cluster had returned to its normal state, and we went home for the day.

Continuing the diagnosis the next morning was kick-started by another identical failure. We quickly got the message queue running again and tried to work out why Rabbit was suffering from so much network traffic. Enabling debug logging on `nova-api` quickly brought understanding. A `tail -f /var/log/nova/nova-api.log` was scrolling by faster than we'd ever seen before. CTRL+C on that, and we could plainly see the contents of a system log spewing failures over and over again—a system log from one of our users' instances.

After finding the instance ID, we headed over to `/var/lib/nova/instances` to find the `console.log`:

```
adm@cc12:/var/lib/nova/instances/instance-00000e05# wc -l console.log
92890453 console.log
adm@cc12:/var/lib/nova/instances/instance-00000e05# ls -sh console.log
5.5G console.log
```

Sure enough, the user had been periodically refreshing the console log page on the dashboard, and the 5 GB file was traversing the rabbit cluster to get to the dashboard.

We called the user and asked her to stop for a while, and she was happy to abandon the horribly broken VM. After that, we started monitoring the size of console logs.

To this day, the issue (*http://opsgui.de/NPFiAx*) doesn't have a permanent resolution, but we look forward to the discussion at the next summit.

Havana Haunted by the Dead

Felix Lee of Academia Sinica Grid Computing Centre in Taiwan contributed this story.

I just upgraded OpenStack from Grizzly to Havana 2013.2-2 using the RDO repository and everything was running pretty well—except the EC2 API.

I noticed that the API would suffer from a heavy load and respond slowly to particular EC2 requests, such as `RunInstances`.

Output from `/var/log/nova/nova-api.log` on Havana:

```
2014-01-10 09:11:45.072 129745 INFO nova.ec2.wsgi.server
[req-84d16d16-3808-426b-b7af-3b90a11b83b0
0c6e7dba03c24c6a9bce299747499e8a 7052bd6714e7460caeb16242e68124f9]
117.103.103.29 "GET
/services/Cloud?AWSAccessKeyId= \
[something]&Action=RunInstances&ClientToken= \
[something]&ImageId=ami-00000001&InstanceInitiatedShutdownBehavior=terminate...
HTTP/1.1" status: 200 len: 1109 time: 138.5970151
```

This request took more than two minutes to process, but it executed quickly on another coexisting Grizzly deployment using the same hardware and system configuration.

Output from `/var/log/nova/nova-api.log` on Grizzly:

```
2014-01-08 11:15:15.704 INFO nova.ec2.wsgi.server
[req-ccac9790-3357-4aa8-84bd-cdaab1aa394e
ebbd729575cb404081a45c9ada0849b7 8175953c209044358ab5e0ec19d52c37]
117.103.103.29 "GET
/services/Cloud?AWSAccessKeyId= \
[something]&Action=RunInstances&ClientToken= \
[something]&ImageId=ami-00000007&InstanceInitiatedShutdownBehavior=terminate...
HTTP/1.1" status: 200 len: 931 time: 3.9426181
```

While monitoring system resources, I noticed a significant increase in memory consumption while the EC2 API processed this request. I thought it wasn't handling memory properly—possibly not releasing memory. If the API received several of these requests, memory consumption quickly grew until the system ran out of RAM and began using swap. Each node has 48 GB of RAM, and the `nova-api` process would consume all of it within minutes. Once this happened, the entire system would become unusably slow until I restarted the `nova-api` service.

So, I found myself wondering what changed in the EC2 API on Havana that might cause this to happen. Was it a bug or normal behavior that I now need to work around?

After digging into the nova code, I noticed two areas in `api/ec2/cloud.py` potentially impacting my system:

```
        instances = self.compute_api.get_all(context,
                                             search_opts=search_opts,
                                             sort_dir='asc')

        sys_metas = self.compute_api.get_all_system_metadata(
            context, search_filts=[{'key': ['EC2_client_token']},
                                   {'value': [client_token]}])
```

Since my database contained many records—over 1 million metadata records and over 300,000 instance records in "deleted" or "errored" states—each search took ages. I decided to clean up the database by first archiving a copy for backup and then performing some deletions using the MySQL client. For example, I ran the following SQL command to remove rows of instances deleted for more than a year:

```
mysql> delete from nova.instances where deleted=1 and terminated_at < (NOW() -
INTERVAL 1 YEAR);
```

Performance increased greatly after deleting the old records, and my new deployment continues to behave well.

APPENDIX C
Working with Roadmaps

The good news: OpenStack has unprecedented transparency when it comes to providing information about what's coming up. The bad news: each release moves very quickly. The purpose of this appendix is to highlight some of the useful pages to track, and take an educated guess at what is coming up in the Icehouse release and perhaps further afield.

OpenStack follows a six month release cycle, typically releasing in April/May and October/November each year. At the start of each cycle, the community gathers in a single location for a design summit. At the summit, the features for the coming releases are discussed, prioritized, and planned. Figure C-1 shows an example release cycle, with dates showing milestone releases, code freeze, and string freeze dates, along with an example of when the summit occurs. Milestones are interim releases within the cycle that are available as packages for download and testing. Code freeze is putting a stop to adding new features to the release. String freeze is putting a stop to changing any strings within the source code.

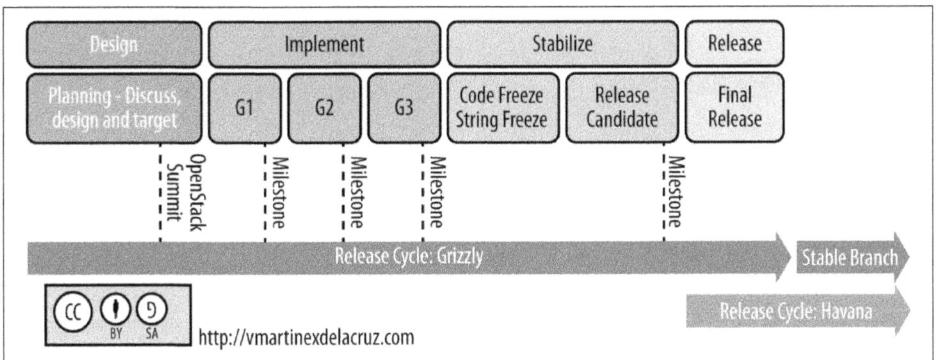

Figure C-1. Release cycle diagram

Information Available to You

There are several good sources of information available that you can use to track your OpenStack development desires.

Release notes are maintained on the OpenStack wiki, and also shown here:

Series	Status	Releases	Date
Icehouse	Under development, release schedule (*http://opsgui.de/1eLzG51*)	2014.1 (*http://opsgui.de/NPFhMW*)	Apr 17, 2014
Havana	Current stable release, security-supported	2013.2 (*http://opsgui.de/1eLzHFY*)	Apr 4, 2013
		2013.2.1 (*http://opsgui.de/NPFjEI*)	Dec 16, 2013
Grizzly	Security-supported	2013.1 (*http://opsgui.de/1eLzK4A*)	Apr 4, 2013
		2013.1.1 (*http://opsgui.de/NPFlw8*)	May 9, 2013
		2013.1.2 (*http://opsgui.de/1eLzMtp*)	Jun 6, 2013
		2013.1.3 (*http://opsgui.de/NPFks3*)	Aug 8, 2013
		2013.1.4 (*http://opsgui.de/1eLzNgP*)	Oct 17, 2013
Folsom	Community-supported	2012.2 (*http://opsgui.de/NPFmjO*)	Sep 27, 2012
		2012.2.1 (*http://opsgui.de/1eLzOBB*)	Nov 29, 2012
		2012.2.2 (*http://opsgui.de/NPFobr*)	Dec 13, 2012
		2012.2.3 (*http://opsgui.de/1eLzPpd*)	Jan 31, 2013
		2012.2.4 (*http://opsgui.de/NPFos2*)	Apr 11, 2013
Essex	Community-supported	2012.1 (*http://opsgui.de/1eLzSRP*)	Apr 5, 2012
		2012.1.1 (*http://opsgui.de/NPFqjB*)	Jun 22, 2012
		2012.1.2 (*http://opsgui.de/1eLzUsX*)	Aug 10, 2012
		2012.1.3 (*http://opsgui.de/NPFqQs*)	Oct 12, 2012
Diablo	Deprecated	2011.3 (*http://opsgui.de/1eLzVwW*)	Sep 22, 2011
		2011.3.1 (*http://opsgui.de/NPFsYy*)	Jan 19, 2012

Series	Status	Releases	Date
Cactus	Deprecated	2011.2 (*http://opsgui.de/1eLzYsI*)	Apr 15, 2011
Bexar	Deprecated	2011.1 (*http://opsgui.de/NPFtvH*)	Feb 3, 2011
Austin	Deprecated	2010.1 (*http://opsgui.de/1eLA1Vm*)	Oct 21, 2010

Here are some other resources:

- A breakdown of current features under development, with their target milestone (*http://opsgui.de/NPFvnh*)
- A list of all features, including those not yet under development (*http://opsgui.de/1eLA2IT*)
- Rough-draft design discussions ("etherpads") from the last design summit (*http://opsgui.de/NPFwaQ*)
- List of individual code changes under review (*http://opsgui.de/1eLA43u*)

Influencing the Roadmap

OpenStack truly welcomes your ideas (and contributions) and highly values feedback from real-world users of the software. By learning a little about the process that drives feature development, you can participate and perhaps get the additions you desire.

Feature requests typically start their life in Etherpad, a collaborative editing tool, which is used to take coordinating notes at a design summit session specific to the feature. This then leads to the creation of a blueprint on the Launchpad site for the particular project, which is used to describe the feature more formally. Blueprints are then approved by project team members, and development can begin.

Therefore, the fastest way to get your feature request up for consideration is to create an Etherpad with your ideas and propose a session to the design summit. If the design summit has already passed, you may also create a blueprint directly. Read this blog post about how to work with blueprints (*http://opsgui.de/NPFy2x*) the perspective of Victoria Martínez, a developer intern.

The roadmap for the next release as it is developed can be seen at Releases (*http://opsgui.de/1eLA7wg*).

To determine the potential features going in to future releases, or to look at features implemented previously, take a look at the existing blueprints such as OpenStack Compute (nova) Blueprints (*http://opsgui.de/NPFxf5*), OpenStack Identity (keystone) Blueprints (*http://opsgui.de/1eLA8An*), and release notes.

Aside from the direct-to-blueprint pathway, there is another very well-regarded mechanism to influence the development roadmap: the user survey. Found at *http://openstack.org/user-survey*, it allows you to provide details of your deployments and needs, anonymously by default. Each cycle, the user committee analyzes the results and produces a report, including providing specific information to the technical committee and technical leads of the projects.

Aspects to Watch

You want to keep an eye on the areas improving within OpenStack. The best way to "watch" roadmaps for each project is to look at the blueprints that are being approved for work on milestone releases. You can also learn from PTL webinars that follow the OpenStack summits twice a year.

Driver Quality Improvements

A major quality push has occurred across drivers and plug-ins in Block Storage, Compute, and Networking. Particularly, developers of Compute and Networking drivers that require proprietary or hardware products are now required to provide an automated external testing system for use during the development process.

Easier Upgrades

One of the most requested features since OpenStack began (for components other than Object Storage, which tends to "just work"): easier upgrades. From Grizzly onward (and significantly improved in Havana), internal messaging communication is versioned, meaning services can theoretically drop back to backward-compatible behavior. This allows you to run later versions of some components, while keeping older versions of others.

In addition, a lot of focus has been placed on database migrations. These are now better managed, including the use of the Turbo Hipster tool, which tests database migration performance on copies of real-world user databases.

These changes have facilitated the first proper OpenStack upgrade guide, found in Chapter 18, and will continue to improve in Icehouse.

Deprecation of Nova Network

With the introduction of the full software-defined networking stack provided by OpenStack Networking (neutron) in the Folsom release, development effort on the initial networking code that remains part of the Compute component has gradually lessened. While many still use `nova-network` in production, there has been a long-term plan to remove the code in favor of the more flexible and full-featured OpenStack Networking.

An attempt was made to deprecate `nova-network` during the Havana release, which was aborted due to the lack of equivalent functionality (such as the FlatDHCP multi-host high-availability mode mentioned in this guide), lack of a migration path between versions, insufficient testing, and simplicity when used for the more straightforward use cases `nova-network` traditionally supported. Though significant effort has been made to address these concerns, `nova-network` will not be deprecated in the Icehouse release. In addition, the Program Technical Lead of the Compute project has indicated that, to a limited degree, patches to `nova-network` will now again begin to be accepted.

This leaves you with an important point of decision when designing your cloud. OpenStack Networking is robust enough to use with a small number of limitations (IPv6 support, performance issues in some scenarios) and provides many more features than `nova-network`. However, if you do not have the more complex use cases that can benefit from fuller software-defined networking capabilities, or are uncomfortable with the new concepts introduced, `nova-network` may continue to be a viable option for the next 12 to 18 months.

Similarly, if you have an existing cloud and are looking to upgrade from `nova-network` to OpenStack Networking, you should have the option to delay the upgrade for this period of time. However, each release of OpenStack brings significant new innovation, and regardless of your use of networking methodology, it is likely best to begin planning for an upgrade within a reasonable timeframe of each release.

As mentioned, there's currently no way to cleanly migrate from `nova-network` to neutron. We recommend that you keep a migration in mind and what that process might involve for when a proper migration path is released. If you must upgrade, please be aware that both service and instance downtime is likely unavoidable.

Replacement of Open vSwitch Plug-in with Modular Layer 2

The Modular Layer 2 plug-in is a framework allowing OpenStack Networking to simultaneously utilize the variety of layer-2 networking technologies found in complex real-world data centers. It currently works with the existing Open vSwitch, Linux Bridge, and Hyper-V L2 agents and is intended to replace and deprecate the monolithic plug-ins associated with those L2 agents.

Compute V3 API

The third version of the Compute API was broadly discussed and worked on during the Havana and Icehouse release cycles. Current discussions indicate that the V2 API will remain for many releases, but this is a great time to evaluate the Compute API and provide comments while it is being defined. Of particular note is the decision that the V3 API will not support XML messages—being JSON only. This was based on the poor testing of existing XML responses in the V2 API and the lack of effort to continue to develop and maintain an entire second response type. Feedback on this and any such change is welcome by responding to the user survey (*http://opsgui.de/1eLAaba*).

OpenStack on OpenStack (TripleO)

This project continues to improve and you may consider using it for greenfield deployments.

Data Processing (Sahara)

A much-requested answer to big data problems, a dedicated team has been making solid progress on a Hadoop-as-a-Service project.

Bare-Metal Deployment (Ironic)

Though bare-metal deployment has been widely lauded, and development continues, the project to replace the Compute bare-metal driver will not graduate in Icehouse. A particular blueprint to follow is Migration Path from Nova's BM Driver (*http://opsgui.de/NPFBex*), which tracks the ability to move to the new project from an existing bare-metal deployment.

Database as a Service (Trove)

The OpenStack community has had a database-as-a-service tool in development for some time, and we will finally see the first integrated release of it in Icehouse. Initially, it will only support MySQL, with further options available in Juno onward, but it should be able to deploy database servers out of the box in a highly available way from this release.

Messaging as a Service (Marconi)

A service to provide queues of messages and notifications has entered "incubation," meaning if the upcoming development cycles are successful, it will be released in Juno.

Scheduler Improvements

Both Compute and Block Storage rely on schedulers to determine where to place virtual machines or volumes. In Havana, the Compute scheduler underwent significant improvement, while in Icehouse the scheduler in Block Storage is slated for a boost. Further down the track, an effort started this cycle that aims to create a holistic scheduler covering both will come to fruition.

Block Storage Improvements

The team discussed many areas of work at the Icehouse summit, including volume migration support, Ceph integration, and access control for volumes.

Toward a Python SDK

Though many successfully use the various python-*client code as an effective SDK for interacting with OpenStack, consistency between the projects and documentation availability waxes and wanes. To combat this, an effort to improve the experience (*http://opsgui.de/1eLAaYU*) has started. Cross-project development efforts in OpenStack have a checkered history, such as the unified client project (*http://opsgui.de/NPFBLH*) having several false starts. However, the early signs for the SDK project are promising, and we expect to see results during the Juno cycle.

APPENDIX D

Icehouse Preview

The Icehouse release of OpenStack was made available April 17, 2014, a few days before this book went to print! It was built by 112 different companies. Over 1,200 contributors submitted a patch to the collection of projects for more than 17,000 commits. All in all, this release had more than 113,000 reviews on those commits.

Here is a preview of the features being offered for the first time for each project. Not all of these features are fully documented in the official documentation, but we wanted to share the list here.

A few themes emerge as you investigate the various blueprints implemented and bugs fixed:

- Projects now consider migration and upgrades as part of the "gated" test suite.
- Projects do not have a common scheduler yet, but are testing and releasing various schedulers according to real-world uses.
- Projects are enabling more notifications and custom logging.
- Projects are adding in more location-awareness.
- Projects are tightly integrating with advancements in orchestration.
- The Block Storage, Compute, and Networking projects implemented the `x-openstack-request-id` header to more efficiently trace request flows across OpenStack services by logging mappings of request IDs as they cross service boundaries.

These sections offer listings of features added, hand-picked from a total of nearly 350 blueprints implemented across ten projects in the integrated Icehouse release. For even more details about the Icehouse release including upgrade notes, refer to the release notes at *https://wiki.openstack.org/wiki/ReleaseNotes/Icehouse*.

Block Storage (cinder)

31 blueprints

- When using absolute limits command, let user know the currently used resources, similar to Compute.
- Notifications for volume attach and detach.
- Deprecate the chance and simple schedulers.
- Retyping volumes enabled—HP LeftHand, SolidFire.
- Volume metadata stored on backup.
- Let operators log the reasons that the Block Storage service was disabled.
- Dell EqualLogic volumes can now be extended.
- Support for qos_specs for SolidFire driver; creation and management of qos separate from volume-types.
- Quota settings for deletion.
- Backup recovery API for import and export.
- EMC VNX Direct Driver added.
- Fibre Channel Volume Driver added.
- HP MSA2040 driver added.
- Enhancements to 3PAR driver such as migrate volume natively and the qos-specs feature.
- IBM SONAS and Storwize v7000 Unified Storage Systems drivers added.
- HP LeftHand driver enhancements.
- TSM Backup Driver enhancements.

Common (oslo)

22 blueprints

- Standalone rootwrap implementation.
- Messages can be localized for i18n support.
- Notifications are configurable.

Compute (nova)

65 blueprints

Limited live upgrades are now supported. This enables deployers to upgrade controller infrastructure first, and subsequently upgrade individual compute nodes without requiring downtime of the entire cloud to complete.

Hyper-V driver added RDP console support.

Libvirt (KVM) driver additions:

- The Libvirt compute driver now supports providing modified kernel arguments to booting compute instances. The kernel arguments are retrieved from the `os_command_line` key in the image metadata as stored in Glance, if a value for the key was provided. Otherwise, the default kernel arguments are used.
- The Libvirt driver now supports using VirtIO SCSI (virtio-scsi) instead of VirtIO Block (virtio-blk) to provide block device access for instances. Virtio SCSI is a para-virtualized SCSI controller device designed as a future successor to VirtIO Block and aiming to provide improved scalability and performance.
- The Libvirt Compute driver now supports adding a Virtio RNG device to compute instances to provide increased entropy. Virtio RNG is a paravirtual random number generation device. It allows the compute node to provide entropy to the compute instances in order to fill their entropy pool. The default entropy device used is /dev/random; however, use of a physical hardware RNG device attached to the host is also possible. The use of the Virtio RNG device is enabled using the hw_rng property in the metadata of the image used to build the instance.
- The Libvirt driver now allows the configuration of instances to use video driver other than the default (cirros). This allows the specification of different video driver models, different amounts of video RAM, and different numbers of heads. These values are configured by setting the `hw_video_model`, `hw_video_vram`, and `hw_video_head` properties in the image metadata. Currently supported video driver models are `vga`, `cirrus`, `vmvga`, `xen` and `qxl`.
- Watchdog support has been added to the Libvirt driver. The watchdog device used is `i6300esb`. It is enabled by setting the `hw_watchdog_action` property in the image properties or flavor extra specifications (`extra_specs`) to a value other than `disabled`. Supported `hw_watchdog_action` property values, which denote the action for the watchdog device to take in the event of an instance failure, are `poweroff`, `reset`, `pause`, and `none`.
- The High Precision Event Timer (HPET) is now disabled for instances created using the Libvirt driver. The use of this option was found to lead to clock drift in Windows guests when under heavy load.

- The Libvirt driver now supports waiting for an event from Neutron during instance boot for better reliability. This requires a suitably new Neutron that supports sending these events, and avoids a race between the instance expecting networking to be ready and the actual plumbing that is required.

VMware driver additions:

- The VMware Compute drivers now support the virtual machine diagnostics call. Diagnostics can be retrieved using the `nova diagnostics` *`INSTANCE`* command, where *`INSTANCE`* is replaced by an instance name or instance identifier.
- The VMware Compute drivers now support booting an instance from an ISO image.
- The VMware Compute drivers now support the aging of cached images.

XenServer driver additions:

- Added initial support for PCI pass-through.
- Maintained group B status through the introduction of the XenServer CI (*http://opsgui.de/1gwRjq3*).
- Improved support for ephemeral disks (including migration and resize up of multiple ephemeral disks).
- Support for vcpu_pin_set, essential when you pin CPU resources to Dom0.
- Numerous performance and stability enhancements.

API changes:

- In OpenStack Compute, the `OS-DCF:diskConfig` API attribute is no longer supported in V3 of the nova API.
- The Compute API currently supports both XML and JSON formats. Support for the XML format is now deprecated and will be retired in a future release.
- The Compute API now exposes a mechanism for permanently removing decommissioned compute nodes. Previously these would continue to be listed even where the Compute Service had been disabled and the system re-provisioned. This functionality is provided by the `ExtendedServicesDelete` API extension.
- Separated the V3 API admin_actions plug-in into logically separate plug-ins so operators can enable subsets of the functionality currently present in the plug-in.
- The Compute Service now uses the tenant identifier instead of the tenant name when authenticating with OpenStack Networking (Neutron). This improves support for the OpenStack Identity API v3, which allows non-unique tenant names.

- The Compute API now exposes the hypervisor IP address, allowing it to be retrieved by administrators using the `nova hypervisor-show` command.

Scheduler updates:

- The scheduler now includes an initial implementation of a caching scheduler driver. The caching scheduler uses the existing facilities for applying scheduler filters and weights but caches the list of available hosts. When a user request is passed to the caching scheduler it attempts to perform scheduling based on the list of cached hosts, with a view to improving scheduler performance.
- A new scheduler filter, `AggregateImagePropertiesIsolation`, has been introduced. The new filter schedules instances to hosts based on matching namespaced image properties with host aggregate properties. Hosts that do not belong to any host aggregate remain valid scheduling targets for instances based on all images. The new Compute Service configuration keys `aggregate_image_properties_isolation_namespace` and `aggregate_image_properties_isolation_separator` are used to determine which image properties are examined by the filter.
- Weight normalization in OpenStack Compute is now a feature. Weights are normalized, so there is no need to artificially inflate multipliers. The maximum weight that a weigher will put for a node is 1.0 and the minimum is 0.0.
- The scheduler now supports server groups. The following types are supported—anti-affinity and affinity filters. That is, a server that is deployed will be done according to a predefined policy.

Other features:

- Notifications are now generated upon the creation and deletion of keypairs.
- Notifications are now generated when an compute host is enabled, disabled, powered on, shut down, rebooted, put into maintenance mode and taken out of maintenance mode.
- Compute services are now able to shut down gracefully by disabling processing of new requests when a service shutdown is requested but allowing requests already in process to complete before terminating.
- The Compute Service determines what action to take when instances are found to be running that were previously marked deleted based on the value of the `running_deleted_instance_action` configuration key. A new `shutdown` value has been added. Using this new value allows administrators to optionally keep instances found in this state for diagnostics while still releasing the runtime resources.
- File injection is now disabled by default in OpenStack Compute. Instead it is recommended that the ConfigDrive and metadata server facilities are used to

modify guests at launch. To enable file injection modify the `inject_key` and `inject_partition` configuration keys in `/etc/nova/nova.conf` and restart the compute services. The file injection mechanism is likely to be disabled in a future release.

- A number of changes have been made to the expected format `/etc/nova/nova.conf` configuration file with a view to ensuring that all configuration groups in the file use descriptive names. A number of driver specific flags, including those for the Libvirt driver, have also been moved to their own option groups.

Database Service (trove)

23 blueprints

- Integration with Orchestration.
- Support for Apache Cassandra NoSQL database for Ubuntu.
- Incremental backups for point in time restoration of database.
- Limited support for MongoDB.

Identity (keystone)

26 blueprints

- The Identity API v2 has been prepared for deprecation, but remains stable and supported in Icehouse.

The *OpenStack Operations Guide* does not contain Identity API v3 in either example architecture.

- Users can update their own password.
- The `/v3/OS-FEDERATION/` call allows Identity API to consume federated authentication with Shibboleth for multiple Identity Providers, and mapping federated attributes into OpenStack group-based role assignments.
- The `POST /v3/users/{user_id}/password` call allows API users to update their own passwords.

- The `GET v3/auth/token?nocatalog` call allows API users to opt out of receiving the service catalog when performing online token validation.
- The `/v3/regions` call provides a public interface for describing multi-region deployments.
- `/v3/OS-SIMPLECERT/` now publishes the certificates used for PKI token validation.
- The `/v3/OS-TRUST/trusts` call is now capable of providing limited-use delegation via the `remaining_uses` attribute of trusts.
- Deployers can now define arbitrary limits on the size of collections in API responses (for example, GET /v3/users might be configured to return only 100 users, rather than 10,000). Clients will be informed when truncation has occurred.
- Backwards compatibility for `keystone.middleware.auth_token` has been removed. The `auth_token` middleware module is no longer provided by the keystone project itself, and must be imported from `keystoneclient.middleware.auth_token` instead.
- The `s3_token middleware` module is no longer provided by the keystone project itself, and must be imported from `keystoneclient.middleware.s3_token` instead. Backwards compatibility for `keystone.middleware.s3_token` is slated for removal in Juno.
- Default token download lasts 1 hour instead of 24 hours. This effectively reduces the number of tokens that must be persisted at any one time, and (for PKI deployments) reduces the overhead of the token revocation list.
- Middleware changes:
  - The `keystone.contrib.access.core.AccessLogMiddleware` middleware has been deprecated in favor of either the eventlet debug access log or Apache httpd access log and may be removed in the K release.
  - The `keystone.contrib.stats.core.StatsMiddleware` middleware has been deprecated in favor of external tooling and may be removed in the K release.
  - The `keystone.middleware.XmlBodyMiddleware` middleware has been deprecated in favor of support for "application/json" only and may be removed in the K release.
- A v3 API version of the EC2 Credential system has been implemented. To use this, the following section needs to be added to `keystone-paste.ini`:

```
[filter:ec2_extension_v3]
paste.filter_factory = keystone.contrib.ec2:Ec2ExtensionV3.factory
```

Also, `ec2_extension_v3` needs to be added to the pipeline variable in the `[pipeline:api_v3]` section of `keystone-paste.ini`.

- Trust notification for third parties. Identity now emits Cloud Audit Data Federation (CADF) event notifications in response to authentication events.
- KVS drivers are now capable of writing to persistent key-value stores such as Redis, Cassandra, or MongoDB.
- Notifications (*http://opsgui.de/RmoxzD*) are now emitted in response to create, update and delete events on roles, groups, and trusts.
- The LDAP driver for the assignment backend now supports group-based role assignment operations.
- Identity now publishes token revocation events in addition to providing continued support for token revocation lists. Token revocation events are designed to consume much less overhead (when compared to token revocation lists) and will enable Identity to eliminate token persistence during the Juno release.

Image Service (glance)

10 blueprints

- Can limit the number of additional image locations to pull from storage.
- Upload an image policy now for v1 API.
- ISO Image support.
- NFS as a backend storage facility for images.
- Image location support.
- Image owners in v2 API.
- Retry failed image download with Object Storage (swift) as backend.
- Allow modified kernel arguments.

Networking (neutron)

43 blueprints

- Migration paths for deprecated plug-ins.
- Quotas extended to VIPs, pools, members, and health monitors.
- Hyper-V agent security groups.
- Least routers scheduler.

- Operational status for floating IP addresses.
- Open Daylight plug-in.
- Big Switch plug-in enhancements—DHCP scheduler support.
- MidoNet plug-in enhancement.
- One Convergence plug-in.
- Nuage plug-in.
- IBM SDN-VE plug-in.
- Brocade mechanism driver for ML2.
- Remote L2 gateway integration.
- LBaaS driver from Embrane, Radware.
- VPNaaS for Cisco products.
- NEC plug-in enhanced to support packet filtering by Programmable Flow Controllers (PFC).
- Plumgrid plug-in enables provider network extension.

Object Storage (swift)

15 blueprints

- Logging at the warning level for when an object is quarantined.
- Better container synchronization support across multiple clusters while enabling a single endpoint.
- New gatekeeper middleware guarding the system metadata.
- Discoverable capabilities added to /info API response so end user can be informed of cluster limits on names, metadata, and object's size.
- Account-level access control lists (ACLs) with x-Account-Access-Control header.

OpenStack dashboard (horizon)

40 blueprints

- Translated user interfaces added for German, Hindi, and Serbian.
- Live migration tasks can be performed in the dashboard.
- Users can set public container access for Object Storage objects from the dashboard.

- Users can create "directories" to organize their stored objects.

Orchestration (heat)

53 blueprints

- Adds Identity API v3 support.
- Enables a Database as a Service resource.
- Provides a stack filtering capability.
- Provides a management API.
- Provides a cloud-init resource for templates to use.

Telemetry (ceilometer)

21 blueprints

- Add alarm support for HBase.
- Addition of time-constrained alarms, providing flexibility to set the bar higher or lower depending on time of day or day of the week.
- Enabled derived rate-based meters for disk and network, more suited to threshold-oriented alarming.
- Support for collecting metrics of VMs deployed on VMware vCenter.
- Exclude alarms on data points where not enough data is gathered to be significant.
- Enable API access to sampled data sets.
- New sources of metrics:
  - Neutron north-bound API on SDN controller
  - VMware vCenter Server API
  - SNMP daemons on baremetal hosts
  - OpenDaylight REST APIs

APPENDIX E

Resources

OpenStack

- OpenStack Configuration Reference (*http://opsgui.de/NPGtjs*)
- OpenStack Install Guide for Debian 7.0 (*http://opsgui.de/1eLBGtX*)
- OpenStack Install Guide for Red Hat Enterprise Linux, CentOS, and Fedora (*http://opsgui.de/NPGvrs*)
- OpenStack Install Guide for openSUSE, SUSE Linux Enterprise Server (*http://opsgui.de/1eLBI50*)
- OpenStack Install Guide for Ubuntu 12.04 (LTS) Server (*http://opsgui.de/NPGunp*)
- OpenStack Cloud Administrator Guide (*http://opsgui.de/1eLBL0N*)
- *OpenStack Cloud Computing Cookbook* (Packt Publishing) (*http://opsgui.de/NPGwvz*)

Cloud (General)

- "The NIST Definition of Cloud Computing" (*http://opsgui.de/1eLBLOv*)

Python

- *Dive Into Python* (Apress) (*http://opsgui.de/NPGxQd*)

Networking

- *TCP/IP Illustrated, Volume 1: The Protocols, 2/E* (Pearson) (*http://opsgui.de/1eLBNWl*)
- *The TCP/IP Guide* (No Starch Press) (*http://opsgui.de/NPGzYr*)
- "A `tcpdump` Tutorial and Primer" (*http://opsgui.de/1eLBOJS*)

Systems Administration

- *UNIX and Linux Systems Administration Handbook* (Prentice Hall) (*http://opsgui.de/NPGyDR*)

Virtualization

- *The Book of Xen* (No Starch Press) (*http://opsgui.de/1eLBQSb*)

Configuration Management

- Puppet Labs Documentation (*http://opsgui.de/NPGzrj*)
- *Pro Puppet* (Apress) (*http://opsgui.de/1eLBRFD*)

Glossary

Use this glossary to get definitions of OpenStack-related words and phrases.

To add to this glossary, fork the `openstack/openstack-manuals` repository (*https://github.com/openstack/openstack-manuals*) and update the source files through the OpenStack contribution process.

absolute limit
: Impassable limits for guest VMs. Settings include total RAM size, maximum number of vCPUs, and maximum disk size.

access control list
: A list of permissions attached to an object. An ACL specifies which users or system processes have access to objects. It also defines which operations can be performed on specified objects. Each entry in a typical ACL specifies a subject and an operation. For instance, the ACL entry `(Alice, delete)` for a file gives Alice permission to delete the file.

access key
: Alternative term for an Amazon EC2 access key. See EC2 access key.

account
: The Object Storage context of an account. Do not confuse with a user account from an authentication service, such as Active Directory, /etc/passwd, OpenLDAP, OpenStack Identity Service, and so on.

account auditor
: Checks for missing replicas and incorrect or corrupted objects in a specified Object Storage account by running queries against the backend SQLite database.

account database
: A SQLite database that contains Object Storage accounts and related metadata and that the accounts server accesses.

account reaper
: An Object Storage worker that scans for and deletes account databases and that the account server has marked for deletion.

account server
: Lists containers in Object Storage and stores container information in the account database.

account service
: An Object Storage component that provides account services such as list, create, modify, and audit. Do not confuse with OpenStack Identity Service, OpenLDAP, or similar user-account services.

accounting
: The Compute Service provides accounting information through the event notification and system usage data facilities.

ACL
See access control list.

active/active configuration
In a high-availability setup with an active/active configuration, several systems share the load together and if one fails, the load is distributed to the remaining systems.

Active Directory
Authentication and identity service by Microsoft, based on LDAP. Supported in OpenStack.

active/passive configuration
In a high-availability setup with an active/passive configuration, systems are set up to bring additional resources online to replace those that have failed.

address pool
A group of fixed and/or floating IP addresses that are assigned to a project and can be used by or assigned to the VM instances in a project.

admin API
A subset of API calls that are accessible to authorized administrators and are generally not accessible to end users or the public Internet. They can exist as a separate service (keystone) or can be a subset of another API (nova).

admin server
In the context of the Identity Service, the worker process that provides access to the admin API.

Advanced Message Queuing Protocol (AMQP)
The open standard messaging protocol used by OpenStack components for intra-service communications, provided by RabbitMQ, Qpid, or ZeroMQ.

Advanced RISC Machine (ARM)
Lower power consumption CPU often found in mobile and embedded devices. Supported by OpenStack.

alert
The Compute Service can send alerts through its notification system, which includes a facility to create custom notification drivers. Alerts can be sent to and displayed on the horizon dashboard.

allocate
The process of taking a floating IP address from the address pool so it can be associated with a fixed IP on a guest VM instance.

Amazon Kernel Image (AKI)
Both a VM container format and disk format. Supported by Image Service.

Amazon Machine Image (AMI)
Both a VM container format and disk format. Supported by Image Service.

Amazon Ramdisk Image (ARI)
Both a VM container format and disk format. Supported by Image Service.

Anvil
A project that ports the shell script-based project named DevStack to Python.

Apache
The Apache Software Foundation supports the Apache community of open-source software projects. These projects provide software products for the public good.

Apache License 2.0
All OpenStack core projects are provided under the terms of the Apache License 2.0 license.

Apache Web Server
The most common web server software currently used on the Internet.

API
Application programming interface.

API endpoint
The daemon, worker, or service that a client communicates with to access an API. API endpoints can provide any number of services, such as authentication, sales data, performance metrics, Compute VM commands, census data, and so on.

API extension
: Custom modules that extend some OpenStack core APIs.

API extension plug-in
: Alternative term for a Networking plug-in or Networking API extension.

API key
: Alternative term for an API token.

API server
: Any node running a daemon or worker that provides an API endpoint.

API token
: Passed to API requests and used by OpenStack to verify that the client is authorized to run the requested operation.

API version
: In OpenStack, the API version for a project is part of the URL. For example, `example.com/nova/v1/foobar`.

applet
: A Java program that can be embedded into a web page.

Application Programming Interface (API)
: A collection of specifications used to access a service, application, or program. Includes service calls, required parameters for each call, and the expected return values.

application server
: A piece of software that makes available another piece of software over a network.

Application Service Provider (ASP)
: Companies that rent specialized applications that help businesses and organizations provide additional services with less cost.

arptables
: Tool used for maintaining Address Resolution Protocol packet filter rules in the Linux kernel firewall modules. Used along with iptables, ebtables, and ip6tables in Compute to provide firewall services for VMs.

associate
: The process associating a Compute floating IP address with a fixed IP address.

Asynchronous JavaScript and XML (AJAX)
: A group of interrelated web development techniques used on the client-side to create asynchronous web applications. Used extensively in horizon.

ATA over Ethernet (AoE)
: A disk storage protocol tunneled within Ethernet.

attach
: The process of connecting a VIF or vNIC to a L2 network in Networking. In the context of Compute, this process connects a storage volume to an instance.

attachment (network)
: Association of an interface ID to a logical port. Plugs an interface into a port.

auditing
: Provided in Compute through the system usage data facility.

auditor
: A worker process that verifies the integrity of Object Storage objects, containers, and accounts. Auditors is the collective term for the Object Storage account auditor, container auditor, and object auditor.

Austin
: Project name for the initial release of OpenStack.

auth node
: Alternative term for an Object Storage authorization node.

authentication
: The process that confirms that the user, process, or client is really who they say they are through private key, secret token, password, fingerprint, or similar method.

authentication token
: A string of text provided to the client after authentication. Must be provided by the

user or process in subsequent requests to the API endpoint.

AuthN
The Identity Service component that provides authentication services.

authorization
The act of verifying that a user, process, or client is authorized to perform an action.

authorization node
An Object Storage node that provides authorization services.

AuthZ
The Identity Service component that provides high-level authorization services.

Auto ACK
Configuration setting within RabbitMQ that enables or disables message acknowledgment. Enabled by default.

auto declare
A Compute RabbitMQ setting that determines whether a message exchange is automatically created when the program starts.

availability zone
An Amazon EC2 concept of an isolated area that is used for fault tolerance. Do not confuse with an OpenStack Compute zone or cell.

AWS
Amazon Web Services.

backend
Interactions and processes that are obfuscated from the user, such as Compute volume mount, data transmission to an iSCSI target by a daemon, or Object Storage object integrity checks.

backend catalog
The storage method used by the Identity Service catalog service to store and retrieve information about API endpoints that are available to the client. Examples include a SQL database, LDAP database, or KVS backend.

backend store
The persistent data store used to save and retrieve information for a service, such as lists of Object Storage objects, current state of guest VMs, lists of usernames, and so on. Also, the method that the Image Service uses to get and store VM images. Options include Object Storage, local file system, S3, and HTTP.

bandwidth
The amount of available data used by communication resources, such as the Internet. Represents the amount of data that is used to download things or the amount of data available to download.

bare
An Image Service container format that indicates that no container exists for the VM image.

base image
An OpenStack-provided image.

Bexar
A grouped release of projects related to OpenStack that came out in February of 2011. It included Compute (nova) and Object Storage (swift) only.

binary
Information that consists solely of ones and zeroes, which is the language of computers.

bit
A bit is a single digit number that is in base of 2 (either a zero or one). Bandwidth usage is measured in bits per second.

bits per second (BPS)
The universal measurement of how quickly data is transferred from place to place.

block device
A device that moves data in the form of blocks. These device nodes interface the devices, such as hard disks, CD-ROM drives, flash drives, and other addressable regions of memory.

block migration
A method of VM live migration used by KVM to evacuate instances from one host to another with very little downtime during a user-initiated switchover. Does not require shared storage. Supported by Compute.

Block Storage
The OpenStack core project that enables management of volumes, volume snapshots, and volume types. The project name of Block Storage is cinder.

BMC
Baseboard Management Controller. The intelligence in the IPMI architecture, which is a specialized micro-controller that is embedded on the motherboard of a computer and acts as a server. Manages the interface between system management software and platform hardware.

bootable disk image
A type of VM image that exists as a single, bootable file.

Bootstrap Protocol (BOOTP)
A network protocol used by a network client to obtain an IP address from a configuration server. Provided in Compute through the dnsmasq daemon when using either the FlatDHCP manager or VLAN manager network manager.

browser
Any client software that enables a computer or device to access the Internet.

builder file
Contains configuration information that Object Storage uses to reconfigure a ring or to re-create it from scratch after a serious failure.

button class
A group of related button types within horizon. Buttons to start, stop, and suspend VMs are in one class. Buttons to associate and disassociate floating IP addresses are in another class, and so on.

byte
Set of bits that make up a single character; there are usually 8 bits to a byte.

CA
Certificate Authority or Certification Authority. In cryptography, an entity that issues digital certificates. The digital certificate certifies the ownership of a public key by the named subject of the certificate. This enables others (relying parties) to rely upon signatures or assertions made by the private key that corresponds to the certified public key. In this model of trust relationships, a CA is a trusted third party for both the subject (owner) of the certificate and the party relying upon the certificate. CAs are characteristic of many public key infrastructure (PKI) schemes.

cache pruner
A program that keeps the Image Service VM image cache at or below its configured maximum size.

Cactus
An OpenStack grouped release of projects that came out in the spring of 2011. It included Compute (nova), Object Storage (swift), and the Image Service (glance).

CALL
One of the RPC primitives used by the OpenStack message queue software. Sends a message and waits for a response.

capability
Defines resources for a cell, including CPU, storage, and networking. Can apply to the specific services within a cell or a whole cell.

capacity cache
A Compute backend database table that contains the current workload, amount of free RAM, and number of VMs running on each host. Used to determine on which VM a host starts.

capacity updater
: A notification driver that monitors VM instances and updates the capacity cache as needed.

CAST
: One of the RPC primitives used by the OpenStack message queue software. Sends a message and does not wait for a response.

catalog
: A list of API endpoints that are available to a user after authentication with the Identity Service.

catalog service
: An Identity Service that lists API endpoints that are available to a user after authentication with the Identity Service.

ceilometer
: The project name for the Telemetry service, which is an integrated project that provides metering and measuring facilities for OpenStack.

cell
: Provides logical partitioning of Compute resources in a child and parent relationship. Requests are passed from parent cells to child cells if the parent cannot provide the requested resource.

cell forwarding
: A Compute option that enables parent cells to pass resource requests to child cells if the parent cannot provide the requested resource.

cell manager
: The Compute component that contains a list of the current capabilities of each host within the cell and routes requests as appropriate.

CentOS
: A Linux distribution that is compatible with OpenStack.

Ceph
: Massively scalable distributed storage system that consists of an object store, block store, and POSIX-compatible distributed file system. Compatible with OpenStack.

CephFS
: The POSIX-compliant file system provided by Ceph.

certificate authority
: A simple certificate authority provided by Compute for cloudpipe VPNs and VM image decryption.

Challenge-Handshake Authentication Protocol (CHAP)
: An iSCSI authentication method supported by Compute.

chance scheduler
: A scheduling method used by Compute that randomly chooses an available host from the pool.

changes since
: A Compute API parameter that downloads changes to the requested item since your last request, instead of downloading a new, fresh set of data and comparing it against the old data.

Chef
: An operating system configuration management tool supporting OpenStack deployments.

child cell
: If a requested resource such as CPU time, disk storage, or memory is not available in the parent cell, the request is forwarded to its associated child cells. If the child cell can fulfill the request, it does. Otherwise, it attempts to pass the request to any of its children.

cinder
: A core OpenStack project that provides block storage services for VMs.

Cisco neutron plug-in
: A Networking plug-in for Cisco devices and technologies, including UCS and Nexus.

cloud architect
A person who plans, designs, and oversees the creation of clouds.

cloud computing
A model that enables access to a shared pool of configurable computing resources, such as networks, servers, storage, applications, and services, that can be rapidly provisioned and released with minimal management effort or service provider interaction.

cloud controller
Collection of Compute components that represent the global state of the cloud; talks to services, such as Identity Service authentication, Object Storage, and node/storage workers through a queue.

cloud controller node
A node that runs network, volume, API, scheduler, and image services. Each service may be broken out into separate nodes for scalability or availability.

Cloud Data Management Interface (CDMI)
SINA standard that defines a RESTful API for managing objects in the cloud, currently unsupported in OpenStack.

Cloud Infrastructure Management Interface (CIMI)
An in-progress specification for cloud management. Currently unsupported in OpenStack.

cloud-init
A package commonly installed in VM images that performs initialization of an instance after boot using information that it retrieves from the metadata service, such as the SSH public key and user data.

cloudadmin
One of the default roles in the Compute RBAC system. Grants complete system access.

cloudpipe
A compute service that creates VPNs on a per-project basis.

cloudpipe image
A pre-made VM image that serves as a cloudpipe server. Essentially, OpenVPN running on Linux.

CMDB
Configuration Management Database.

command filter
Lists allowed commands within the Compute rootwrap facility.

community project
A project that is not officially endorsed by the OpenStack Foundation. If the project is successful enough, it might be elevated to an incubated project and then to a core project, or it might be merged with the main code trunk.

compression
Reducing the size of files by special encoding, the file can be decompressed again to its original content. OpenStack supports compression at the Linux file system level but does not support compression for things such as Object Storage objects or Image Service VM images.

Compute
The OpenStack core project that provides compute services. The project name of Compute Service is nova.

Compute API
The `nova-api` daemon provides access to nova services. Can communicate with other APIs, such as the Amazon EC2 API.

compute controller
The Compute component that chooses suitable hosts on which to start VM instances.

compute host
Physical host dedicated to running compute nodes.

compute node
A node that runs the `nova-compute` daemon that manages VM instances that

provide a wide range of services, such as web applications and analytics.

Compute Service
: Name for the Compute component that manages VMs.

compute worker
: The Compute component that runs on each compute node and manages the VM instance life cycle, including run, reboot, terminate, attach/detach volumes, and so on. Provided by the `nova-compute` daemon.

concatenated object
: A set of segment objects that Object Storage combines and sends to the client.

conductor
: In Compute, conductor is the process that proxies database requests from the compute process. Using conductor improves security because compute nodes do not need direct access to the database.

consistency window
: The amount of time it takes for a new Object Storage object to become accessible to all clients.

console log
: Contains the output from a Linux VM console in Compute.

container
: Organizes and stores objects in Object Storage. Similar to the concept of a Linux directory but cannot be nested. Alternative term for an Image Service container format.

container auditor
: Checks for missing replicas or incorrect objects in specified Object Storage containers through queries to the SQLite backend database.

container database
: A SQLite database that stores Object Storage containers and container metadata. The container server accesses this database.

container format
: A wrapper used by the Image Service that contains a VM image and its associated metadata, such as machine state, OS disk size, and so on.

container server
: An Object Storage server that manages containers.

container service
: The Object Storage component that provides container services, such as create, delete, list, and so on.

controller node
: Alternative term for a cloud controller node.

core API
: Depending on context, the core API is either the OpenStack API or the main API of a specific core project, such as Compute, Networking, Image Service, and so on.

core project
: An official OpenStack project. Currently consists of Compute (nova), Object Storage (swift), Image Service (glance), Identity (keystone), Dashboard (horizon), Networking (neutron), and Block Storage (cinder). The Telemetry module (ceilometer) and Orchestration module (heat) are integrated projects as of the Havana release. In the Icehouse release, the Database module (trove) gains integrated project status.

cost
: Under the Compute distributed scheduler, this is calculated by looking at the capabilities of each host relative to the flavor of the VM instance being requested.

credentials
: Data that is only known to or accessible by a user and used to verify that the user is who he says he is. Credentials are presented to the server during authentication. Examples include a password, secret key, digital certificate, and fingerprint.

Crowbar
: An open source community project by Dell that aims to provide all necessary services to quickly deploy clouds.

current workload
: An element of the Compute capacity cache that is calculated based on the number of build, snapshot, migrate, and resize operations currently in progress on a given host.

customer
: Alternative term for tenant.

customization module
: A user-created Python module that is loaded by horizon to change the look and feel of the dashboard.

daemon
: A process that runs in the background and waits for requests. May or may not listen on a TCP or UDP port. Do not confuse with a worker.

DAC
: Discretionary access control. Governs the ability of subjects to access objects, while enabling users to make policy decisions and assign security attributes. The traditional UNIX system of users, groups, and read-write-execute permissions is an example of DAC.

dashboard
: The web-based management interface for OpenStack. An alternative name for horizon.

data encryption
: Both Image Service and Compute support encrypted virtual machine (VM) images (but not instances). In-transit data encryption is supported in OpenStack using technologies such as HTTPS, SSL, TLS, and SSH. Object Storage does not support object encryption at the application level but may support storage that uses disk encryption.

database ID
: A unique ID given to each replica of an Object Storage database.

database replicator
: An Object Storage component that copies changes in the account, container, and object databases to other nodes.

deallocate
: The process of removing the association between a floating IP address and a fixed IP address. Once this association is removed, the floating IP returns to the address pool.

Debian
: A Linux distribution that is compatible with OpenStack.

deduplication
: The process of finding duplicate data at the disk block, file, and/or object level to minimize storage use—currently unsupported within OpenStack.

default panel
: The default panel that is displayed when a user accesses the horizon dashboard.

default tenant
: New users are assigned to this tenant if no tenant is specified when a user is created.

default token
: An Identity Service token that is not associated with a specific tenant and is exchanged for a scoped token.

delayed delete
: An option within Image Service so that an image is deleted after a predefined number of seconds instead of immediately.

delivery mode
: Setting for the Compute RabbitMQ message delivery mode; can be set to either transient or persistent.

deprecated auth
: An option within Compute that enables administrators to create and manage users

through the `nova-manage` command as opposed to using the Identity Service.

developer
: One of the default roles in the Compute RBAC system and the default role assigned to a new user.

device ID
: Maps Object Storage partitions to physical storage devices.

device weight
: Distributes partitions proportionately across Object Storage devices based on the storage capacity of each device.

DevStack
: Community project that uses shell scripts to quickly build complete OpenStack development environments.

DHCP
: Dynamic Host Configuration Protocol. A network protocol that configures devices that are connected to a network so that they can communicate on that network by using the Internet Protocol (IP). The protocol is implemented in a client-server model where DHCP clients request configuration data, such as an IP address, a default route, and one or more DNS server addresses from a DHCP server.

Diablo
: A grouped release of projects related to OpenStack that came out in the fall of 2011, the fourth release of OpenStack. It included Compute (nova 2011.3), Object Storage (swift 1.4.3), and the Image Service (glance).

direct consumer
: An element of the Compute RabbitMQ that comes to life when a RPC call is executed. It connects to a direct exchange through a unique exclusive queue, sends the message, and terminates.

direct exchange
: A routing table that is created within the Compute RabbitMQ during RPC calls; one is created for each RPC call that is invoked.

direct publisher
: Element of RabbitMQ that provides a response to an incoming MQ message.

disassociate
: The process of removing the association between a floating IP address and fixed IP and thus returning the floating IP address to the address pool.

disk encryption
: The ability to encrypt data at the file system, disk partition, or whole-disk level. Supported within Compute VMs.

disk format
: The underlying format that a disk image for a VM is stored as within the Image Service backend store. For example, AMI, ISO, QCOW2, VMDK, and so on.

dispersion
: In Object Storage, tools to test and ensure dispersion of objects and containers to ensure fault tolerance.

Django
: A web framework used extensively in horizon.

DNS
: Domain Name Server. A hierarchical and distributed naming system for computers, services, and resources connected to the Internet or a private network. Associates a human-friendly names to IP addresses.

DNS record
: A record that specifies information about a particular domain and belongs to the domain.

dnsmasq
: Daemon that provides DNS, DHCP, BOOTP, and TFTP services, used by the Compute VLAN manager and FlatDHCP manager.

domain
: Separates a website from other sites. Often, the domain name has two or more parts that are separated by dots. For example, yahoo.com, usa.gov, harvard.edu, or mail.yahoo.com.

  A domain is an entity or container of all DNS-related information containing one or more records.

Domain Name Service (DNS)
: In Compute, the support that enables associating DNS entries with floating IP addresses, nodes, or cells so that hostnames are consistent across reboots.

Domain Name System (DNS)
: A system by which Internet domain name-to-address and address-to-name resolutions are determined.

  DNS helps navigate the Internet by translating the IP address into an address that is easier to remember For example, translating 111.111.111.1 into www.yahoo.com.

  All domains and their components, such as mail servers, utilize DNS to resolve to the appropriate locations. DNS servers are usually set up in a master-slave relationship such that failure of the master invokes the slave. DNS servers might also be clustered or replicated such that changes made to one DNS server are automatically propagated to other active servers.

download
: The transfer of data, usually in the form of files, from one computer to another.

DRTM
: Dynamic root of trust measurement.

durable exchange
: The Compute RabbitMQ message exchange that remains active when the server restarts.

durable queue
: A Compute RabbitMQ message queue that remains active when the server restarts.

Dynamic Host Configuration Protocol (DHCP)
: A method to automatically configure networking for a host at boot time. Provided by both Networking and Compute.

Dynamic HyperText Markup Language (DHTML)
: Pages that use HTML, JavaScript, and Cascading Style Sheets to enable users to interact with a web page or show simple animation.

EBS boot volume
: An Amazon EBS storage volume that contains a bootable VM image, currently unsupported in OpenStack.

ebtables
: Used in Compute along with arptables, iptables, and ip6tables to create firewalls and to ensure isolation of network communications.

EC2
: The Amazon commercial compute product, similar to Compute.

EC2 access key
: Used along with an EC2 secret key to access the Compute EC2 API.

EC2 API
: OpenStack supports accessing the Amazon EC2 API through Compute.

EC2 Compatibility API
: A Compute component that enables OpenStack to communicate with Amazon EC2.

EC2 secret key
: Used along with an EC2 access key when communicating with the Compute EC2 API; used to digitally sign each request.

Elastic Block Storage (EBS)
: The Amazon commercial block storage product.

encryption
: OpenStack supports encryption technologies such as HTTPS, SSH, SSL, TLS, digital certificates, and data encryption.

endpoint
: See API endpoint.

endpoint registry
: Alternative term for an Identity Service catalog.

endpoint template
: A list of URL and port number endpoints that indicate where a service, such as Object Storage, Compute, Identity, and so on, can be accessed.

entity
: Any piece of hardware or software that wants to connect to the network services provided by Networking, the network connectivity service. An entity can make use of Networking by implementing a VIF.

ephemeral image
: A VM image that does not save changes made to its volumes and reverts them to their original state after the instance is terminated.

ephemeral volume
: Volume that does not save the changes made to it and reverts to its original state when the current user relinquishes control.

Essex
: A grouped release of projects related to OpenStack that came out in April 2012, the fifth release of OpenStack. It included Compute (nova 2012.1), Object Storage (swift 1.4.8), Image (glance), Identity (keystone), and Dashboard (horizon).

ESX
: An OpenStack-supported hypervisor.

ESXi
: An OpenStack-supported hypervisor.

ebtables
: Filtering tool for a Linux bridging firewall, enabling filtering of network traffic passing through a Linux bridge. Used to restrict communications between hosts and/or nodes in OpenStack Compute along with iptables, arptables, and ip6tables.

ETag
: MD5 hash of an object within Object Storage, used to ensure data integrity.

euca2ools
: A collection of command-line tools for administering VMs; most are compatible with OpenStack.

Eucalyptus Kernel Image (EKI)
: Used along with an ERI to create an EMI.

Eucalyptus Machine Image (EMI)
: VM image container format supported by Image Service.

Eucalyptus Ramdisk Image (ERI)
: Used along with an EKI to create an EMI.

evacuate
: The process of migrating one or all virtual machine (VM) instances from one host to another, compatible with both shared storage live migration and block migration.

exchange
: Alternative term for a RabbitMQ message exchange.

exchange type
: A routing algorithm in the Compute RabbitMQ.

exclusive queue
: Connected to by a direct consumer in RabbitMQ—Compute, the message can be consumed only by the current connection.

extended attributes (xattrs)
: File system option that enables storage of additional information beyond owner, group, permissions, modification time, and so on. The underlying Object Storage file system must support extended attributes.

extension
Alternative term for an API extension or plug-in. In the context of Identity Service, this is a call that is specific to the implementation, such as adding support for OpenID.

extra specs
Specifies additional requirements when Compute determines where to start a new instance. Examples include a minimum amount of network bandwidth or a GPU.

FakeLDAP
An easy method to create a local LDAP directory for testing Identity Service and Compute. Requires Redis.

fan-out exchange
Within RabbitMQ and Compute, it is the messaging interface that is used by the scheduler service to receive capability messages from the compute, volume, and network nodes.

Fedora
A Linux distribution compatible with OpenStack.

Fibre Channel
Storage protocol similar in concept to TCP/IP; encapsulates SCSI commands and data.

Fibre Channel over Ethernet (FCoE)
The fibre channel protocol tunneled within Ethernet.

fill-first scheduler
The Compute scheduling method that attempts to fill a host with VMs rather than starting new VMs on a variety of hosts.

filter
The step in the Compute scheduling process when hosts that cannot run VMs are eliminated and not chosen.

firewall
Used to restrict communications between hosts and/or nodes, implemented in Compute using iptables, arptables, ip6tables, and etables.

Firewall-as-a-Service (FWaaS)
A Networking extension that provides perimeter firewall functionality.

fixed IP address
An IP address that is associated with the same instance each time that instance boots, is generally not accessible to end users or the public Internet, and is used for management of the instance.

Flat Manager
The Compute component that gives IP addresses to authorized nodes and assumes DHCP, DNS, and routing configuration and services are provided by something else.

flat mode injection
A Compute networking method where the OS network configuration information is injected into the VM image before the instance starts.

flat network
The Network Controller provides virtual networks to enable compute servers to interact with each other and with the public network. All machines must have a public and private network interface. A flat network is a private network interface, which is controlled by the `flat_interface` option with flat managers.

FlatDHCP Manager
The Compute component that provides dnsmasq (DHCP, DNS, BOOTP, TFTP) and radvd (routing) services.

flavor
Alternative term for a VM instance type.

flavor ID
UUID for each Compute or Image Service VM flavor or instance type.

floating IP address
An IP address that a project can associate with a VM so that the instance has the same public IP address each time that it boots. You create a pool of floating IP addresses and assign them to instances as

they are launched to maintain a consistent IP address for maintaining DNS assignment.

Folsom
A grouped release of projects related to OpenStack that came out in the fall of 2012, the sixth release of OpenStack. It includes Compute (nova), Object Storage (swift), Identity (keystone), Networking (neutron), Image Service (glance), and Volumes or Block Storage (cinder).

FormPost
Object Storage middleware that uploads (posts) an image through a form on a web page.

frontend
The point where a user interacts with a service; can be an API endpoint, the horizon dashboard, or a command-line tool.

gateway
Hardware or software that translates between two different protocols.

glance
A core project that provides the OpenStack Image Service.

glance API server
Processes client requests for VMs, updates Image Service metadata on the registry server, and communicates with the store adapter to upload VM images from the backend store.

glance registry
Alternative term for the Image Service image registry.

global endpoint template
The Identity Service endpoint template that contains services available to all tenants.

GlusterFS
A file system designed to aggregate NAS hosts, compatible with OpenStack.

golden image
A method of operating system installation where a finalized disk image is created and then used by all nodes without modification.

Graphic Interchange Format (GIF)
A type of image file that is commonly used for animated images on web pages.

Graphics Processing Unit (GPU)
Choosing a host based on the existence of a GPU is currently unsupported in OpenStack.

Green Threads
The cooperative threading model used by Python; reduces race conditions and only context switches when specific library calls are made. Each OpenStack service is its own thread.

Grizzly
Project name for the seventh release of OpenStack.

guest OS
An operating system instance running under the control of a hypervisor.

Hadoop
Apache Hadoop is an open source software framework that supports data-intensive distributed applications.

handover
An object state in Object Storage where a new replica of the object is automatically created due to a drive failure.

hard reboot
A type of reboot where a physical or virtual power button is pressed as opposed to a graceful, proper shutdown of the operating system.

Havana
Project name for the eighth release of OpenStack.

heat
An integrated project that aims to orchestrate multiple cloud applications for OpenStack.

horizon
OpenStack project that provides a dashboard, which is a web interface.

horizon plug-in
A plug-in for the OpenStack dashboard (horizon).

host
A physical computer, not a VM instance (node).

host aggregate
A method to further subdivide availability zones into hypervisor pools, a collection of common hosts.

Host Bus Adapter (HBA)
Device plugged into a PCI slot, such as a fibre channel or network card.

HTTP
Hypertext Transfer Protocol. HTTP is an application protocol for distributed, collaborative, hypermedia information systems. It is the foundation of data communication for the World Wide Web. Hypertext is structured text that uses logical links (hyperlinks) between nodes containing text. HTTP is the protocol to exchange or transfer hypertext.

HTTPS
Hypertext Transfer Protocol Secure (HTTPS) is a communications protocol for secure communication over a computer network, with especially wide deployment on the Internet. Technically, it is not a protocol in and of itself; rather, it is the result of simply layering the Hypertext Transfer Protocol (HTTP) on top of the SSL/TLS protocol, thus adding the security capabilities of SSL/TLS to standard HTTP communications.

Hyper-V
One of the hypervisors supported by OpenStack.

hyperlink
Any kind of text that contains a link to some other site, commonly found in documents where clicking on a word or words opens up a different website.

Hypertext Transfer Protocol (HTTP)
The protocol that tells browsers where to go to find information.

Hypertext Transfer Protocol Secure (HTTPS)
Encrypted HTTP communications using SSL or TLS; most OpenStack API endpoints and many inter-component communications support HTTPS communication.

hypervisor
Software that arbitrates and controls VM access to the actual underlying hardware.

hypervisor pool
A collection of hypervisors grouped together through host aggregates.

IaaS
Infrastructure-as-a-Service. IaaS is a provisioning model in which an organization outsources physical components of a data center, such as storage, hardware, servers, and networking components. A service provider owns the equipment and is responsible for housing, operating and maintaining it. The client typically pays on a per-use basis. IaaS is a model for providing cloud services.

Icehouse
Project name for the ninth release of OpenStack.

ID number
Unique numeric ID associated with each user in Identity Service, conceptually similar to a Linux or LDAP UID.

Identity API
Alternative term for the Identity Service API.

Identity backend
: The source used by Identity Service to retrieve user information; an OpenLDAP server, for example.

Identity Service
: The OpenStack core project that provides a central directory of users mapped to the OpenStack services they can access. It also registers endpoints for OpenStack services. It acts as a common authentication system. The project name of the Identity Service is keystone.

Identity Service API
: The API used to access the OpenStack Identity Service provided through keystone.

IDS
: Intrusion Detection System.

image
: A collection of files for a specific operating system (OS) that you use to create or rebuild a server. OpenStack provides prebuilt images. You can also create custom images, or snapshots, from servers that you have launched. Custom images can be used for data backups or as "gold" images for additional servers.

Image API
: The Image Service API endpoint for management of VM images.

image cache
: Used by Image Service to obtain images on the local host rather than re-downloading them from the image server each time one is requested.

image ID
: Combination of a URI and UUID used to access Image Service VM images through the image API.

image membership
: A list of tenants that can access a given VM image within Image Service.

image owner
: The tenant who owns an Image Service virtual machine image.

image registry
: A list of VM images that are available through Image Service.

Image Service
: An OpenStack core project that provides discovery, registration, and delivery services for disk and server images. The project name of the Image Service is glance.

Image Service API
: Alternative name for the glance image API.

image status
: The current status of a VM image in Image Service, not to be confused with the status of a running instance.

image store
: The backend store used by Image Service to store VM images, options include Object Storage, local file system, S3, or HTTP.

image UUID
: UUID used by Image Service to uniquely identify each VM image.

incubated project
: A community project may be elevated to this status and is then promoted to a core project.

ingress filtering
: The process of filtering incoming network traffic. Supported by Compute.

injection
: The process of putting a file into a virtual machine image before the instance is started.

instance
: A running VM, or a VM in a known state such as suspended, that can be used like a hardware server.

instance ID
Alternative term for instance UUID.

instance state
The current state of a guest VM image.

instance type
Describes the parameters of the various virtual machine images that are available to users; includes parameters such as CPU, storage, and memory. Alternative term for flavor.

instance type ID
Alternative term for a flavor ID.

instance UUID
Unique ID assigned to each guest VM instance.

interface ID
Unique ID for a Networking VIF or vNIC in the form of a UUID.

Internet Service Provider (ISP)
Any business that provides Internet access to individuals or businesses.

ironic
OpenStack project that provisions bare metal, as opposed to virtual, machines.

IP address
Number that is unique to every computer system on the Internet. Two versions of the Internet Protocol (IP) are in use for addresses: IPv4 and IPv6.

IP Address Management (IPAM)
The process of automating IP address allocation, deallocation, and management. Currently provided by Compute, melange, and Networking.

IPL
Initial Program Loader.

IPMI
Intelligent Platform Management Interface. IPMI is a standardized computer system interface used by system administrators for out-of-band management of computer systems and monitoring of their operation. In layman's terms, it is a way to manage a computer using a direct network connection, whether it is turned on or not; connecting to the hardware rather than an operating system or login shell.

ip6tables
Tool used to set up, maintain, and inspect the tables of IPv6 packet filter rules in the Linux kernel. In OpenStack Compute, ip6tables is used along with arptables, ebtables, and iptables to create firewalls for both nodes and VMs.

iptables
Used along with arptables and ebtables, iptables create firewalls in Compute. iptables are the tables provided by the Linux kernel firewall (implemented as different Netfilter modules) and the chains and rules it stores. Different kernel modules and programs are currently used for different protocols: iptables applies to IPv4, ip6tables to IPv6, arptables to ARP, and ebtables to Ethernet frames. Requires root privilege to manipulate.

iSCSI
The SCSI disk protocol tunneled within Ethernet, supported by Compute, Object Storage, and Image Service.

ISO9960
One of the VM image disk formats supported by Image Service.

itsec
A default role in the Compute RBAC system that can quarantine an instance in any project.

Java
A programming language that is used to create systems that involve more than one computer by way of a network.

JavaScript
A scripting language that is used to build web pages.

JavaScript Object Notation (JSON)
: One of the supported response formats in OpenStack.

Jenkins
: Tool used to run jobs automatically for OpenStack development.

Juno
: Project name for the 10th release of OpenStack.

kernel-based VM (KVM)
: An OpenStack-supported hypervisor.

keystone
: The project that provides OpenStack Identity services.

Kickstart
: A tool to automate system configuration and installation on Red Hat, Fedora, and CentOS-based Linux distributions.

large object
: An object within Object Storage that is larger than 5 GB.

Launchpad
: The collaboration site for OpenStack.

Layer-2 network
: Term used for OSI network architecture for the data link layer.

libvirt
: Virtualization API library used by OpenStack to interact with many of its supported hypervisors.

Linux bridge
: Software that enables multiple VMs to share a single physical NIC within Compute.

Linux Bridge neutron plug-in
: Enables a Linux bridge to understand a Networking port, interface attachment, and other abstractions.

Linux containers (LXC)
: An OpenStack-supported hypervisor.

live migration
: The ability within Compute to move running virtual machine instances from one host to another with only a small service interruption during switchover.

load balancer
: A load balancer is a logical device that belongs to a cloud account. It is used to distribute workloads between multiple back-end systems or services, based on the criteria defined as part of its configuration.

load balancing
: The process of spreading client requests between two or more nodes to improve performance and availability.

Load-Balancing-as-a-Service (LBaaS)
: Enables Networking to distribute incoming requests evenly between designated instances.

management API
: Alternative term for an admin API.

management network
: A network segment used for administration, not accessible to the public Internet.

manager
: Logical groupings of related code, such as the Block Storage volume manager or network manager.

manifest
: Used to track segments of a large object within Object Storage.

manifest object
: A special Object Storage object that contains the manifest for a large object.

marconi
: OpenStack project that provides a queue service to applications.

melange
: Project name for OpenStack Network Information Service. To be merged with Networking.

membership
: The association between an Image Service VM image and a tenant. Enables images to be shared with specified tenants.

membership list
: A list of tenants that can access a given VM image within Image Service.

memcached
: A distributed memory object caching system that is used by Object Storage for caching.

memory overcommit
: The ability to start new VM instances based on the actual memory usage of a host, as opposed to basing the decision on the amount of RAM each running instance thinks it has available. Also known as RAM overcommit.

message broker
: The software package used to provide AMQP messaging capabilities within Compute. Default package is RabbitMQ.

message bus
: The main virtual communication line used by all AMQP messages for inter-cloud communications within Compute.

message queue
: Passes requests from clients to the appropriate workers and returns the output to the client after the job completes.

Meta-Data Server (MDS)
: Stores CephFS metadata.

migration
: The process of moving a VM instance from one host to another.

multinic
: Facility in Compute that allows each virtual machine instance to have more than one VIF connected to it.

Modular Layer 2 (ML2) neutron plug-in
: Can concurrently use multiple layer-2 networking technologies, such as 802.1Q and VXLAN, in Networking.

Monitor (LBaaS)
: LBaaS feature that provides availability monitoring using the `ping` command, TCP, and HTTP/HTTPS GET.

Monitor (Mon)
: A Ceph component that communicates with external clients, checks data state and consistency, and performs quorum functions.

multi-factor authentication
: Authentication method that uses two or more credentials, such as a password and a private key. Currently not supported in Identity Service.

MultiNic
: Facility in Compute that enables a virtual machine instance to have more than one VIF connected to it.

Nebula
: Released as open source by NASA in 2010 and is the basis for Compute.

netadmin
: One of the default roles in the Compute RBAC system. Enables the user to allocate publicly accessible IP addresses to instances and change firewall rules.

NetApp volume driver
: Enables Compute to communicate with NetApp storage devices through the NetApp OnCommand Provisioning Manager.

network
: A virtual network that provides connectivity between entities. For example, a collection of virtual ports that share network connectivity. In Networking terminology, a network is always a layer-2 network.

Network Address Translation (NAT)
: The process of modifying IP address information while in transit. Supported by Compute and Networking.

network controller
: A Compute daemon that orchestrates the network configuration of nodes, including

IP addresses, VLANs, and bridging. Also manages routing for both public and private networks.

Network File System (NFS)
A method for making file systems available over the network. Supported by OpenStack.

network ID
Unique ID assigned to each network segment within Networking. Same as network UUID.

network manager
The Compute component that manages various network components, such as firewall rules, IP address allocation, and so on.

network node
Any compute node that runs the network worker daemon.

network segment
Represents a virtual, isolated OSI layer-2 subnet in Networking.

Network Time Protocol (NTP)
A method of keeping a clock for a host or node correct through communications with a trusted, accurate time source.

network UUID
Unique ID for a Networking network segment.

network worker
The `nova-network` worker daemon; provides services such as giving an IP address to a booting nova instance.

Networking
A core OpenStack project that provides a network connectivity abstraction layer to OpenStack Compute. The project name of Networking is neutron.

Networking API
API used to access OpenStack Networking. Provides an extensible architecture to enable custom plug-in creation.

neutron
A core OpenStack project that provides a network connectivity abstraction layer to OpenStack Compute.

neutron API
An alternative name for Networking API.

neutron manager
Enables Compute and Networking integration, which enables Networking to perform network management for guest VMs.

neutron plug-in
Interface within Networking that enables organizations to create custom plug-ins for advanced features, such as QoS, ACLs, or IDS.

Nexenta volume driver
Provides support for NexentaStor devices in Compute.

No ACK
Disables server-side message acknowledgment in the Compute RabbitMQ. Increases performance but decreases reliability.

node
A VM instance that runs on a host.

non-durable exchange
Message exchange that is cleared when the service restarts. Its data is not written to persistent storage.

non-durable queue
Message queue that is cleared when the service restarts. Its data is not written to persistent storage.

non-persistent volume
Alternative term for an ephemeral volume.

nova
OpenStack project that provides compute services.

Nova API
Alternative term for the Compute API.

nova-network
A Compute component that manages IP address allocation, firewalls, and other network-related tasks. This is the legacy networking option and an alternative to Networking.

object
A BLOB of data held by Object Storage; can be in any format.

object auditor
Opens all objects for an object server and verifies the MD5 hash, size, and metadata for each object.

object expiration
A configurable option within Object Storage to automatically delete objects after a specified amount of time has passed or a certain date is reached.

object hash
Uniquely ID for an Object Storage object.

object path hash
Used by Object Storage to determine the location of an object in the ring. Maps objects to partitions.

object replicator
An Object Storage component that copies an object to remote partitions for fault tolerance.

object server
An Object Storage component that is responsible for managing objects.

Object Storage
The OpenStack core project that provides eventually consistent and redundant storage and retrieval of fixed digital content. The project name of OpenStack Object Storage is swift.

Object Storage API
API used to access OpenStack Object Storage.

Object Storage Device (OSD)
The Ceph storage daemon.

object versioning
Allows a user to set a flag on an Object Storage container so that all objects within the container are versioned.

Oldie
Term for an Object Storage process that runs for a long time. Can indicate a hung process.

Open Cloud Computing Interface (OCCI)
A standardized interface for managing compute, data, and network resources, currently unsupported in OpenStack.

Open Virtualization Format (OVF)
Standard for packaging VM images. Supported in OpenStack.

Open vSwitch neutron plug-in
Provides support for Open vSwitch in Networking.

OpenLDAP
An open source LDAP server. Supported by both Compute and Identity Service.

OpenStack
OpenStack is a cloud operating system that controls large pools of compute, storage, and networking resources throughout a data center, all managed through a dashboard that gives administrators control while empowering their users to provision resources through a web interface. OpenStack is an open source project licensed under the Apache License 2.0.

openSUSE
A Linux distribution that is compatible with OpenStack.

operator
The person responsible for planning and maintaining an OpenStack installation.

Orchestration
An integrated project that orchestrates multiple cloud applications for OpenStack. The project name of Orchestration is heat.

orphan
In the context of Object Storage, this is a process that is not terminated after an upgrade, restart, or reload of the service.

parent cell
If a requested resource, such as CPU time, disk storage, or memory, is not available in the parent cell, the request is forwarded to associated child cells.

partition
A unit of storage within Object Storage used to store objects. It exists on top of devices and is replicated for fault tolerance.

partition index
Contains the locations of all Object Storage partitions within the ring.

partition shift value
Used by Object Storage to determine which partition data should reside on.

pause
A VM state where no changes occur (no changes in memory, network communications stop, etc); the VM is frozen but not shut down.

PCI passthrough
Gives guest VMs exclusive access to a PCI device. Currently supported in OpenStack Havana and later releases.

persistent message
A message that is stored both in memory and on disk. The message is not lost after a failure or restart.

persistent volume
Changes to these types of disk volumes are saved.

personality file
A file used to customize a Compute instance. It can be used to inject SSH keys or a specific network configuration.

Platform-as-a-Service (PaaS)
Provides to the consumer the ability to deploy applications through a programming language or tools supported by the cloud platform provider. An example of Platform-as-a-Service is an Eclipse/Java programming platform provided with no downloads required.

plug-in
Software component providing the actual implementation for Networking APIs, or for Compute APIs, depending on the context.

policy service
Component of Identity Service that provides a rule-management interface and a rule-based authorization engine.

port
A virtual network port within Networking; VIFs / vNICs are connected to a port.

port UUID
Unique ID for a Networking port.

preseed
A tool to automate system configuration and installation on Debian-based Linux distributions.

private image
An Image Service VM image that is only available to specified tenants.

private IP address
An IP address used for management and administration, not available to the public Internet.

private network
The Network Controller provides virtual networks to enable compute servers to interact with each other and with the public network. All machines must have a public and private network interface. A private network interface can be a flat or VLAN network interface. A flat network interface is controlled by the flat_interface with flat managers. A VLAN network interface is controlled by the `vlan_interface` option with VLAN managers.

project
: A logical grouping of users within Compute; defines quotas and access to VM images.

project ID
: User-defined alphanumeric string in Compute; the name of a project.

project VPN
: Alternative term for a cloudpipe.

provider
: An administrator who has access to all hosts and instances.

proxy node
: A node that provides the Object Storage proxy service.

proxy server
: Users of Object Storage interact with the service through the proxy server, which in turn looks up the location of the requested data within the ring and returns the results to the user.

public API
: An API endpoint used for both service-to-service communication and end-user interactions.

public image
: An Image Service VM image that is available to all tenants.

public IP address
: An IP address that is accessible to end-users.

public network
: The Network Controller provides virtual networks to enable compute servers to interact with each other and with the public network. All machines must have a public and private network interface. The public network interface is controlled by the `public_interface` option.

Puppet
: An operating system configuration-management tool supported by OpenStack.

Python
: Programming language used extensively in OpenStack.

QEMU Copy On Write 2 (QCOW2)
: One of the VM image disk formats supported by Image Service.

Qpid
: Message queue software supported by OpenStack; an alternative to RabbitMQ.

quarantine
: If Object Storage finds objects, containers, or accounts that are corrupt, they are placed in this state, are not replicated, cannot be read by clients, and a correct copy is re-replicated.

Quick EMUlator (QEMU)
: QEMU is a generic and open source machine emulator and virtualizer.

: One of the hypervisors supported by OpenStack, generally used for development purposes.

quota
: In Compute and Block Storage, the ability to set resource limits on a per-project basis.

RabbitMQ
: The default message queue software used by OpenStack.

Rackspace Cloud Files
: Released as open source by Rackspace in 2010; the basis for Object Storage.

RADOS Block Device (RBD)
: Ceph component that enables a Linux block device to be striped over multiple distributed data stores.

radvd
: The router advertisement daemon, used by the Compute VLAN manager and FlatDHCP manager to provide routing services for VM instances.

RAM filter
The Compute setting that enables or disables RAM overcommitment.

RAM overcommit
The ability to start new VM instances based on the actual memory usage of a host, as opposed to basing the decision on the amount of RAM each running instance thinks it has available. Also known as memory overcommit.

rate limit
Configurable option within Object Storage to limit database writes on a per-account and/or per-container basis.

raw
One of the VM image disk formats supported by Image Service; an unstructured disk image.

rebalance
The process of distributing Object Storage partitions across all drives in the ring; used during initial ring creation and after ring reconfiguration.

reboot
Either a soft or hard reboot of a server. With a soft reboot, the operating system is signaled to restart, which enables a graceful shutdown of all processes. A hard reboot is the equivalent of power cycling the server. The virtualization platform should ensure that the reboot action has completed successfully, even in cases in which the underlying domain/VM is paused or halted/stopped.

rebuild
Removes all data on the server and replaces it with the specified image. Server ID and IP addresses remain the same.

Recon
An Object Storage component that collects metrics.

record
Belongs to a particular domain and is used to specify information about the domain. There are several types of DNS records. Each record type contains particular information used to describe the purpose of that record. Examples include mail exchange (MX) records, which specify the mail server for a particular domain; and name server (NS) records, which specify the authoritative name servers for a domain.

record ID
A number within a database that is incremented each time a change is made. Used by Object Storage when replicating.

Red Hat Enterprise Linux (RHEL)
A Linux distribution that is compatible with OpenStack.

reference architecture
A recommended architecture for an OpenStack cloud.

region
A discrete OpenStack environment with dedicated API endpoints that typically shares only the Identity Service (keystone) with other regions.

registry
Alternative term for the Image Service registry.

registry server
An Image Service that provides VM image metadata information to clients.

Reliable, Autonomic Distributed Object Store (RADOS)
A collection of components that provides object storage within Ceph. Similar to OpenStack Object Storage.

Remote Procedure Call (RPC)
The method used by the Compute RabbitMQ for intra-service communications.

replica
Provides data redundancy and fault tolerance by creating copies of Object Storage objects, accounts, and containers so that they are not lost when the underlying storage fails.

replica count
The number of replicas of the data in an Object Storage ring.

replication
The process of copying data to a separate physical device for fault tolerance and performance.

replicator
The Object Storage backend process that creates and manages object replicas.

request ID
Unique ID assigned to each request sent to Compute.

rescue image
A special type of VM image that is booted when an instance is placed into rescue mode. Allows an administrator to mount the file systems for an instance to correct the problem.

resize
Converts an existing server to a different flavor, which scales the server up or down. The original server is saved to enable rollback if a problem occurs. All resizes must be tested and explicitly confirmed, at which time the original server is removed.

RESTful
A kind of web service API that uses REST, or Representational State Transfer. REST is the style of architecture for hypermedia systems that is used for the World Wide Web.

ring
An entity that maps Object Storage data to partitions. A separate ring exists for each service, such as account, object, and container.

ring builder
Builds and manages rings within Object Storage, assigns partitions to devices, and pushes the configuration to other storage nodes.

Role Based Access Control (RBAC)
Provides a predefined list of actions that the user can perform, such as start or stop VMs, reset passwords, and so on. Supported in both Identity Service and Compute and can be configured using the horizon dashboard.

role
A personality that a user assumes to perform a specific set of operations. A role includes a set of rights and privileges. A user assuming that role inherits those rights and privileges.

role ID
Alphanumeric ID assigned to each Identity Service role.

rootwrap
A feature of Compute that allows the unprivileged "nova" user to run a specified list of commands as the Linux root user.

round-robin scheduler
Type of Compute scheduler that evenly distributes instances among available hosts.

routing key
The Compute direct exchanges, fanout exchanges, and topic exchanges use this key to determine how to process a message; processing varies depending on exchange type.

RPC driver
Modular system that allows the underlying message queue software of Compute to be changed. For example, from RabbitMQ to ZeroMQ or Qpid.

rsync
Used by Object Storage to push object replicas.

RXTX cap
Absolute limit on the amount of network traffic a Compute VM instance can send and receive.

RXTX quota
Soft limit on the amount of network traffic a Compute VM instance can send and receive.

Ryu neutron plug-in
Enables the Ryu network operating system to function as a Networking OpenFlow controller.

S3
Object storage service by Amazon; similar in function to Object Storage, it can act as a backend store for Image Service VM images.

sahara
OpenStack project that provides a scalable data-processing stack and associated management interfaces.

scheduler manager
A Compute component that determines where VM instances should start. Uses modular design to support a variety of scheduler types.

scoped token
An Identity Service API access token that is associated with a specific tenant.

scrubber
Checks for and deletes unused VMs; the component of Image Service that implements delayed delete.

secret key
String of text known only by the user; used along with an access key to make requests to the Compute API.

secure shell (SSH)
Open source tool used to access remote hosts through an encrypted communications channel, SSH key injection is supported by Compute.

security group
A set of network traffic filtering rules that are applied to a Compute instance.

segmented object
An Object Storage large object that has been broken up into pieces. The re-assembled object is called a concatenated object.

server
Computer that provides explicit services to the client software running on that system, often managing a variety of computer operations.

A server is a VM instance in the Compute system. Flavor and image are requisite elements when creating a server.

server image
Alternative term for a VM image.

server UUID
Unique ID assigned to each guest VM instance.

service
An OpenStack service, such as Compute, Object Storage, or Image Service. Provides one or more endpoints through which users can access resources and perform operations.

service catalog
Alternative term for the Identity Service catalog.

service ID
Unique ID assigned to each service that is available in the Identity Service catalog.

service registration
An Identity Service feature that enables services, such as Compute, to automatically register with the catalog.

service tenant
Special tenant that contains all services that are listed in the catalog.

service token
An administrator-defined token used by Compute to communicate securely with the Identity Service.

session backend
: The method of storage used by horizon to track client sessions, such as local memory, cookies, a database, or memcached.

session persistence
: A feature of the load-balancing service. It attempts to force subsequent connections to a service to be redirected to the same node as long as it is online.

session storage
: A horizon component that stores and tracks client session information. Implemented through the Django sessions framework.

shared IP address
: An IP address that can be assigned to a VM instance within the shared IP group. Public IP addresses can be shared across multiple servers for use in various high-availability scenarios. When an IP address is shared to another server, the cloud network restrictions are modified to enable each server to listen to and respond on that IP address. You can optionally specify that the target server network configuration be modified. Shared IP addresses can be used with many standard heartbeat facilities, such as keepalive, that monitor for failure and manage IP failover.

shared IP group
: A collection of servers that can share IPs with other members of the group. Any server in a group can share one or more public IPs with any other server in the group. With the exception of the first server in a shared IP group, servers must be launched into shared IP groups. A server may be a member of only one shared IP group.

shared storage
: Block storage that is simultaneously accessible by multiple clients, for example, NFS.

Sheepdog
: Distributed block storage system for QEMU, supported by OpenStack.

Simple Cloud Identity Management (SCIM)
: Specification for managing identity in the cloud, currently unsupported by OpenStack.

Single-root I/O Virtualization (SR-IOV)
: A specification that, when implemented by a physical PCIe device, enables it to appear as multiple separate PCIe devices. This enables multiple virtualized guests to share direct access to the physical device, offering improved performance over an equivalent virtual device. Currently supported in OpenStack Havana and later releases.

SmokeStack
: Runs automated tests against the core OpenStack API; written in Rails.

snapshot
: A point-in-time copy of an OpenStack storage volume or image. Use storage volume snapshots to back up volumes. Use image snapshots to back up data, or as "gold" images for additional servers.

soft reboot
: A controlled reboot where a VM instance is properly restarted through operating system commands.

SolidFire Volume Driver
: The Block Storage driver for the SolidFire iSCSI storage appliance.

SPICE
: The Simple Protocol for Independent Computing Environments (SPICE) provides remote desktop access to guest virtual machines. It is an alternative to VNC. SPICE is supported by OpenStack.

spread-first scheduler
: The Compute VM scheduling algorithm that attempts to start a new VM on the host with the least amount of load.

SQL-Alchemy
: An open source SQL toolkit for Python, used in OpenStack.

SQLite
: A lightweight SQL database, used as the default persistent storage method in many OpenStack services.

StackTach
: Community project that captures Compute AMQP communications; useful for debugging.

static IP address
: Alternative term for a fixed IP address.

StaticWeb
: WSGI middleware component of Object Storage that serves container data as a static web page.

storage backend
: The method that a service uses for persistent storage, such as iSCSI, NFS, or local disk.

storage node
: An Object Storage node that provides container services, account services, and object services; controls the account databases, container databases, and object storage.

storage manager
: A XenAPI component that provides a pluggable interface to support a wide variety of persistent storage backends.

storage manager backend
: A persistent storage method supported by XenAPI, such as iSCSI or NFS.

storage services
: Collective name for the Object Storage object services, container services, and account services.

strategy
: Specifies the authentication source used by Image Service or Identity Service.

subdomain
: A domain within a parent domain. Subdomains cannot be registered. Subdomains enable you to delegate domains. Subdomains can themselves have subdomains, so third-level, fourth-level, fifth-level, and deeper levels of nesting are possible.

SUSE Linux Enterprise Server (SLES)
: A Linux distribution that is compatible with OpenStack.

suspend
: Alternative term for a paused VM instance.

swap
: Disk-based virtual memory used by operating systems to provide more memory than is actually available on the system.

swawth
: An authentication and authorization service for Object Storage, implemented through WSGI middleware; uses Object Storage itself as the persistent backing store.

swift
: An OpenStack core project that provides object storage services.

swift All in One (SAIO)
: Creates a full Object Storage development environment within a single VM.

swift middleware
: Collective term for Object Storage components that provide additional functionality.

swift proxy server
: Acts as the gatekeeper to Object Storage and is responsible for authenticating the user.

swift storage node
: A node that runs Object Storage account, container, and object services.

sync point
: Point in time since the last container and accounts database sync among nodes within Object Storage.

sysadmin
: One of the default roles in the Compute RBAC system. Enables a user to add other users to a project, interact with VM images that are associated with the project, and start and stop VM instances.

system usage
: A Compute component that, along with the notification system, collects metrics and usage information. This information can be used for billing.

Telemetry
: An integrated project that provides metering and measuring facilities for OpenStack. The project name of Telemetry is ceilometer.

TempAuth
: An authentication facility within Object Storage that enables Object Storage itself to perform authentication and authorization. Frequently used in testing and development.

Tempest
: Automated software test suite designed to run against the trunk of the OpenStack core project.

TempURL
: An Object Storage middleware component that enables creation of URLs for temporary object access.

tenant
: A group of users; used to isolate access to Compute resources. An alternative term for a project.

Tenant API
: An API that is accessible to tenants.

tenant endpoint
: An Identity Service API endpoint that is associated with one or more tenants.

tenant ID
: Unique ID assigned to each tenant within the Identity Service. The project IDs map to the tenant IDs.

token
: An alpha-numeric string of text used to access OpenStack APIs and resources.

token services
: An Identity Service component that manages and validates tokens after a user or tenant has been authenticated.

tombstone
: Used to mark Object Storage objects that have been deleted; ensures that the object is not updated on another node after it has been deleted.

topic publisher
: A process that is created when a RPC call is executed; used to push the message to the topic exchange.

Torpedo
: Community project used to run automated tests against the OpenStack API.

transaction ID
: Unique ID assigned to each Object Storage request; used for debugging and tracing.

transient
: Alternative term for non-durable.

transient exchange
: Alternative term for a non-durable exchange.

transient message
: A message that is stored in memory and is lost after the server is restarted.

transient queue
: Alternative term for a non-durable queue.

trove
: OpenStack project that provides database services to applications.

Ubuntu
: A Debian-based Linux distribution.

unscoped token
: Alternative term for an Identity Service default token.

updater
: Collective term for a group of Object Storage components that processes queued and failed updates for containers and objects.

user
: In Identity Service, each user is associated with one or more tenants, and in Compute can be associated with roles, projects, or both.

user data
: A blob of data that can be specified by the user when launching an instance. This data can be accessed by the instance through the metadata service or config drive. Commonly used for passing a shell script that is executed by the instance on boot.

User Mode Linux (UML)
: An OpenStack-supported hypervisor.

VIF UUID
: Unique ID assigned to each Networking VIF.

Virtual Central Processing Unit (vCPU)
: Subdivides physical CPUs. Instances can then use those divisions.

Virtual Disk Image (VDI)
: One of the VM image disk formats supported by Image Service.

Virtual Hard Disk (VHD)
: One of the VM image disk formats supported by Image Service.

virtual IP
: An Internet Protocol (IP) address configured on the load balancer for use by clients connecting to a service that is load balanced. Incoming connections are distributed to backend nodes based on the configuration of the load balancer.

virtual machine (VM)
: An operating system instance that runs on top of a hypervisor. Multiple VMs can run at the same time on the same physical host.

virtual network
: An L2 network segment within Networking.

Virtual Network Computing (VNC)
: Open source GUI and CLI tools used for remote console access to VMs. Supported by Compute.

Virtual Network InterFace (VIF)
: An interface that is plugged into a port in a Networking network. Typically a virtual network interface belonging to a VM.

virtual port
: Attachment point where a virtual interface connects to a virtual network.

virtual private network (VPN)
: Provided by Compute in the form of cloudpipes, specialized instances that are used to create VPNs on a per-project basis.

virtual server
: Alternative term for a VM or guest.

virtual switch (vSwitch)
: Software that runs on a host or node and provides the features and functions of a hardware-based network switch.

virtual VLAN
: Alternative term for a virtual network.

VirtualBox
: An OpenStack-supported hypervisor.

VLAN manager
: A Compute component that provides dnsmasq and radvd and sets up forwarding to and from cloudpipe instances.

VLAN network
: The Network Controller provides virtual networks to enable compute servers to interact with each other and with the public network. All machines must have a public and private network interface. A VLAN network is a private network interface, which is controlled by the `vlan_interface` option with VLAN managers.

VM disk (VMDK)
One of the VM image disk formats supported by Image Service.

VM image
Alternative term for an image.

VM Remote Control (VMRC)
Method to access VM instance consoles using a web browser. Supported by Compute.

VMware API
Supports interaction with VMware products in Compute.

VMware NSX Neutron plug-in
Provides support for VMware NSX in Neutron.

VNC proxy
A Compute component that provides users access to the consoles of their VM instances through VNC or VMRC.

volume
Disk-based data storage generally represented as an iSCSI target with a file system that supports extended attributes; can be persistent or ephemeral.

Volume API
An API on a separate endpoint for attaching, detaching, and creating block storage for compute VMs.

volume controller
A Block Storage component that oversees and coordinates storage volume actions.

volume driver
Alternative term for a volume plug-in.

volume ID
Unique ID applied to each storage volume under the Block Storage control.

volume manager
A Block Storage component that creates, attaches, and detaches persistent storage volumes.

volume node
A Block Storage node that runs the `cinder-volume` daemon.

volume plug-in
Provides support for new and specialized types of backend storage for the Block Storage volume manager.

Volume Service API
Alternative term for the Compute volume API.

volume worker
A cinder component that interacts with backend storage to manage the creation and deletion of volumes and the creation of compute volumes, provided by the `cinder-volume` daemon.

vSphere
An OpenStack-supported hypervisor.

weighing
A Compute process that determines the suitability of the VM instances for a job for a particular host. For example, not enough RAM on the host, too many CPUs on the host, and so on.

weight
Used by Object Storage devices to determine which storage devices are suitable for the job. Devices are weighted by size.

weighted cost
The sum of each cost used when deciding where to start a new VM instance in Compute.

worker
A daemon that listens to a queue and carries out tasks in response to messages. For example, the `cinder-volume` worker manages volume creation and deletion on storage arrays.

Xen API
The Xen administrative API, which is supported by Compute.

Xen Cloud Platform (XCP)
An OpenStack-supported hypervisor.

Xen Storage Manager Volume Driver
: A Block Storage volume plug-in that enables communication with the Xen Storage Manager API.

XenServer
: An OpenStack-supported hypervisor.

ZeroMQ
: Message queue software supported by OpenStack. An alternative to RabbitMQ. Also spelled 0MQ.

Zuul
: Tool used in OpenStack development to ensure correctly ordered testing of changes in parallel.

Index

Symbols

A

B

C

D

J

K

L

M

N

O

P

Q

R

S

T

U

V

W

X

Z

Colophon

The animal on the cover of *OpenStack Operations Guide* is a crested agouti (*Dasyprocta cristata*), a rodent found in the South American countries of Guyana and Suriname. *Cristata* is derived from the Portuguese word *crista*, meaning "crest." Presumably, this refers to a thick collar of fur around the animal's neck. However, its classification is in question—in 1978, scientist A.M. Husson theorized that the crested agouti was the same species as the red-rumped agouti (*Dasyprocta leporina*), which occupies the same geographic range. Because the matter has not been definitively resolved, it is difficult to determine the abundance and range of the species, so it is officially categorized as Data Deficient by the IUCN.

Agoutis are related to guinea pigs, though the agouti is generally larger and has longer legs. They also have very short hairless tails and coarse fur. Their diet consists of fruit, nuts, roots, and leaves, which they eat by sitting on their hind legs and holding the food in their front paws. Agoutis are among the few species (including macaws) that can open Brazil nuts without tools. Using their sharp teeth, they gnaw through the hard outer capsule to reach the nuts inside.

Many of the animals on O'Reilly covers are endangered; all of them are important to the world. To learn more about how you can help, go to *http://animals.oreilly.com*.

The cover image is from Beeton's *Dictionary of Natural History*. The cover fonts are URW Typewriter and Guardian Sans. The text font is Adobe Minion Pro; the heading font is Adobe Myriad Condensed; and the code font is Dalton Maag's Ubuntu Mono.

Milton Keynes UK
Ingram Content Group UK Ltd.
UKHW011829070824
446675UK00007B/108

9 781491 946954